HIDDEN
WISDOM
in the Holy Bible

Volume II

HIDDEN WISDOM
in the Holy Bible

Volume II

Geoffrey Hodson

Wheaton, Ill. U.S.A.
Madras, India/London, England

The Theosophical Publishing House
P.O. Box 270
Wheaton, Illinois 60189-0270

A publication of the Theosophical Publishing House,
a department of the Theosophical Society in America.

*This publication made possible with
the assistance of the Kern Foundation*

Library of Congress Cataloging-in-Publication Data

(Revised for vol. 2)

Hodson, Geoffrey.
    Hidden wisdom in the Holy Bible.

    Includes bibliographical references and index.
    1. Jesus Christ—Theosophical interpretations.
2. Bible—Miscellanea. 3. Symbolism in the Bible. 4. Prodigal son
(Parable)—Miscellanea. I. Title.
BS534.H67 1993   220.6'4   92-56484
ISBN 0-8356-0705-4

            9 8 7 6 5 4 3 2 1 * 94 95 96 97 98 99

    This edition is printed on acid-free paper that meets the
    American National Standards Institute Z39.48 Standard

    Printed in the United States of America by Versa Press

This work is dedicated to Philo Judaeus,
the great Alexandrian sage.

Acknowledgments

I acknowledge with gratitude the help in the production of this work received from my wife, Sandra, who at dictation wrote out all the original interpretations of biblical passages, and is continuing to do so; my valued literary assistant, Myra G. Fraser; my friend Nell K. Griffith, who for many years cared for my domestic needs and assisted in typing from the first draft of the manuscript; also from Mrs. Margaret Fisher of Columbus, Ohio, U.S.A., who retyped a considerable portion of this book.

Contents

Part Four
Moses and the Exodus

Publisher's Note

Geoffrey Hodson's *The Hidden Wisdom of the Holy Bible* is a Theosophical classic which demonstrates the method of uncovering the teachings of the Ageless Wisdom concealed within the stories and metaphors of the Old and New Testaments. Since its original four-volume form is unwieldy and repetitious and since Hodson's style is difficult for modern readers, we have prepared a two-volume abridgment of Hodson's work. Our aim in this edition is to make this classic of Theosophical literature accessible to contemporary readers.

Volume I of this series contains much of the material in Hodson's original Volume I. Its purpose is to lay out and demonstrate succinctly Hodson's method of biblical interpretation. Volume II of the series provides selections from Hodson's interpretations of key scriptural episodes, such as the Creation, the Flood, the Life of Joseph, and the Exodus, chosen from the material in the original Volumes II, III, and IV.

Care has been taken to modernize Hodson's style while remaining faithful to his method. Quotations from the King James Version are now identified by chapter and verse in parenthesis in the text. Definitions of Theosophical and Sanskrit terms formerly given in footnotes have been integrated into the text, and information about Hodson's sources now appears in a Bibliography at the back of the book. Definitions of terms which Hodson did not define and which may be unclear to readers have been taken mainly from *The Theosophical Glossary* (TG) by H. P. Blavatsky and from the *Occult Glossary* (OG) by G. de Purucker. Some definitions are also from Blavatsky's *The Secret Doctrine* (SD).

In the interest of readability, a boxed summary in prose of each biblical chapter discussed by Hodson precedes the first chapter of his discussion; most passages which Hodson comments on directly are quoted in full from the King James Version. Readers are invited to consult a text of the Bible for complete versions of all passages discussed. Students of biblical literature should also be aware that Hodson took most of the Hebrew words and their translations (given in quotation marks) used in his discussions from *The Unknown God,* by F. J. Mayers, which is based in part on Fabre d'Olivet's *The Hebraic Tongue Restored.* They are not from *Strong's Concordance.*

Hodson's spelling, punctuation, and usage have also been modernized. In keeping with modern conventions, gender-specific terms such as *man* and *mankind* have been replaced by gender-neutral terms such as *human being, humanity,* and *humankind.* Masculine pronouns referring to the Deity have also been eliminated. Chapter titles and subheadings have been changed to make them more descriptive of the contents.

It is our hope that this book, as well as other volumes in the Theosophical Heritage Classics series, will bring the Ageless Wisdom to a new audience of readers as well as to those who have always found sustenance in drinking from its deep well of spiritual truth.

Preface to Volume II

In the first volume of this series, the theory is advanced that many of the narratives recounted in both the Old and the New Testaments, as also in the inspired portions of the scriptures and mythologies of other ancient peoples, contain far more than is apparent on the surface. Undermeanings are said to have been deliberately introduced and are conveyed by the use of a system—widely recognized in ancient times—of so narrating actual events that they also reveal underlying laws governing the emanation, involution and evolution of both universe and humanity. To this end the characters of the people in such stories are made to personify Intelligences, forces, procedures and stages of development in the unfolding universe and the spiritual, intellectual, psychological and physical components of every human being.

Acceptance of this view gives to world scriptures a far deeper significance than if they were regarded as narratives of physical events alone. This approach also helps to explain the inclusion of passages which either contradict known scientific and historical facts, or else repel because recording criminal, immoral or very cruel actions.

If I seem to apologize too much for condemning the literal meaning of certain passages and advancing possible hidden meanings—and I have been so charged by one reviewer of my first volume—it is because I remember and do not wish to hurt or harm those to whom orthodox beliefs mean much in their religious life. Having suffered myself from atheistic iconoclasm, I wish to lead my readers along a more pleasant pathway to what I have come to regard as truth, preferring to win over and persuade to further examination than entirely to crush.

Many biblical passages do indeed present grave difficulties, particularly when deeds are stated to have been performed either, as in the Old Testament, at the instance of the Supreme Deity or, as in mythology, even by deities themselves. Many such textual problems are resolved when the classical keys of interpretation are applied, and this volume of this work offers some of the results of study of the scriptures and mythologies of ancient peoples as if the sages of old had recorded them in the sacred language of allegory and symbol.

Geoffrey Hodson
Auckland, New Zealand, 1966.

Introduction

The basis for some of the proffered interpretations of the Bible given in this book is that Ageless Wisdom to which the Greeks gave the title *Theosophia,* derived from the two Greek words *Theo* and *sophia* – divine wisdom.

The first known literary use of this Greek word is found in the writings of the Neoplatonists in the second century of the Christian era, who employed it to connote the truths revealed to humanity by evolutionary elders at the dawn of human life on this planet. These truths have been added to, checked and rechecked down to the present day by an unbroken succession of Adept investigators. This term, Adept, refers to an initiate of the fifth degree in the greater Mysteries, a master in the science of esoteric philosophy, a perfected human, an exalted being who has attained complete mastery over the purely human nature and possesses knowledge and power commensurate with lofty evolutionary stature. Such fulfillment of human destiny is thus described by St. Paul: "Till we all come in the unity of the faith, and of the knowledge of the Son of God, unto a perfect man, unto the measure of the stature of the fullness of Christ" (Eph. 4:13). Certain Adepts remain on Earth in physical bodies in order to assist humanity, and are presumably referred to by St. Paul as "just men made perfect" (Heb. 12:23). The Lord Christ referred to a far more lofty destiny for humanity, saying: "Ye therefore shall be perfect, as your heavenly Father is perfect" (Matt. 5:48 [Revised Version of the Bible (RV)]).

The full fruits of the processes of Adept research and revelation have been preserved by the still living hierophants and initiates of the greater Mysteries. In their doctrinal aspect these Mysteries consist of a vast body of teaching which embraces every conceivable subject to which the human mind can be turned. The fundamental principles of religion, philosophy, art, science and politics are contained within this Wisdom of the Ages. From the time of the closing of the Neoplatonic and Gnostic schools to the last quarter of the nineteenth century, save for the few Alchemists, Kabbalists, Rosicrucians, esoterically instructed Masons and the Christian mystics, Theosophy was little known in the Western world. Before then it was studied in various forms by the Platonists, the Pythagoreans, the Egyptians and the Chaldeans, while in India and China it has been preserved down the ages in unbroken continuity. It is the wisdom of the *Upanishads* and the *Vedas,* the very heart of Hinduism, Buddhism, Taoism and Islam. By means of allegory and symbol it is revealed in the Christian scriptures, the literal reading of which has blinded many Christians to their deeper significance.

The study of comparative religion does in fact reveal the existence of certain doctrines which are common to all world faiths. Although differently presented in each, when collected and blended into a whole these teachings constitute a basic body of revealed Truth which can be studied independently of all religious systems. Each world religion reveals an arc of the circle of Eternal Wisdom. Theosophy, although as yet only partially revealed to humanity, is the full circle of Truth. Age by age, at the direction of Those who are the guardians of knowledge and its accompanying power, aspects of this all-inclusive body of ideas are revealed to humans through world religions and philosophies. The theme of this book is that certain power-bestowing aspects of Theosophia have always been partially concealed under a veil of allegory and symbol. This is because such knowledge can bestow theurgic, hypnotic and other powers susceptible of misuse. Rightly used, however, it can be of great value to humanity and since the present is an age when many are searching deeply for a philosophy of life which will support them when in danger, stress and need, the time has now arrived, I believe, when the outer layers of this veil may usefully, if but partially, be drawn aside. The interpretations of the scriptures which now begin are based upon these convictions. Here, then, is an attempt to lift the mysterious veil of the temple which one day for all people, we may hope, will be "rent in twain from the top to the bottom" (Matt. 27:51).

Cosmogenesis

Since some of the concepts of the cosmogony of esoteric philosophy are included in the interpretations of the book of Genesis which now follow, a brief statement of them may prove helpful, especially to those contacting these ideas for the first time.

The concept of creation as the emergence and subsequent development of a universe and its contents is regarded in esoteric philosophy as being less the result of a single act of creation, followed by natural evolution, than a process of emanation guided by intelligent Forces under immutable law. The creation or emergence of universes from nothing is not an acceptable concept, the cosmos being regarded as emanating from an all-containing, sourceless Source, the Absolute.

For example, the first five verses of the book of Genesis describe the opening phases of the process of creation as follows:

In the beginning God created the heaven and the earth.

And the earth was without form, and void; and darkness was upon the face of the deep. And the Spirit of God moved upon the face of the waters.

And God said, Let there be light: and there was light.

And God saw the light, that it was good: and God divided the light from the darkness.

And God called the light Day, and the darkness He called Night. And the evening and the morning were the first day.

Thus originally there existed duality in unity, namely the "Spirit of God" as the masculine creative potency on the one hand and the "face of the deep" as the feminine creative potency on the other. Primarily there was a dual principle, a positive and a negative, Spirit-matter. During the long creative "Night," which in Sanskrit is called *Pralaya* (period of repose), there was darkness upon the face of the deep. The whole of boundless space was dark and quiescent. Then, it is stated, a change occurred. The "Spirit of God," having emerged from Absolute Existence, moved upon the face of the waters. The "Great Breath" breathed upon the "Great Deep," whereupon emanation began to occur and manifestation (*Manvantara*) was initiated.

Thus, behind and beyond and within all is the eternal and infinite Parent from within which the temporary and the finite emerge, or are born. That boundless self-existence is variously referred to as the Absolute, the Changeless, the eternal All, the causeless Cause, the rootless Root. This is non-Being, negative Existence, no-Thing, *Ain* (as the Kabbalist says), an impersonal Unity without attributes conceivable by human beings.

In esoteric philosophy the term "God" in its highest meaning refers to a supreme, eternal and indefinable Reality. This Absolute is inconceivable, ineffable and unknowable. Its revealed existence is postulated in three terms: an absolute Existence, an absolute Consciousness and an absolute Bliss. Infinite consciousness is regarded as inherent in the Supreme Being as a dynamic force that manifests the potentialities held in its own infinitude, and calls into being forms out of its own formless depths. From That, the Absolute, emerged an active, creative power and intelligence to become formative Deity, the *Demiurgos* (the supernal Power which built the universe – the third manifested Logos [TG]) of the universe-to-be. The illumined sages thus taught that the eternal One, which is potentially twofold (Spirit-matter), is subject to cyclic, rhythmic Motion, a primordial Third which is also eternal. Under certain conditions the relationship of the conjoined Spirit-matter changes from passive unity into active duality – distinct positive and negative potencies.

Thus, when "interior" Motion causes previously unified, quiescent Spirit-Matter to become oppositely polarized or creatively active, then there is activity, light, "Day"; for these two (universal Spirit and universal Matter) produce a third, a "Son," which becomes the presiding Deity, the Logos, the Architect of the resultant universe. A finite principle has now emerged from the Infinite. Universal Spirit-Matter-Motion have become focused into a Being who is beyond normal human comprehension. This is the One Alone, the "only-begotten Son" (originally from a Greek Eucharistic hymn; when correctly translated, "alone begotten" or emanated from a unified, single Source), being of "one substance with the Father," which in this case is the Absolute, the Uncreated. By this "Son," the Cosmic Christ, all worlds are fashioned, "He" being the Emanator, Architect, Sustainer and Regenerator of universes and all that they will ever contain.

This formative Logos is the first objective emanation of the Absolute. It is the principle of divine thought, now to be remade manifest in an individual sense, first as the Logos of the whole cosmos, secondly as the solar Deity of a single Solar System, and thirdly as the Logos of the soul of every human being – the dweller in the innermost. These Three are One, indivisible, an integral part of each other, a whole. In the beginning, when newly formed, the First, the One Alone, is purely spiritual and intellectual. Ultimately, as we have seen, It becomes manifested as both the presiding Power, Life and Intelligence transcendent beyond all that objectively exists and the indwelling and transforming Divine Life immanent within all nature, all beings and all things.

These, in outline, are some of the cosmogonical ideas to be found in esoteric philosophy. Further expositions of them will be found in the interpretations of the book of Genesis which follow.

A Mistranslated Word

In interpreting the Bible, beginning with Genesis, attention is drawn to a single important word which appears in the original Hebrew text. This word is *tho* and translated from the Hebrew means "symbolic." Especially note the following three commentaries on the presence of this word in the Hebrew text, and also the way in which it is translated in Genesis 2:4 in the Revised Version of the Bible [the King James Version also makes a similar omission].

> These are the generations of the heaven and the earth when they were created. In the day that the Lord God made earth and heaven. . .
> *(RV)*

F. J. Mayers writes in his book *The Unknown God:*

> The first thing we notice when we compare the above version with the original Hebrew text, is that the latter contains a word which is not translated at all in the English. It was also ignored in the Latin translation. The translators apparently did not know what to do with it. The Hebrew Text reads: 'aelleh *tho*-ledoth.' The little word 'tho,' which translators have passed over, denotes 'symbolic.' It may be applied to a *book,* a fable, a hieroglyph, a discourse, or anything else which is of a 'symbolic' nature. The translators of the 'Septuagint' did not ignore the word, but they 'by-passed' its real meaning . . . and translated it merely by the word 'book'; that avoided raising awkward questions. What the whole phrase really stated quite clearly was, that the 'generations' or 'productions' of the heavens and the earth . . . would be described *in symbolic* language. It is particularly illuminating that the writer of Genesis should himself tell us this in advance. He takes the ground from under the feet of those who are continually seeking to 'literalize' and 'de-spiritualize' the Bible. . . .

Fabre d'Olivet, in *The Hebraic Tongue Restored* states: "The root 'tho' contains every idea of sign, of symbol, of hieroglyphic character. . . ."

Nayan Louise Redfield, the translator of *The Hebraic Tongue Restored,* writes in his Foreword:

> He [Fabre d'Olivet] asserts plainly and fearlessly that the Genesis of Moses was symbolically expressed and ought not to be taken in

a purely literal sense. Saint Augustine recognized this, and Origen avers that "if one takes the history of the creation in the literal sense, it is absurd and contradictory.". . .

According to the Essenian tradition, every word in this *Sepher of Moses* [Genesis] contains three meanings—the positive or simple, the comparative or figurative, the superlative or hieratic. When one has penetrated to this last meaning, all things are disclosed through a radiant illumination and the soul of that one attains to heights which those bound to the narrow limits of the positive meaning and satisfied with the letter which killeth, never know.

The learned Maimonides says "Employ you (sic) reason, and you will be able to discern what is said allegorically, figuratively and hyperbolically, and what is meant literally."

PART ONE

Creation

1

In the Beginning

Genesis 1

In the beginning God created the heavens and the Earth. From a flooded Earth, void and without life, the Creator said, "Let there be light," and it was in this light that creation was brought into being.

God began with the waters, drawing them together into seas, allowing the land to appear, and causing the clouds to form. The Creator spoke, and the Earth became green with grass and trees and herbs. That these might grow God looked to the heavens and set there the sun, moon and stars.

Turning again to the seas God spoke, and they brought forth abundant life in the form of fish and whales and sea creatures, and God created birds to grace the shores.

To the dry land God said, "Bring forth!" and it obeyed, yielding wild animals, cattle and other living things. Yet, in all this beauty something was lacking, and it was then that man and woman were created, made in the image of God. They were loved above all creation and God gave the Earth into their keeping.

And having completed this great work in six days, God beheld all of creation and saw that it was very good.

In the beginning God created the heaven and the earth.
And the earth was without form, and void; and darkness was upon the
face of the deep. And the Spirit of God moved upon the face of the
waters. *(Gen. 1:1–2)*

The Bible opens with these verses of affirmation that an intelligent, self-knowing group of formative agencies of cosmic evolutionary stature (*Elohim*) was responsible for the direction of the form-producing impulse which arose in precosmic space. Wherever the term "God" is used in Genesis the word in the original text is the Hebrew Elohim, meaning not a single Being, but an order of creative Intelligences. The terms "the heaven" and "the earth" refer to the separation of primordial substance (heavens) from the manifested universe (the Earth).

J. Ralston Skinner, in a passage quoted by H. P. Blavatsky in Vol. VII of her *Collected Writings* (p. 261), writes: "It is made to be read 'B'rashith bârâ Elohim'. . . , 'In the beginning God created the heavens and the earth.'" Skinner notes that Elohim is a plural noun, but the form of the verb "bârâ" (meaning "created" in Hebrew) is third person singular [in other words, the number of Deity(ies) in the subject and the verb does not match grammatically]. Skinner adds that Nachmanides called attention to the fact that the text might also be read as "B'rash ithbârâ Elohim". . . , which translated means "In the head (source or beginning) created itself (or developed) Gods, the heavens and the earth," which is more grammatically correct.

The term "God" as used in these verses is thus not singular but plural in its implications. Although the original directive Intelligence—the precursor and Source of Universal Mind—arose in a unitary state from its root in precosmic space, immediately as that agency became outward-turned, the rule of number obtained: One alone cannot manifest; three are essential to the production of any result. This is as true of cosmic manifestation as of microcosmic or human creation, whether intellectual or physical. No germinal essence is a unit, each at its simplest being a triplicity of potentials, namely the positive, the negative and their productive interaction. So also is the seed of a cosmos which, though a unit in *Pralaya* (period of quiescence, either planetary or universal), displays a number at the outset of *Manvantara* (period of activity or manifestation). The term *God,* therefore, as used in these verses is to be understood, as in Kabbalism, to refer to the group of intelligent, productive agencies inherent in and emanated from precosmic space, the Elohim. The first chapter of Genesis is, in consequence, called the Elohistic and the second the Yahwistic.

The question is sometimes asked, even by children: If God made all things, who made God? Esoteric philosophy answers, No one; for the Demiurgos (the supernal Power which built the universe) or active

Logos is an emanation from the immutable Infinite, the Boundless, the Absolute, which cannot will, think or act until it has become partially manifest as finite. This it does by the projection of a ray which penetrates into infinite space, there to become the Architect of the resultant universe.

The kabbalistic perspective on Genesis-like cosmogony is expressed by J. F. C. Fuller as follows: "There was a time when Heaven and Earth did not exist, but only an unlimited Space in which reigned absolute immobility. All the visible things and all that which possesses existence were born in that Space from a powerful principle, which existed by Itself, and from Itself developed Itself, and which made the heavens revolve and preserved the universal life; a principle as to which philosophy declares we know not the name."

God—the Totality of Existence

The term "God," therefore, carries a number of implications. It includes physical nature; the evolutionary impulse imparted to it; the irresistible formative force which bestows the attribute of self-reproduction and the capacity to express it; the creative Intelligences—the Elohim—which direct the manifestations and the operations of that force; the divine thought or ideation of the whole cosmos from its beginning to its end; and the sound of the creative "Voice" (*Logos*) by which that ideation is impressed upon precosmic substance. These, together with all seeds, beings, forces and laws, including those of expansion, alternation, cyclic progression and harmonious equipoise, constitute that totality of existence to which alone may be given with any measure of fitness the majestic and awe-inspiring title "God."

If so vast a synthesis may be designated a Being, then that Being is so complex, so all-inclusive, as to be beyond the comprehension of the human mind and the possibility of restriction to any single form. The idea of God also includes everlasting law, everlasting will, everlasting life and everlasting mind.

In nonmanifestation God is quiescent, in manifestation objectively active. Behind both quiescence and activity exists That which is eternal and unchanging, the Absolute, self-existent All. The divine Creator referred to by various names in the world's cosmogonies is the active expression of that eternal, incomprehensible One Alone.

Emanation, Not Creation

The word "create" also has its particular significance. The production of something previously nonexistent in any state is not to be understood or implied by this word. To emanate or make manifest more truly describes the process; for cosmos is inherent in Chaos (the primordial, pre-atomic condition in which matter existed before the first atoms and planes of nature were created [TG]), the difference being not of substance but of condition. Formlessness and darkness describe Chaos. Form and light describe cosmos. Both conditions are inherent in precosmic *substans*.

The verses of Genesis should therefore be translated as follows: "At the dawn of the return of Manvantara, the group of creative Intelligences (Elohim) resumed activity, with the result that the seed of Cosmos inherent in Chaos commenced to unfold according to natural law." This process is continuous throughout the period of manifestation, for the universe is a perpetual becoming, not a static condition of being. This applies equally to the primordial elements, to the substances derived from them, to the forms of nature and to their ensouling life. All grows or expands from less to more from the dawn of the first "day" of emanation to the evening of the last or seventh "day."

In Genesis 1:2 is presented the primordial trinity, namely Spirit (not an entity but formless and immaterial spiritual substance), space (waters) and motion. The essential triplicity of the creative agencies is perfectly described. "The Spirit of God" is the masculine potency within the seed of cosmos preexistent in Chaos. "The waters" and "the deep" are symbols or hierograms for the feminine potency, and the movement of the former upon or within the latter is the third potency essential to manifestation. In terms of electricity, it is the current which passes between positive and negative poles. Thus in the first two verses of Genesis the creative necessities are symbolically introduced and creative activity is allegorically described.

And God said, Let there be light: and there was light. *(Gen. 1:3)*

Again a threefold agency is described here, but it is an agency differing from the first. Whereas the original triplicity is integral, comprising the whole of existence, its successor is productive only and is completed by a product. The latter trinity of Genesis consists first of ideation—the thought of light; second of active productive power—

speech; and third of the product—Universal Mind, here called light. This light should be regarded as the divine Intelligence, the first emanation of the Supreme, that light which according to the Gospel of John is the life of humanity. It is not to be confused with the light of the sun, which is a focus or lens by which the rays of the primordial light become materialized and concentrated upon our solar system and produce all the correlations of forces. The criticism often made by those who read the Bible literally that light appeared three days before the sun is thus disposed of.

Progression from the germinal to the active state is thus indicated. The manifesting process has not only been initiated, but has also become effective. Light is described as the first product of the generative act, and this light is born of ideation and power, or thought and speech, the true parents of cosmos. Yet these three are not separate existences, but one; for speech is thought expressed in sound, and the product, light, was inherent in divine thought.

These masculine and feminine creative potencies, together with motion, preexisted within the germinal seed. The first activity to occur within that seed is ideation, or the arising of the concept of the eternal design. This process is followed by the expression of that archetype in terms of power or energy, the product being divine Intelligence symbolized as light. Thus six agencies are introduced in the first three verses. Two stages are also described, the precosmic and the primary cosmic, the preexistent and the first manifested existence.

Light, An Expression of the First Active Logos

The first-born light contains the potencies of its parents and grandparents, namely power, thought (the parents), and feminine and masculine potency endowed with motion (the grandparents). The first light, therefore, is itself a complete creative power, a synthesis of the total essentials for manifestation, the Cosmic Christos or Son by whom "all things were made" (John 1:3). By light, self-existing as a unitary synthesis, the sevenfold creative agency is completed. The *Adonai* [Heb.— Lord or Yahweh, YHWH] is made manifest as Elohim.

The first light may therefore be defined as the active *Verbum* or *Logos* (the Word; a divine spiritual Entity; manifested Deity; the outward expression or effect of the ever-concealed Cause—speech is the Logos of thought), the potent, creative agency whose arising from latency in the cosmic seed is the mark, the sign and the demonstration that Pralaya has given place to Manvantara. This first light is the highest manifested Deity, and to it alone, with all that is implied, may justly and truly be given the name "God."

No personalization of That, which becomes Creator or Manifestor according to law, is either philosophically sound or spiritually reverent. Though the producer of life-imbued form, it is itself essentially formless, as its symbol—"light"—accurately portrays. Even in action as a manifesting agency its symbol is speech, or the potency and activity of thought-sound, which again is formless.

A further definition of God as presented in these verses of Genesis might be that it is a single, a threefold and a sevenfold directive Agency, originally inherent in precosmic *substans* and now active throughout the whole field of creative activity. This activity is infallibly guided by numerical necessity. God as the first light is therefore not almighty, being subject to mathematical law, which is the absolute, if abstract, Monarch of the cosmos. The dual title "Logos-Law" best depicts the true parental Deity of which the present cosmos is the product or "Son."

> And God saw the light, that it was good: and God divided the light from the darkness. *(Gen. 1:4)*

External awareness is postulated here as an essential of cosmic formative procedure. The primordial Parent, having awakened from pralayic sleep, first becomes active in terms of light, for light and darkness respectively are symbols of spiritual activity and quiescence. In one interpretation, light in the allegorical language is descriptive of a condition of consciousness, a state of being in which Spirit predominates over matter. Darkness on the other hand symbolizes the dominance of matter over Spirit. The first phrase of this verse is therefore repetitive, and says that precosmic night or Pralaya had given place to cosmic day or Manvantara, but adds that the newly awakened creative Agency was now aware of that change and henceforth entered consciously upon its official activity.

The subsequent division of light from darkness described in the second phrase of the verse is the first biblical reference to alternation. The primary pair consists of precosmos and cosmos, allegorically called night and day, darkness and light, respectively. During the darkness no activity except absolute, and therefore incognizable, activity exists and only darkness—to the finite mind—is prevalent, alternation being confined to cosmos, for once cosmos appears alternation is inseparable from it. This is because a contrasting pair—quiescence and activity or absolute and finite existence—has come into being. These two constitute the darkness and the light which are automatically divided from each other when cosmos appears.

The term "God," therefore, here also refers to essential, inescapable law under which duality must be prevalent whenever there is finiteness. From these first "parents" all successive and subordinate dualities arise, and continue in a descending scale down to the smallest living things. Thus alternation may truly be stated to be both the law of existence and the essential condition of awareness. The moment light exists, darkness is known as its inseparable opposite.

> And God called the light Day, and the darkness He called Night. And the evening and the morning were the first day. *(Gen. 1:5)*

This verse repeats the above-mentioned law of alternation and affirms divine awareness of its operation; for naming and name in the allegorical language describe conscious, demiurgic activity by mind and will, thought and power, to produce individuality out of that which was formerly universal. A name is definitive and separative. Once anything is named it has individuality and is therefore separated from other individualities.

By naming the new cosmos, or the area in it, the Logos limits the universe and marks out an area in which creative activity is to be confined. This insulation also is achieved, or automatically occurs, by the combined operation of consciousness and sound. In this verse, therefore, the external limits of the universe-to-be are defined and marked out. Within those limits the precisely ordained frequencies of oscillation of the creative power must eventually rule.

As the genesis and propagation of the universal "egg"—symbol of all new creations, whether cosmic, universal or solar—these frequencies are apportioned by numerical law. They are affirmed by Universal Mind as expressive of both the underlying character and the potential attainment of the new universe. The first sentence of the verse, therefore, describes these two processes.

The second sentence, referring to evening and morning, reintroduces the property of time, mentioned in the opening words of the chapter. Subdivisions of time are thus affirmed as being inseparable from the change from Chaos to cosmos. The words "in the beginning" (*b'resheth*

—at first, in principle) actually mean the beginning, or rather the reemergence of all things. Evening and morning of the first day refer to the opening and the close of the first creative epoch or "day."

The use of the word "first" suggests a succession, thus introducing the subject of symbolical numbers. As indicated in Volume I of this work, numbers in the symbolical language carry meanings beyond their numerical significance. Each number has its own metaphysical meanings, one of which includes the living Intelligence which it also represents.

Every creative "day," for example, has its Deity or number; for numbers in this connection are living Intelligences emanated from the One, meaning the finite but universal Intelligence which is the active, but not absolute, Parent of all. In terms of formative Intelligences, when the first of the seven has completed its day of activity, has produced its inevitable effects, it withdraws to give place to its sibling, who is the second in the succession.

> And God said, Let there be a firmament in the midst of the waters, and let it divide the waters from the waters. *(Gen. 1:6)*

In this verse the defining and insulating process is carried out in primordial substance, symbolized by waters, as earlier it has been carried out in primordial thought. The waters which were under the firmament, which represents the manifested visible universe, were divided from the waters which were above the firmament, meaning the invisible, superphysical planes of nature.

The term "firmament" (literally a rarifying) here refers to the enveloping shell or membrane in which the fetal physical universe is enclosed, and which separates substance without from substance within.

> And God made the firmament, and divided the waters which were under the firmament from the waters which were above the firmament: and it was so.
> And God called the firmament Heaven. And the evening and the morning were the second day. *(Gen. 1:7–8)*

The first verse allegorically describes the establishment of the membrane by the action of creative thought and will expressed as sound. The further establishment (by means of naming) of the limits of the selected creative area is partly described here in the second verse. This may be likened to the natural process of the hardening into a shell or skin of the outer layer of an enclosing fetal membrane. In universal creative processes this shell is descriptively referred to as a "Ring-pass-not," the outermost edge or limits marked out by the Logos within which its System is to appear, and the frontiers to which awareness is limited. The verse shows that this is part of the activity of the second number or creative Intelligence, while its completion marks the successful fulfillment of that second number's work or "day."

Numbered days and nights therefore have a dual significance. They refer to both the existence and activity of the creative Intelligence connoted by the number, and also to the condition of substance resulting from its completed work throughout the numbered "day" or creative epoch.

2

Nature in All Her Kingdoms

> And God said, Let the waters under the heaven be gathered together
> unto one place and let the dry land appear: and it was so. *(Gen. 1:9)*

In this opening description of the third cycle or "day" of creative
activity, the first of many errors—if I may presume to say so—appears
in the book of Genesis. This consists of the erroneous merging into
one cycle of two distinct processes which are in reality separated from
each other by a vast period of time. Actually, each process occupies
its own complete cycle from morning to evening of a creative "day."
As explained, creative "days" are separated from each other by
"nights."

The original authors, being initiates of the Mysteries of Chaldea,
must have known this truth. The error, therefore, must either be
deliberate in order to conceal from full revelation the then secret
knowledge of septenary cycles and subcycles, or else be a mistake
made by less well-informed or uninitiated authors or translators.
Whatever the explanation, a miscomputation was made and must be
corrected for and by every student of cosmogony.

Manifestation of Primordial Substance

Verse nine introduces the division of intrauniversal water, or primordial substance, into two states—liquid and solid. It also allows
for the establishment in the demiurgic Mind the thought of the mineral
kingdom, followed by the slow process of the embodiment of that
formative thought in appropriately densified substance. This occupies
a complete cycle of "day" and "night."

The intermediate mineral stage between the division of the waters and the fashioning of the plant kingdom is omitted. Furthermore fire is not introduced until the appearance of the sun. This creative act is placed in the fourth "day," mineral and plant having erroneously and impossibly preceded it. The account, therefore, is sadly muddled. The emergence of the plant kingdom should rightly be placed in the cycle which would have followed the establishment of the mineral kingdom.

> And God called the dry land Earth; and the gathering together of the waters called he Seas: and God saw that it was good. *(Gen. 1:10)*

The Earth period or cycle occupied a whole "day," and was the work of one of the seven creative Intelligences. Esoteric cosmogenesis states that the universe within the divine thought became manifest as spiritual fire. Condensation and densification eventually produced the element rather than the solid substance of earth, the noumenon (the unchanging essence from which the phenomenon arises; antithesis of phenomenon – Kant) of the mineral kingdom. Earth and water, meaning the solid and liquid states, then existed at the same time though separated one from the other, and it is to this coexistence that the verse refers. The naming of the two elements signifies their objective manifestation, each at its own individual level. The phrase "and God saw that it was good" refers to the end of the cycle, when the designated work had been brought to its highest pitch for that period.

> And God said, Let the earth bring forth grass, the herb yielding seed, and the fruit tree yielding fruit after his kind, whose seed is in itself, upon the earth: and it was so. *(Gen. 1:11)*

This verse refers to the plant Manvantara or Chain of the Planetary Scheme. As the seed of the whole universe existed in precosmic substance (*Mulaprakriti* – undifferentiated substance), so also do the seeds of all living beings and their natural forms ever potentially exist within the matter of the universe (*Prakriti* – nature or matter, as opposed to Spirit). As this becomes densified through all the stages on the descending arc down to the physical, the living divine seeds are densified also.

According to esoteric philosophy when the element of earth, however tenuous, ultimately comes into objective existence at its atomic level, amongst its atoms are master atoms which comprise the noumena of the physical seeds. When at last the dense, solid condition is reached, the master atoms constitute those seeds from which the first organic growth occurs. The plant kingdom then becomes manifest, occupies a whole cycle, and continues its development in those which follow.

Just as the seed is in the fruit, so all seeds are present within the mother-substance from which everything is born. The statement that each plant yields fruit after its own kind simply refers to the divine order under which manifestation occurs. This order might be described as numerical law, abstract and everlasting, omnipotent and omnipresent, the supreme deific Power or creative Agency. Under this governing law the Elohim carry out their work of making manifest through the seven planes or divisions of matter the primary creative idea or archetype, which is the seed from which the whole universe is evolved.

These Intelligences make manifest the archetype or seed-thought under the absolute rule of numerical law, as we have seen. Though the whole order of the Elohim plays its part in all cycles and in all manifestation, one component order is predominant in each cycle according to its office and function. There are seven in all, and they are indirectly designated by their numbers and their "days" by the authors of Genesis.

> And God said, Let there be lights in the firmament of the heaven to divide the day from the night; and let them be for signs, and for seasons, and for days, and years:
> And let them be for lights in the firmament of the heaven to give light upon the earth: and it was so.
> And God made two great lights; the greater light to rule the day, and the lesser light to rule the night: he made the stars also.
> And God set them in the firmament of the heaven to give light upon the earth,
> And to rule over the day and over the night, and to divide the light from the darkness: and God saw that it was good.
> And the evening and the morning were the fourth day. *(Gen. 1:14–19)*

The making of the first lights — sun, moon and stars — after the passage of three days and three nights and the creation of the plant kingdom (if such was the original statement) is clearly a chronological error. In the earliest available Hebrew original text, the words *shemesh,* "sun," and *iarech,* "moon," are not used. The abstract expression *maoroth,* "sources of enlightenment," is the word employed. This suggests not only sources of physical light, but of mental and spiritual enlightenment also.

The five opening verses of the book of Genesis describe the production and appearance of the first cycle, that of light. This refers to the emergence of the finite from the Absolute, of cosmos from Chaos. The second creation of light referred to in verses fourteen through eighteen alludes to the appearance of suns in individual Solar Systems within the cosmos. Actually Schemes, Chains, and even Rounds are inextricably mixed up in this exoterically imperfect but nevertheless deeply esoteric cosmogony.

The appearance of the physical sun should come first in the account of the manifestation of a single Solar System. The suggestion of a moon to rule the night as the sun rules the day, and the later creation of the stars, is a relic and an adaptation from Chaldean astrometaphysical esotericism. Indeed, this whole account of creation in Genesis is borrowed from Chaldea, where it was taught that sun, moon and stars were the physical bodies of great creative Intelligences of varying evolutionary stature in the esoteric hierarchy of the universe — the *Dhyan Chohans* (the divine Intelligences charged with the supervision of the cosmos) of Hinduism.

Elohim—Creative Intelligences

Thus intimately associated with the physical sun, moon and stars were and are great archangels. In the *Zend-Avesta* — the sacred books of the Parsees — they are referred to as *Amshashpends,* who are none other than types of the Sephiroth or Elohim. The Amshashpends are the seven Planetary Logoi, as well as the creative Hosts who carry out their will. There are six angels or divine Forces, personified as gods, who attend upon *Ahura Mazda* (the personified Deity, the principle of universal Divine Light of the Parsees), considered the synthesis and the seventh of these gods.

These archangels are the true creative Agents who take up their stations and carry out their functions in an ordered succession as the process of the production of the universe continues. It is these Beings who as directive Intelligences preside over Manvantaras or "days."

The verses under consideration describe that synthesis of the elohistic Hosts who is the solar Logos, the spiritual Sun behind the physical orb. At the dawn of Creation the solar Logos, with a physical heart which is the visible sun, assumes the stations, superphysical and physical, at the center of the new Solar System, and through the Elohim rules over all Manvantaras, major and minor. Pralayas alternate with these Manvantaras, and throughout the periods of nonactivity members of a special order of the Elohim are said to contain and preserve within themselves all the seeds of life. Then, in the new cycle, these seeds are delivered to the solar Logos and the Elohim for further evolution. This constitutes part of the deeply esoteric mystery teaching allegorically revealed in the story of Noah and the Ark, and similar Flood legends.

The reference to the stars takes thought beyond a single Solar System, and may perhaps be regarded as indicating that similar processes are occurring universally during *Maha-Manvantara* (the major, total period of universal activity which includes numberless inner cycles, finite and conditioned, or minor periods of Manvantaras [TG]; also the period of the lifetime of a Planet during its seven Rounds [*Occult Glossary*—OG]). The whole of the cosmogony of Genesis, like all esoteric cosmogonies, refers primarily to the noumena or essential nature of universes, Solar Systems, Suns and Planets, as also to the planes and kingdoms of nature. These, as we have already seen, include their ensouling principles, which are made objectively manifest by great creative Intelligences, members of the Hosts of the Logos, the Numbers, the Lords of the Divine Face, the embodiments of formative Powers, Principles and Orders—the Elohim in the fullest meaning of the term.

The physical manifestation or outer appearance of nature in all her kingdoms refers to the material clothing or densified auras of these Mighty Ones. In esoteric cosmogony the true fashioners of universes according to the divine idea are these Beings, "the Fiery Lives" (Beings of the seventh and highest subdivision of the plane of matter, corresponding in the individual with the One Life of the universe, though only on that plane of matter—*The Secret Doctrine* [SD] 1:306, 3:125), major and minor. Their emergence, assumption of office and embarkation upon appropriate activity and function are of the most profound significance. They should be thought of not only as Beings with bodies and auras, but also as centers of power, life, consciousness and law. They, their radiance and their spheres of influence and activity, constitute the ensouling principle of every order of Creation, whether it be a universe, a solar system, a planet, a plane or a kingdom of nature.

In the Elohim, who constitute a vast hierarchy of spiritual Beings— Planetary and Solar Spirits or Dhyan Chohans—the illusion of self-separated existence as experienced by the human pre-initiate has entirely disappeared. An initiate undergoes a phychospirited transformation, attains realization of the oneness of all life and receives ceremonial admission to the greater Mysteries. A new evolutionary stage is reached. They know themselves for what they truly are— component centers of the Power, Life and Consciousness of the one synthesis of all Beings, the supreme directive Intelligence in nature, the Solar Logos. Thus, although referred to as the Hosts of the Logos, we have seen that the Elohim may also be described as a unity, a summation and a synthesis embracing and including all divine Intelligences charged with the supervision of cosmos.

This essential oneness of all spiritual Beings is the heart of esoteric philosophy and the key to all cosmogonies. Universes are the bodies and the auras of resplendent Beings. Humanity is on the evolutionary path, and the universe is the field of this evolution. Cosmological systems are designed in order to teach humanity to know both the current environment and its future activities in it. These activities will be to conceive, build and perfect universes with their suns, planets, planes and kingdoms of nature; for the human being is a pilgrim God and this is his or her destiny.

> And God said, Let the waters bring forth abundantly the moving creature that hath life, and fowl that may fly above the earth in the open firmament of heaven.
> And God created great whales, and every living creature that moveth, which the waters brought forth abundantly, after their kind, and every winged fowl after his kind: and God saw that it was good.
> And God blessed them, saying, Be fruitful, and multiply, and fill the waters in the seas, and let fowl multiply in the earth.
> And the evening and the morning were the fifth day. *(Gen. 1:20–23)*

If restored to a correct chronological position, the emergence of fish, reptiles and, far later, birds from primeval slime would follow the production by nature of her plant kingdom. These verses record this process and, reducing description to an ascetic minimum, affirm the presence of procreative and self-productive powers.

Nature—Living Product of an Infinite Creative Potency

The instruction to be fruitful and multiply is of profound esoteric, as well as natural, significance. Nature is here shown to be what she really is, a self-perpetuating, living, conscious product of an infinite power now made finite. Both universal Spirit and universal substance noumenally and phenomenally possess and contain the fiery energy by which all things are made. This is the true, immanent Logos, omnipresent, all-pervading, inherent in both the Soul and the substance of the universe. When to the order of created things are added beings with the power of free motion, procreation becomes a consciously exercised power. The inherent reproductive capacity attains to conscious self-expression in the first creatures endowed with the power of motion, for movement is an attribute of the life-force. Locked up and held fast in the mineral, it is active there only against immense resistance. The production of molecular and chemical combinations, and therefore substances, within and from the one substance is its sole activity in the mineral kingdom of nature.

In the plant kingdom much freer motion occurs, and therefore far fuller activity. Sentiency as possessed by animals has, however, not yet been attained by the life-force in this mineral phase of its active manifestation. No allegorical command to create is therefore given to the plant kingdom, for no power of conscious response has yet been developed. The first animal forms do possess the power consciously to procreate, and may rightly be thus described in the text as receiving from the creative "Word" a verbal command to exercise it.

> And God said, Let the earth bring forth the living creature after his kind, cattle, and creeping thing, and beast of the earth after his kind: and it was so.
> And God made the beast of the earth after his kind, and cattle after their kind, and every thing that creepeth upon the earth after his kind: and God saw that it was good. *(Gen. 1:24–25)*

The land reptiles and later the mammalia followed the first denizens of water and air. Ultimately, as described in the verses which follow, the most significant event—the appearance of humans—occurs. Nature reaches her highest achievement in the production of human beings.

3

In the Image of God

> And God said, Let us make man in our image, after our likeness: and
> let them have dominion over the fish of the sea, and over the fowl
> of the air, and over the cattle, and over all the earth, and over every
> creeping thing that creepeth upon the earth.
> So God created man in his own image, in the image of God created
> he him; male and female created he them. *(Gen. 1:26–27)*

In verse twenty-six, three statements are made. First, God decides
to make humanity and announces that decision. Second, humanity is
to be made in the likeness of God, the plural pronoun "our" suggesting
that plurality is used by the Deity (Elohim) in reference to Itself, the
totality of Intelligences. Third, humanity (also referred to as "them")
is to have dominion over all preceding orders of creation. Clearly,
as stated, the pronoun "our" refers to Elohim, a plural name which
in English translations erroneously tends to be regarded as singular
and to be used with a singular verb. Note that after using the words
"our image" in verse twenty-six, the statement is made in verse twenty-
seven that Elohim created humanity (*Adam* in Heb.) in "his" own
image, which suggests Elohim as a unity. While this may seem to
be contradictory, it is not so in reality; for all divine attributes, powers
and formative Intelligences are summed up in "Elohim," which makes
a united whole of the active, manifesting God. From this point of
view, at least, both plural and singular attributions are admissible.

Throughout this cosmogony the mental decision of Deity and its
verbal expression are continually put forth as essential to the process
of the emanation and fashioning of a universe. God first conceives
mentally and then expresses vocally the name of whatever is about

19

to be produced. This consigns to allegory the process of creation by sound or the "Word," and personifies the various formative agencies, the Elohim, as one Being. It must always be remembered that the "Creator" is no single Being alone, and the importance of this fact justifies its many repetitions in this volume. Although a totality in unity, God should rather be described as the collective, natural agencies, forces and Intelligences which arise from within and emanate from the Absolute at the dawn of Manvantara. The use of the plural pronouns "us" and "our" in verse twenty-six is therefore highly suggestive, and indeed exact.

Humans—Models of the Totality of Nature

The decision attributed to the Deity to make humanity in "his own image" introduces a profound and fundamental truth concerning humankind—namely that the spiritual, intellectual, psychical and physical nature of humanity is a miniature replica of the whole Order of created beings and things. Humans, according to esoteric philosophy, are models of the totality of nature, containing within themselves the collective aggregate of all that ever has existed, that does at any time exist and that ever will exist throughout the eternity of eternities. This concept is also to be found in Kabbalism, where it is formulated somewhat as follows: Humanity may be regarded as a symbolic transparency through which the secrets of the cosmos may be discerned.

Humanity may also be looked upon as the waist of an hourglass through which passes the sand (creative power) from the upper receptacle—the past—into the lower which represents the future. All must pass through the human kingdom; for potentially all exists within each individual, however great the degree of latency may be in this present epoch and however germinal as yet the possibility of the emanation and formation of future universes and cosmoi. Humanity is a microcosm, a miniature reproduction of the macrocosm, and is therefore rightly said to be made in the image of the Creator. The Chinese philosopher Lao Tzu expressed this in his famous phrase: "The universe is a man on a large scale."

In Genesis humanity, as nature's highest product up to that time, is also stated to have dominion over all earlier creations. At this point it is important to make clear the fact that humanity, said to be conceived and formed in the likeness of God, is not a new and separate production. Humanity preexisted as Monad (the divine Spirit of each human); and as an individual intelligence in human form it is the product of the slow process of the involution and evolution of the radiated ray or "thread" (current of spiritual life-force; a golden thread of continuous life upon which the seed atoms or nuclei of the seven bodies of humanity are "strung" — *A Study in Consciousness*, A. Besant) of Monadic life through elemental, plant and animal kingdoms. There are three premineral kingdoms which are passed through by the radiated Monadic ray on the involutionary or descending arc. Arrival at the mineral kingdom marks the stage of deepest descent into matter. Thereafter the upward or evolutionary arc is entered upon, with the plant kingdom being the next embodiment of the ascending Monadic life. This phase is followed by entry into and passage through the animal, human and superhuman kingdoms. In the elemental, plant, and animal kingdoms, however, the deific potencies locked up and latent in the Monad experience diffuse and diverse manifestation as part of a Group Soul (the preindividualized manifestation of the human Monads when evolving through the mineral, the plant and the animal kingdoms of nature) embodied in many forms.

Nature's greatest miracle takes place when the summit — mental, psychical and physical — of animal development is reached. The Monadic ray is then singly focused — rather like the sun's rays when brought to a point of light beneath a magnifying glass — into one intellectual principle, to constitute a new-formed spiritual Soul, a now-born higher human Self. It is this Monad-Ego, and not the temporary physical personality, which is made in the likeness of its Creator; for it contains within itself the potentialities of the collective agencies and forces — the Elohim — as well as of all from which they emanate and could ever produce.

Such is the immortal, imperishable and eternal human, made in the image of her or his Creator; embodied in vehicles of flesh, emotion and mind; and made manifest in the three grossest densities of substance. As a totality, a unit, a consciousness with infinite potentialities, humanity is indeed greater than all preceding products of nature and in this sense only, I believe, may be said to have dominion over them.

In verse twenty-seven the most fundamental fact concerning humankind is first reiterated, demonstrating its importance in the minds of those inspired sages who discovered and gave to humanity the truths upon which the book of Genesis is founded. This Ageless Wisdom teaches that human as Monad is an infinite manifestation of the deific power, which in humans is as yet largely germinal, although becoming increasingly active. The means by which these latent potentialities in humans become active powers are then indicated. These means partly consist of successive incarnations in male and female bodies on Earth, in and through which the necessary masculine and feminine experience is gained and the dual evolution attained; for the human Monad develops from within itself the attributes of the first divine, creative Pair, the positive and negative potencies, as the result of the interaction of which the universe appears. Separate modes of manifestation—in the opposite sexes—are essential to the development of this threefold capacity inherent in the spiritual Soul of humans. Nature, if her purpose is to be fulfilled, must produce two separate physical organisms with the distinct experiences and functions of man and of woman; for only thus may the twofold expression and development be gained and human evolutionary progress be achieved.

An Initiatory Interpretation

> And God blessed them, and God said unto them, Be fruitful, and multiply, and replenish the earth, and subdue it: and have dominion over the fish of the sea, and over the fowl of the air, and over every living thing that moveth upon the earth. *(Gen. 1:28)*

While the more general significance of this verse is plainly apparent, it can also be interpreted as guidance to those who are passing through advanced phases of evolution. Admittedly no such instruction may have been intended; nevertheless the verse may possibly be thus interpreted in conformity with the method used by the writers of the sacred language of allegory and symbol.

As observed elsewhere in this work, there are two phases of unfoldment of very great importance in the evolution of the human Monad. One of these is its attainment of individual self-existence as the spiritual Soul of a human being, the immortal Self in its vesture of light. The second development occurs much later in human evolution. After a considerable number of incarnations in successive civilizations and nations, realization of spiritual identity with the Logos, and through the Logos with all that lives, begins to be attained. This profoundly affects the outlook of the physical personality. Love for the life in all beings, service to that life in sentient forms, and a reduction of the sense of separated selfhood, eventually to the vanishing point, find expression in the enlightened human. When this phase becomes sufficiently established in both the inner and the outer individualities, a spiritual Teacher guides the neophyte's further development and eventually presents her or him as a candidate for initiation into the still existing greater Mysteries, and for admission to the Great White Brotherhood of initiates and Adepts which exists from eternity to eternity.

One of the several possible interpretations of the scriptures and mythologies of ancient peoples — as previously mentioned — reveals the guidance and training thus received. Since, when applied, these bestow great mental and thaumaturgical powers, they are concealed from the profane by the use of symbolic language. Since the resultant knowledge could be of great value in both the worldly and the spiritual life, digressions from the main textual theme are, as now, occasionally made in order to include it in these volumes.

Reference to Chapter 7 of Volume I of this work will show that in the cipher of the Bible, physical objects, inanimate and animate, and certain key words have a special significance. Among these the Earth itself and the members of the subhuman kingdoms of nature are used to symbolize humanity's more earthy and animal characteristics.

Thus interpreted, this verse may usefully be regarded as direction to the candidate for initiation to subdue her or his lower nature. In this sense the references to the Earth, the sea and its denizens, the air and the birds and to "every living thing that moveth upon the earth" are to the undesirable aspects (earthy and animal-like) of the candidate's purely human characteristics, which it is humanity's task and destiny wholly to transmute into their corresponding higher attributes. This is especially important to the aspirant to the spiritual life who is hastening beyond the normal speed the evolution of the spiritual Self to the stature of the perfect human.

> And God said, Behold I have given you every herb bearing seed, which is upon the face of all the earth, and every tree, in the which is the fruit of a tree yielding seed; to you it shall be for meat. *(Gen. 1:29)*

This verse can be more easily interpreted in a purely physical sense. A statement is made of the ideal food for the human physical body — nature's plan for the nutriment of humankind. Plants are said to be the source of that food, and from this it may be assumed that divergence from the divine plan is fraught with peril to both the Soul and the body of humans. Presumably the danger partly arises from the inevitable infliction of unnecessary pain and the act of killing sentient beings, the animals; for such actions must constitute crimes against that perfect harmony which is a fundamental law of nature. The discord generated by cruelty reacts upon humanity as suffering. When, furthermore, humans disobey the command given in the verse to use as food selected products of the plant kingdom, the severity of the reaction is even greater. One form which this may take is to produce in the human body susceptibility to and suffering from disease.

Thus divine and natural ordinances are given for the well-being of the human physical body and the purity and stainlessness of the human Soul. Departure from these spiritual and physical rules of life may be assumed in large measure to contribute to the sufferings of humanity. To have dominion over the animals does not mean to exploit and oppress them. Rather the verse states the relative positions of humanity and the members of the lower kingdoms on the ladder of evolution.

> And to every beast of the earth, and to every fowl of the air, and to every thing that creepeth upon the earth, wherein there is life, I have given every green herb for meat: and it was so.
> And God saw every thing that he had made, and, behold, it was very good. And the evening and the morning were the sixth day. *(Gen. 1:30-31)*

The first of these two verses further indicates that not only humanity, but also all creatures were originally intended to be plant feeders. Departure by humans from this ordinance may have its place among the factors which changed the face of nature so radically from the original harmony and harmlessness of the Garden of Eden, the primeval world, to the tragic discordance of the post-Eden period. Indeed, it might almost be permissible to see in the increase of meat-eating and of cruelty to animals in more modern times primal causes of the steadily mounting human suffering from disease and war.

The completion of the whole work of Creation in six days is a chronological error. According to esoteric philosophy the total number of major Manvantaras and Pralayas, or successive periods of evolutionary activity and of rest—the "days" and "nights" in Genesis—should be seven. This point is further discussed in the commentary on verse two of the second chapter of Genesis.

4

The Seventh Day

Genesis 2

Having ended the work of Creation, God rested from labor on the seventh day.

In the beginning, before ever a plant grew or rain fell, God fashioned a man from the soil, giving him life. For this man, Adam, God planted a garden, beautiful and lush with fruit trees and all manner of plants. In the center of this garden in Eden grew a tree whose fruit held the key to the knowledge of good and evil. Watered by four great rivers, the garden thrived, and God gave it into the man's keeping, providing all of this for Adam's pleasure. Only the fruit of the tree of knowledge of good and evil was withheld from him.

In time God saw that the man was lonely; so for company God created the animals and birds, and while these were all wonderful, the man was lonely still. Thus, while Adam slept, God removed a rib from him and fashioned it into a woman. When Adam saw her, he was happy at last, for now he had a true companion—she was part of him and he of her. And in happiness they lived in the garden and walked through it unclothed, in unashamed innocence.

Thus the heavens and the earth were finished, and all the host of them. And on the seventh day God ended his work which he had made; and
    he rested on the seventh day from all his work which he had made.
    (Gen. 2:1–2)

In esoteric cosmogony the completion of the process of objective manifestation or "creation" is achieved only at the end of the seventh cycle (in Genesis called "day"), whether major or minor. The seventh day, the end of the cycle of manifestation, is therefore by no means a day of rest throughout the cosmos. Rather it is the day of culmination, of highest activity, in which all that was initiated on the first day is brought to its greatest possible development, expression and function within the major time-period, or at the end of the seventh day. The full period occupies seven cycles, not six.

The "day" on which God rested refers to the culmination or exhaustion in the dynamic sense, the completed outworking of the original creative impulse. The perfect manifestation of original ideation within a given period has by then been achieved. Thereafter, the whole impulse to produce dies down, having fulfilled itself, and this dying down and reduction of activity to a minimum, followed by its complete cessation, is thus the true meaning of the words "he rested."

At the end of the seventh day all nature sleeps—as in the depth of winter—to awaken no more within the duration of the major cycle. Cosmos fades gradually back into Chaos. Substances or elements return to their primordial Source, which is the one maternal root Substance, the eternal Mother from whom all are born. Evening descends upon the vast cosmic field, to be followed by that final "night" into which the whole Creation descends. Finiteness disappears. Infinity once more prevails. The end of the first chapter of Genesis and the first verse of the second chapter might more correctly be regarded as descriptive of this close of the sevenfold period of activity, which begins with the first dawn of the first "day" and ends with the close of the seventh and the oncoming of "night."

All is then withdrawn into a latent, germinal condition, there to rest in quiescence until the opening of the succeeding epoch or new "day." Thereafter, the whole process will be repeated but with a greater fullness, since the condition at the beginning of the new cycle will be that which obtained at the end of the preceding one.

The Pathways of Forthgoing and Return

As, when once begun, the swing of a pendulum continues, so the succession of cycles and subcycles, once initiated by an impulse arising from within the One Alone, continues according to law as long as that impulse is maintained. When this is no longer given, the swing continues through a decreasing arc until at last the pendulum returns to its preceding motionless state. So also does the cycle-governed cosmos emerge from and return to quiescence, to Chaos, which means root-substance in an equipolarized state, unchanged and therefore at rest. This is the abyss, the great deep—upon which, at the dawn of Manvantara, the great breath is again breathed forth to initiate a new period of creative activity.

> And God blessed the seventh day, and sanctified it because that in it
> he had rested from all his work which God created and made. *(Gen.
> 2:3)*

The third verse may be more literally, if less clearly, translated: "And Elohim blessed the seventh day and hallowed it (blessed in Heb., *ikaddesh,* also means hallowed, consecrated, set apart, dedicated to God), because in it He returned from all His work, which He, the Elohim, had created in order to make." The word "Sabbath" here can literally mean "the returning," and the "seventh day," "the day of full realization." Thus Genesis states that Elohim came forth from the unknown eternal One in order to make the One manifest, knowable through the process of Creation. Having finished the creative work of the eternal One, Elohim returned to the divine unity, the universal Sabbath.

> These are the generations of the heavens and of the earth when they
> were created, in the day that the Lord God made the earth and the
> heavens,
> And every plant of the field before it was in the earth, and every herb
> of the field before it grew: for the Lord God had not caused it to
> rain upon the earth, and there was not a man to till the ground.
> But there went up a mist from the earth, and watered the whole face
> of the ground. *(Gen. 2:4–6)*

The second chapter of Genesis at this point recapitulates the description of certain of the processes of Creation. The first chapter, as I have said, describes the emergence of cosmos from Chaos, form from the eternal formless, and reveals creative principles which apply not only to the Earth and its Solar System, but to all cosmoi; for the basic laws of manifestation and the ordered emergence and development of the successive phases and their evolutionary products do not change. Even though those products ascend to ever higher, more spiritual and more powerful manifestations, the underlying laws are the same. The second chapter, however, deals with a single unit such as a Solar System, a Planetary Scheme, a Chain, a Round or a Globe within the larger universe.

In the main, though not entirely, the processes of condensation, solidification to the mineral level, and the successive emergence of plant, animal and humans upon this planet are described. The presence of the seeds of living things in a latent condition is indicated in the fifth verse, and this may be taken to refer to their primary existence in both divine thought and universal precosmic substance.

> And the Lord God formed man of the dust of the ground, and breathed into his nostrils the breath of life; and man became a living soul. *(Gen. 2:7)*

"Man" in Hebrew is *Adam*. Esoterically, the first letter, *a,* denotes anything primal, the first cause, potential power, Deity. The letter *d* is the sign of multiplication and abundance, and the final *m* is one of unlimited plurality. "Man" is "the spiritual One becoming the material Many, the human principle, the essence of humanity." Dust may be regarded as "the refinement of matter, light, airy." "Breath" in Hebrew can be translated as *nishemath,* "to elevate, to ennoble, being raised to a higher state, becoming an individual human soul."

Verse seven in its literal reading is deceptive, for it somewhat suggests the theory of special creation, which runs counter to that of the cyclic emanation, involution and evolution of all beings and all things, both material and spiritual. Esoterically, however, the order of evolution is not incorrect. The first chapter of Genesis gives the history of the first three Rounds of the present Fourth Chain of Globes, and of the first three Races (types of evolving beings) on Earth in the Fourth Round (see Volume I for an explanation of the meaning of Rounds and Globes), when humanity had already attained conscious life. In the first chapter of Genesis—which deals with the earlier Rounds— animals, fishes and birds are correctly placed before humans, while in the second chapter, which continues the story, humanity is correctly introduced first.

Since evolution is a fact, this verse, in both its exoteric and esoteric readings, may be taken to describe the passage of the human Monad through the mineral (dust), the plant and the animal kingdoms (life), to the attainment of self-conscious individuality or Soulship (humanity). The word "dust" as shown above is somewhat misleading, since the original *aphar* (Heb.) is the present participle of a verb meaning "the process of refining." The threefold nature of humanity—material, psychical and spiritual—is thus described, and especially the fact of humanity's distinguishing characteristic of self-conscious individuality. The breath of life breathed into Adam, the "man of dust," is the nascent, reasoning Soul which in the animal is instinctual only.

> And the Lord God planted a garden eastward in Eden; and there he put the man whom he had formed.
> And out of the ground made the Lord God to grow every tree that is pleasant to the sight, and good for food; the tree of life also in the midst of the garden, and the tree of knowledge of good and evil.
> And a river went out of Eden to water the garden; and from thence it was parted, and became into four heads. *(Gen. 2:8-10)*

The two trees planted in Eden can hardly have been material objects growing in material earth. Rather the words refer to spiritual trees with spiritual qualities—a tree of life and a tree of knowledge of good and evil. More properly they are to be regarded as archetypes or models according to which the material universe emanated and is evolving.

River is *nahar* in Hebrew, "a stream-like movement or current of the life force," and water is *hishekah,* "to make fertile, productive and capable of sustaining life." Thus the original, outflowing life-force is divided into four individual streams, each with its own characteristics. These are less branches or tributaries than starting points for creative activity occurring in their quarter or region of the universe. In verse eight the garden is made to be not the garden *of* Eden, but *in* Eden— apparently a contradiction. Eden, however, is less a location in the physical world than a sphere of activity, an enclosed state of existence within the realm of universal time and space. In this sense, therefore, no contradiction occurs.

The Creation of Man and Woman

> And the Lord God caused a deep sleep to fall upon Adam, and he slept: and he took one of his ribs, and closed up the flesh instead thereof;
> And the rib, which the Lord God had taken from man, made he a woman, and brought her unto the man.
> And Adam said, This is now bone of my bones, and flesh of my flesh: she shall be called Woman, because she was taken out of Man. *(Gen. 2:21-23)*

Adam was first "formed" as a spiritual unity, not physically incarnated (see Gen. 2:7—formed is *iitzer* in Heb.; "[God] gave permanent and homogeneous form to Adam as an individual spiritual entity").

Genesis now proceeds to describe the creation and the evolution of humanity, the second chapter being partly concerned with the change produced in the physical body by evolutionary processes. The first human form, typified by Adam, was androgynous. Gradually, however, as the cycle progressed in which the human form was developed and the masculine-feminine spiritual Soul entered into closer association with that form, a change began to occur. Out of the androgynous organism the single-sexed, separate man and woman of today developed. Adam ("man") alone in the Garden of Eden personifies the first sexually innocent humanity, while Adam and Eve together typify the first separated men and women. The production of Eve from the side and out of a rib of Adam while he slept is an allegorical description of this process.

These verses of Genesis embody the description of both the psychical condition and the bodily development of primitive humanity. Androgynous, Adam was pure—unconscious of sex and innocent of passion. This condition of human purity and innocence is symbolized by the Garden of Eden itself, the state of the soul before the awakening and activity of consciously exercised procreative power. Eden therefore describes the childhood of humanity, and also of every human being up to the stage of puberty.

The expulsion from Eden portrayed in the third chapter of Genesis [see Chapter 5] is an allegory of the passage of every human being through adolescence into adult life. The process, being perfectly natural, involves no sin of either Soul or body, whether for the whole human race or for the individual. In terms of consciousness the story describes the precreative and the procreative stages of human development. Related to physical development the account refers to the evolutionary change from androgyny to reproduction between male and female, with the consequent experience of sexual desire and the expression of procreative power.

Eve Produced from Adam's Rib

As previously mentioned, the formation of Eve from a rib of Adam while he slept in the Garden of Eden is also entirely allegorical. His deep sleep refers to both the nascent mentality and the unawakened, inactive procreative power. Supine and unconscious upon the ground, Adam aptly represents the human race at the first period of the encasement of the Monad in human form. Newly enclosed in dense matter, the first human was "of the earth, earthy." The task was to become accustomed to imprisonment within relatively inert physical substance and gradually to overcome its existence. These first human bodies were gigantic ("there were giants in the earth in those days" – Gen. 6:4; this is also supported by both anthropology and esoteric tradition), with a minimum of nervous organization and activity. Sluggishly and clumsily they moved through tropical vegetation, impelled only by the desire for food and the instinct for self-preservation. The mental torpor of primitive humanity is typified by Adam in deep sleep in the Garden of Eden.

The life-force was present, however, and active within the first physical humans, even though unrecognized. Very gradually a change, both physical and psychical, began to occur. Physically, one sexual faculty began to predominate over the other. Psychically, awareness of opposite polarity was experienced, as either the positive or the negative currents in the life-force became predominant in individuals. These two processes brought an end to the androgynous era and culminated in the establishment upon this planet of separate male and female forms. Since these evolved out of progenitors who up to now had contained the attributes of both sexes, the description of the formation of Eve from the side (rib) of Adam is appropriate as an allegory. The biological fact that as an embryo both sexes contain tissues that could develop into either sex lends support to this theory of human evolution.

The reference to the rib of Adam may also be interpreted as an indication that the procedure of the descent of the Monadic ray into denser and denser forms had culminated in incarnation in solid material bodies. This involved the production by nature of a supporting bony structure, of which the rib of Adam may be taken as a representation. In esoteric anthropology this is said to have occurred in the third sub-race of the Third Root Race (the Lemurian) of the Seven Root Race of humanity (SD). The reference to Adam's rib as the basic substance from which Eve was formed is deeply esoteric. One possible interpretation, tentively advanced, is that the spinal column adn a projecting rib together form a right angle or square. This equal-armed cross has ever been the symbol of the union of desending, positive, fructying Spirit (the vertical) entering negative, receptive, gestatory and all-producing matter (the horizontal). All creation occurs as a result of this process is symbolized by both the cross and the square. In the human skeleton the spinal column and each rib form a right angle. Eve, being feminine, is appropriately formed out of the horizontal arm of this cross.

Thus interpreted, the allegory reveals that as a result of universal processes, the previously combined dual polarity of the life-force was separated into two distinct manifestations. These produced in both the psychical and physical worlds oppositely polarized man and woman. God, as the triune Creator of both Adam and Eve, may therefore be regarded as universal Law and Life acting under the direction of universal Intelligence. As we have seen, this last becomes manifest as—and active in—the hosts of Intelligences, the Elohim, ceaselessly at work throughout the whole of cosmos as builders of forms, directors of consciousness into them, and quickeners of evolutionary development. These builders and their function of inducting the Monads of humans into mortal, material bodies are also personified by the "old serpent" (Rev. 12:9 and 20:2), the Devil in the Garden of Eden. In esoteric philosophy they are referred to as "the Satanic Hierarchy" (see Hodson, *The Kingdom of the Gods,* Part Three, Chapter 5). [See also Hodson *Devas and Men,* Chapter 9, and scattered references in *The Secret Doctrine* for more information about this concept.] Satan's co-partnership with God is suggested by the fact that apart from God, Satan as the Devil is the only recorded visitant to the Garden of Eden before the Fall. The serpent, the Devil and the Satanic Hierarchy are discussed further in Chapter 5.

5

The Expulsion from Eden

Genesis 3

The serpent was a crafty animal who set out to deceive the woman about the forbidden tree of the knowledge of good and evil. Eve was exhorted by the serpent to take the fruit and eat it, saying, "You shall be as gods, knowing good and evil."

The fruit of the tree was pleasing to the eye, and the woman could not resist it. She ate of the fruit and gave some to Adam as well. Having eaten, they beheld their nakedness and made themselves garments of leaves.

In time Adam and Eve heard the Lord God walking through the garden, and they hid themselves. The Lord God called for Adam, but he replied that he was hidden because he was naked. Then God knew that they had eaten of the forbidden tree, and in questioning them learned of the serpent's deceit. Because of this deceit the Lord God cursed the serpent above all animals, condemning it to crawl from place to place. In sadness God then turned to Adam and Eve: for her sin Eve was to have great pain in childbirth, and was also to be ruled over by Adam. Adam's sin caused God to curse the ground—no longer were man and woman to live by the fruit of the garden, and Adam was condemned to plow and plant in the barren ground.

As the final penalty for their sin, Adam and Eve were banished from the garden, never to return—for the Lord God placed at the gate angels and a sword of fire "which turned every way, to keep the way of the tree of life."

Note: *Many of the ideas presented in this chapter are drawn from* The Secret Doctrine *of H. P. Blavatsky, which in its turn consists largely of commentaries on an ancient esoteric work entitled* The Stanzas of Dzyan. *Other similar works have also been consulted. Since these ideas may be strange and new to many Western readers, and are in themselves rather abstruse, pains have been taken to present them from several points of view.*

The third chapter of Genesis relates allegorically the inevitable defilement of the Monad-Egos resulting from both their immersion in the matter of the worlds below them and the conscious exercise in their physical bodies of their power to procreate. The final phases of the pathway of forthgoing are described here. The physical plane has been reached by the divine pilgrim, with the densest of the seven bodies of humans having been assumed. (These bodies are constructed of matter of seven successive degrees of density — the physical, the etheric, the astral or emotional, the lower mental, the higher mental or Causal, the intuitional or Buddhi and the most spiritual, the Monad-Atma.) Bone, flesh, blood and the nervous systems constitute the tomb in which spiritual Will, Wisdom and Intelligence respectively are buried. The nerves, dull in the primitive, sensitized in the saint, are the doorways and windows through which intellect, at first confined, eventually achieves freedom.

The phrase "the Lord God" used in this chapter of Genesis here must be interpreted to include nature herself, the involutionary pressure and all the hosts of Intelligences (Elohim) associated with the forthgoing life-wave bearing its Monadic seeds towards physical incarnation. Actually it is these very agencies which bring about the purported Fall of humanity. Spiritually regarded, these Intelligences are indeed divine and so are correctly referred to as "the Lord God." Looked at from below, as forces bringing about the encasement of the human Monad in limiting forms subject to separateness and sensuality, these self-same agencies can appear devilish, and have therefore been branded as satanic.

The Doctrine of Original Sin

The orthodox doctrine of the "Fall" of humanity as a result of the "sinning" of Adam and Eve in the Garden of Eden (eating of the fruit of the tree of knowledge of good and evil) is not in accord with the teachings of the Ageless Wisdom. The Fall simply refers to the descent of human Monads into physical bodies and the consequent exercise of the natural procreative power in those bodies. As will be more fully expounded later, in principle not the slightest sin was committed by early humanity—nor has it ever been since then—when the process designed by nature for the preservation and development of the human species was exercised. Admittedly, sexuality can be abused, and this can lead to despiritualization, degradation and disease, but this fault cannot justly be attributed to the first humans on Earth nor can it be charged against nature's processes, which are neither pure nor impure, but impersonal and natural. When transmuted to spiritual and intellectual creativity, procreative power can inspire genius, and with further development can endow an esoteric sage with superhuman capacities.

The Temptation by the Devil

The Devil in Eden, by whose machinations Eve and then Adam partook of the fruit of the tree of knowledge of good and evil, plays so significant a role in the great human drama which the Bible unfolds that a digression from the main theme of this chapter of Genesis is useful here.

Who and what then is meant by the Devil? In esoteric philosophy Satan is regarded as a personification of a synthesis of a number of formative forces, processes and Intelligences. The Devil is also a personification of differentiated matter, its inherent life-force, and their combined influence upon human personality. If Spirit and matter are regarded as the positive and negative poles respectively of one energy imbued with intelligence, then their mutual approach will tend to generate electromagnetic attraction, thus awakening into activity the creative fire in both. Matter leads in this awakening and so may be said to lure Spirit into material self-expression. Allegorically, Eve, symbol of universal substance, both answers to the play of the life-force within her substance (the Devil) and tempts and seduces Adam (Spirit).

The Devil—Personification of the Influence of Matter upon Spirit

In this chapter of Genesis the serpent, *na-hash* in Hebrew, stands for "the activity of the basic element of the human personality, namely selfhood." It is a symbol of an inward life principle inherent in every human being, the amoral activity of the self-consciousness of which Adam now becomes aware. Made prominent, the serpent represents more especially the intellectual principle. This is nascent in primitive humanity, but fully awake in those members of the Elohim who, as we have seen, undertake to bring the Monad into a mental vehicle and introduce it to individualized, self-conscious mental life. Resistance to the command of God, and personal action at variance with that command, refer to the attainment of individualized self-thought and self-will.

The actual tempting power, also symbolized by both the serpent itself and its influence, is threefold. It consists first of the felicity experienced by the mind at the temporary union of opposite polarities in man and woman; for this produces in each of the pair an impression of return to the unipolarized condition characteristic of Monadic consciousness. Second, emotional happiness is felt in the expression of love and the fulfillment of desire. Third, the exercise physically of the procreative power induces pleasurable sensation. This threefold experience—mental, emotional and physical—of the action of the creative fire in nature and in humans is the triple lure which, as said, the Satanic Hierarchy of ministers of the solar Logos or "Word" (see John 1:1) employs to induce human Monad-Egos to enter upon the human phase of existence.

Even though thus assisted, the whole process of descent is a perfectly natural one. For a period it does bring suffering, degradation and shame, but it cannot be truthfully described as a tragic Fall. This dogma of original sin appears to have arisen from texts in both the Old and the New Testaments—Gen. 3:6, Ps. 51:5, Isa. 43:27, Rom. 3:9,10,23 and 5:12 and Gal. 3:22. The thirty-nine Articles of Religion of the Anglican Communion state the dogma in the following words:

IX. OF ORIGINAL OR BIRTH-SIN

Original Sin . . . is the fault and corruption of the Nature of every man, that naturally is engendered of the offspring of Adam; whereby man is very far gone from original righteousness, and is of his own nature inclined to evil, so that the flesh lusteth always contrary to the spirit; and therefore in every person born into this world, it deserveth God's wrath and damnation. And this infection of nature doth remain, yea in them that are regenerated; whereby the lust of the flesh, called in Greek, *phronema sarkos* (which some do expound the wisdom, some sensuality, some the affection, some the desire, of the flesh), is not subject to the Law of God. . . .

X. OF FREE-WILL

The condition of Man after the fall of Adam is such, that he cannot turn and prepare himself, by his own natural strength and good works, to faith, and calling upon God: Wherefore we have no power to do good works pleasant and acceptable to God, without the grace of God by Christ preventing us, that we may have that good will, and working with us, when we have that good will.

The views of this body stated here and similar views in other denominations are hardly acceptable to the student of esoteric philosophy; for the supposed original sin is instead regarded as an inevitable concomitant of the involutionary process, and not as a deliberately committed wickedness for which every human being has ever since been condemned to be born in sin. The stain will be left behind and the fruitage will be preserved in the form of full knowledge of, and capacity to wield, the mightiest of all the powers in nature and in humans — the divine power to create universes and all that they contain. The pains of apprenticeship must be endured by the Monad-Ego in the personality before the state of the master builder can be attained.

Eliphas Levi writes in *The History of Magic* (p. 192):

According to the Kabbalists, the true name of Satan is that of Jehovah reversed, for Satan is not a black god but the negation of the Deity. He is the personification of atheism and idolatry. The Devil is not a personality for initiates, but a force created with a good object, though it can be applied to evil: it is really the instrument of liberty.

The Satanic Hierarchy

On the completion of its involutionary and evolutionary passage through the subhuman kingdoms, the Monad attains one of its primary objectives, which is to become a member of the human kingdom of nature. This process is referred to in esoteric philosophy as individualization. It results in the incarnation of a ray of the Monad within a vesture constructed of matter of that realm of nature and level of consciousness at which humans are able to conceive of abstractions and to comprehend underlying principles and laws. This new-formed individuality is referred to as the human Ego. Such Egohood implies the development of the faculty of self-conscious thought, and self-realization as a separate entity. As this phase is entered upon, the function of the Elohim consists of the encasement of the Monad in a mental body. As has already been observed, the resultant acutely separative sense of individuality, or I-am-ness, with its inevitable concomitants of acquisitiveness, pride, egoism and selfishness, is also personified by the Devil.

The work of another order of the purported Satanic Hierarchy is to induct the human Monad-Ego into a vehicle of emotion in which sexual desire can be experienced. The process of descent thereafter culminates in incarnation in physical, "dust-formed" bodies through which the sex impulse can achieve self-conscious expression. The universal life-force, the fire of creation, then finds individual manifestation as human love, desire and procreative activity. Satan is thus seen as a composite personification of matter and of its resistance to Spirit, a hierarchy of Intelligences, and certain creative impulses active within humankind.

The serpentine form of the symbol of the Devil is also deeply significant; for the characteristic mode of manifestation and manner of expression of the generative power in both nature and in humans is undulatory or serpentine. This allurement of the Spirit of humans from primal innocence to sexual experience, and this undulatory current in which the life-force is expressed, are aptly described in the allegory of the temptation of Eve and Adam by the serpent in the Garden of Eden and their subsequent Fall. This deeply esoteric knowledge could be both incomprehensible and potentially dangerous: hence, doubtless, its heavy enveiling in such intricate symbology encompassed by the esoteric concept of kundalini.

The Universal Tree of Life

The Garden of Eden, Adam, Eve, the serpent, the tree, its fruit and the eating of it can be variously interpreted. The tree of knowledge of good and evil (leaving aside its ten Sephirothal implications—see *The Kingdom of the Gods,* Part Three, Chapter 4) growing in the midst of the Garden, with its fruit—proscribed as food—unlike that of the fruit of all the other trees, is the age-old and universal symbol for the intelligence-imbued life-force of the universe. The roots of this divine tree arise from within the substance of precosmic space and draw their sustenance from it. Within every atom of matter of every grade of density, and within every molecular combination, both inorganic and organic, the life-force is present as a component energy. This is symbolized as the sap absorbed by the far-spreading, source-tapping roots of the tree of life. It is the atom-forming, universally manifest, creative energy known in esoteric science as cosmic electricity – primordial Fohat or divine energy and vital force, the primary atomic product of which is the *Mahatattva* or the first differentiation of precosmic space.

Diagrammatically this tree grows downwards with its roots in the heavens or precosmic and cosmic space, *Mulaprakriti* (undifferentiated substance) or *Parabrahman* (the impersonal, nameless, universal and eternal Principle). The trunk of the tree represents the same divine generative power focused into an individualized current. In nature, the macrocosm, it is the specialized life-force of any unit or sub-unit, such as Solar Systems, Planetary Scheme, Chains, Rounds, Globes (in esoteric philosophy a Solar System is said to consist of ten Planetary Schemes, each Scheme is composed of seven Chains of Globes, a Round is one passage of the life-wave around the Globes, and a Chain is seven such passages), and the kingdoms of nature with their species. To each of these there is apportioned an appropriate current of creative life.

In *The Secret Wisdom of the Qabalah* (pp. 72–73), Fuller writes – and I fully concur:

> To the student of the occult it will be apparent that these two trees [the tree of knowledge of good and evil and the tree of life] closely resemble the letter *Shin,* also the caduceus of Hermes with its central rod and its two entwined serpents, and also the Ida, Pingala, and central Sushumna of Hindu Yoga. The whole scheme is symbolized in the Temple of Solomon, the temple itself being the central pillar, whilst its two pylons, Yakhin and Boaz, the white and the black, the right and the left, represent the Tree of Knowledge of Good and Evil – the eternal complementary forces in life without which nothing can be. This symbolism is an excessively ancient one; thus, in the Norse Mythology we find the mystic tree Yggdrasil, the roots of which are in the material world and the branches of which reach up to Asgard, the happy dwelling of the gods. Again, amongst the Akkadians, Chaldeans, and Babylonians we find the World Tree, or Tree of Life, which "stood midway between the Deep and Zikum" – the primordial heaven above. In Hindu mythology there is also a World Tree – the Lingam – and in Buddhist the Bodhi Tree, or Tree of Wisdom under which Buddha sat in meditation.

When the symbol of the tree is used by the allegorists who composed the scriptures and mythologies of the world, the serpent is frequently associated with it. The glyph then consists of the tree of life with a serpent or dragon as guardian, as the Argonauts found at Colchis when searching for the Golden Fleece and Hercules in the garden of the Hesperides, where he sought the golden apples.

In Eden the man and the woman complete the representation of the opposite polarities of the electric, fohatic energy. The tree is also a symbol of esoteric wisdom, the assimilation of which (allegorically described as eating the fruit) indeed makes humanity even as a God. Inversely, the misuse of the resultant power can lead to degradation, and as stated above, this may be one reason for God's command to the first pair that they should not eat of the fruit of the tree of life. In Kabbalism the tree of life is a composite symbol of the entire macrocosm and microcosm. When interpreted, this symbol reveals the whole cosmogonical process and also the relationship between the universe and humanity. The ten Sephiroth, or emanations concerned with phases of involution and evolution, are represented by circles arranged in a geometric design upon the kabbalistic tree of life. The Garden of Eden with all of its contents thus has many interpretations.

In the cosmic sense the Garden of Eden describes the condition of potential fruitfulness and productiveness of the combined primordial Spirit-matter. Eve represents original cosmic substance and Adam primordial creative Spirit, while the tree of life symbolizes the generative current which passes between this pair. The Fall describes the involutionary process, while the Deity and the Devil represent Spirit and matter respectively—the converse and obverse sides of nature.

The Human Tree of Life

The trunk of the tree, in the microcosmic sense, is represented by the spinal column and cord. The spreading branches are the afferent and efferent nerves in the body; the flowers represent the force centers or chakras in the etheric and superphysical bodies, together with their associated nerve centers and glands in the physical body.

In humans the fruits of the tree of knowledge of good and evil are at least twofold. As previously suggested, they consist of the natural products of the evolutionary process, and also of the capacity of an esotericist to use and express the primeval and manifested life principle at any level of consciousness and through any chakra or organ. In nature the fruit represents the varied life-imbued forms which she, with such prodigality, ever continues to produce.

When humans consciously express the generative power in procreation, they symbolically partake of the fruit of the tree of knowledge of good and evil. The statement that Adam was forbidden to do so by the Deity on pain of death on the same day (Gen. 2:17)—a false prophecy, since this did not occur—may be regarded as a cover or blind concealing from the profane a deep esoteric wisdom. This concerns the existence, the source, the nature and the uses—lowest and highest—of the creative life-force by humankind.

> But of the fruit of the tree which is in the midst of the garden, God
> hath said, Ye shall not eat of it, neither shall ye touch it, lest ye
> die. *(Gen. 3:3)*

The terms "death" and "to die" have a particular significance in the symbolic language. Death can refer to spiritual deadness, a state of becoming cut off from or dead to spiritual awareness and power. In this sense the words "death" and "die" do not connote the finality ordinarily attributed to physical death, but refer only to a temporary loss of the illumination and the wisdom of the higher Self. Such a reading is somewhat supported by the fact that sexual excess can produce this mental loss, which will remain as long as the error is continued. If, therefore, the fruit of the tree of knowledge of good and evil is in part the power to procreate, and the danger of death in the above sense exists because of the despiritualizing effect of excess, then the word "die" in Genesis 3:3 may also be regarded as a veiled reference to the fact that excesses can produce such a deadening result.

The Transmutation of the Procreative Power

Adam alone in the Garden of Eden personifies, as we have seen, the passion-free state of the first physical humans on Earth who were androgynous. This innocent condition of the early humans exists in all humanity from the time of birth to the dawn of puberty. The Garden of Eden itself with its totality of created things—plant, animal and human—together with the indwelling Divine Presence, in one interpretation may also be regarded as a symbol of the physical body of humans. Adam and Eve would then represent the oppositely polarized, creative energies, while the tree of life symbolizes the spinal cord and brain.

In terms of outpoured, formative energy, the tree in the midst of the Garden of Eden is thus emblematic of the triple current of the ever-present electrical energy which plays along the center of the spinal cord, symbolized by the trunk. In procreation that force plays downwards into the generative organs. When sublimated and consciously directed by spiritually awakened humans, it flows upwards into the brain and from there onwards to the solar Source. When by the action of the will this transmutation is successfully achieved, the brain cells and organs become highly sensitized to superphysical forces and states of awareness. This makes possible, in full waking consciousness, realization of unity with the Source of all life, the solar Deity.

One of the secrets of initiation (every initiate being symbolically "raised" from a figurative death) concerns the process of this redirection and sublimation of the life-force in humans, success in which makes the initiate immortal and even "as a God." Since that mighty power thus transmuted can be used constructively or destructively, the secret of its nature, control and use is closely guarded within the sanctuaries of the greater Mysteries. Whenever referred to in literature which will become available to the general public, the knowledge is invariably revealed—and thereby concealed—in an allegorical and symbolical manner, as in the myth of the Garden of Eden. The supposed command of the Lord, "Ye shall not eat of it, neither shall ye touch it, lest ye die" (quite obviously impossible to be fulfilled with regard to the human race), in one of its meanings may be regarded as an example of the method by which the secrecy has been preserved.

The puberty of humankind, like individual puberty, causes allegorical expulsion from Eden, which is regained when the pure innocence of childhood becomes the conscious purity of spiritualized humanity. Between the innocence of Eden and full redemption or ascension into Adeptship, humanity passes through a period of bondage in captivity— subservience to materialism, selfishness and sensuality—the phase with which the Old Testament is partly concerned. Additional examples can be found in the bondage of the Israelites in Egypt, the descent of Joseph into the pit and the imprisonment of Samson.

Serpent and Tree as Symbols of Creative Power

The tree of life also symbolizes both the creative and inventive capacity of the human intellect and a responsive condition of matter, these being characteristic of an advanced phase of evolution. The life-force active in the human mind, which thus enfired becomes imbued with the generative impulse, is symbolized by the sap of the tree of life. In this interpretation the serpent is the fohatic force itself, and the tree of life is human consciousness and its vehicles in which that force is active. Together they constitute creative power, macrocosmic and microcosmic. The serpent by itself is emblematic of the undulatory, fohatic, triply polarized formative force in the cosmos, in a universe, in all nature and in every vehicle of human beings. The tree of life is Spirit-impregnated substance, fructified matter, forming the vehicles of any being at any level from a Logos to an amoeba, charged as that matter is with the universal, propellant, vital force.

When inactive the neutral current by itself—the trunk of the tree—represents the latent Divine Presence. When active the positive and negative serpentine currents of the serpent fire (kundalini) are present and in operation. As previously stated, the symbols for this energized condition are the serpent and the tree. Sometimes a single serpent is coiled round the trunk of the tree, while at other times two are present, one on either side of the tree.

The expulsion of Adam and Eve from the Garden as punishment for their supposed "sin" of marital union has other possible meanings. After the exercise of the procreative function, not only is innocence or the Edenic condition lost or closed to Adam and Eve (representing humankind), but the life-force itself becomes temporarily inactive. In this sense the first parents are away from Eden as a state of consciousness, while for the time being their vehicles are no longer empowered by the fiery force. Symbolically and allegorically they are expelled by God, who in this case partly represents natural law. The term "God" may also be taken to refer to the solar Deity, who is the source of the promethean fire which endows nature and humanity with generative potency. It is this divine power that sends humankind forth from the presence of God in Eden, meaning only from the condition of pristine purity, into the evolutionary field for purposes of self-unfoldment and the physical population of a universe.

In the fourth and successive chapters of Genesis the children, the grandchildren and subsequent descendants of Adam and Eve may be regarded as personifying successive sub-races of the Lemurian or Third Root Race, which was the first group of physical, embodied humans on Earth.

The members of the order of angels known as the Cherubim, which were placed at the east of the garden of Eden "to keep the way of the tree of life," represent a hierarchy of the Elohim associated with the positive currents of the life-force. Kabbalistically the Cherubim are pictured as sphinxes and regarded as governors of the four elements in their highest sublimation. They appear to correspond to the *Lipika,* the celestial recorders or scribes, the agents of karma of Hinduism. The hierarchy is concerned with the initiation of the whirling motions by means of which primordial atoms or "holes in space" are formed, presumably using the force which is *Fohat* in Tibetan. This is the essence of cosmic electricity, the ever-present electrical energy and ceaseless formative and destructive power in the universe, the propelling, vital force whose symbol is the *svastika* [an ancient eastern or Native American glyph, with arms that rotate counterclockwise – the arms of the Nazi symbol rotate clockwise]. In Kether ("The Crown," the first Sephira or emanation of Deity of the kabbalistic sephirothal tree which gives birth to the nine others) are thus said to be the beginnings of the whirls, the first stirrings of the divine creative essence. One of the chief duties of the members of this angelic hierarchy is to receive this essence in Kether and carry it to the succeeding hierarchy, the Auphanim or "Wheels," associated with the second Sephira.

At the beginning of creation – according to esoteric philosophy – Fohat, which arises within the central source of life, is directed outward into space upon the involutionary arc, the path of forthgoing of Spirit-light into matter. The consciousness of the Monads follows this fohatic path of forthgoing, being carried by a form of electrical induction outward from the plane of *Adi* (the primeval, the subtlest of the seven planes of nature; Kether) towards the physical world. On arrival there God, allegorically speaking, "made coats of skins" (Gen. 3:21) for Adam and Eve, which means that nature and certain orders of the Elohim produced the physical bodies of humans. Those orders that direct the process of forthgoing, and control the activity of Fohat, are symbolized by the Cherubim with flaming sword "which turned every way, to keep the way of the tree of life." In this sense Eden is the first plane of the manifested cosmos, Adi. There the seeds and potentialities of the whole of the subsequent creation exist from the beginning, and indeed throughout all time. Adi is the plane of the seeds (Monads) in their most sublimated state.

The Monad Descends into Matter

As mentioned in Chapter 4, there are hosts of Intelligences, Elohim, that function to join human Monads to mortal bodies. They are referred to in esoteric philosophy as the Satanic Hierarchy and are also personified by the Devil or serpent in the Garden of Eden.

In the case of human Monads, although they are imbued with the formative fire and impulse, the process of the entry of Spirit into matter is far from being purely automatic. Since Monads are primarily pure, stainless, spiritual beings existing within the life of the Logos, incarnation in matter inevitably involves severe limitations and a loss of complete purity. A deeply esoteric teaching states that Monads shrink from the resultant self-limitation, since from the Monadic point of view the descent involves enslavement and degradation. The adoption of individual mentality, incarnation in a physical body with cerebrospinal system and the dual experience of the delusion of self-separateness and sexual impulses are repellant to the Monad to the extent that it is able to conceive of them. For these and doubtless other reasons, Monads are said to hesitate on the threshold of the individuality which would most adversely affect purely spiritual beings whose innate consciousness is entirely universalized. Admittedly these are all intellectual and purely human reactions which could hardly be expected to reach dwellers in the innermost, sparks within the One Flame. Nevertheless the suggestion is made that in some highly sublimated form the Monads embarking on the pathway of forthgoing are aware of such implications inseparable from that procedure. At the same time, however, Monadic life is drawn towards matter by the operation of the law of polarity, or attraction and repulsion.

The Ageless Wisdom, source of these concepts, also advances the teaching that certain of the hosts of human Monads, thus hesitating to embark upon the great pilgrimage through matter, attempted to resist the universal creative and expansive impulse. This shrinking and this resistance together are said to constitute one of the esoteric and spiritually historical realities behind the allegory of the "war in heaven" (Rev. 12:7). It may also be regarded in more general terms as the conflict between Spirit and matter, whether cosmic or microcosmic, universal or human. In humans, this struggle only ends when the outer terrestrial nature has been brought into complete conformity with the Spirit within. Every candidate for the higher initiations must win—and so end—this war by slaying every unspiritual attribute still remaining in the lower nature. Thus St. George slew the dragon—as did so many other heroines and heroes of world mythologies. The labors of Hercules doubtless possess the same mystical significance.

In summary, the rebellious angels were none other than the Monads of humans who hesitated to surrender their universality and their unstained ascetic purity in obedience to the cosmic evolutionary impulse, process and purpose. Eventually the rebels were obliged by that impulse to descend into generation. Karmic disability is said to have followed, influencing some of them to become servants of the dark face, rebels against society and scourges of the rest of humankind on this Earth in its Fourth Round. Furthermore, an actual war was waged on Earth in the days of Atlantis when these servants, the black magicians and sorcerers, attacked their Adept guardians.

While all human Monads felt aversion, all did not rebel. Assistance was required, however, in embarking upon the path of forthgoing (see Volume I, Chapter 11) and in accomplishing descent into the deeper densities of matter. The necessary allurement or temptation to participate in the vast involutionary and evolutionary activity initiated at creative dawn is described in allegory in the account of the temptation of Eve by Satan. Members of the Elohim, full-formed because evolved from preceding cycles of manifestation, undertook this work (and may still be undertaking it in this or other Solar Systems) of induction into mental, emotional and physical bodies. The Devil is a personification of this order of Intelligences, as also of their functions.

Thus the tree of life within Eden, in a limited interpretation, is the life-force in nature in a state of balance or equipoise. The serpent associated with it represents the twin currents, positive and negative, with the tree trunk as third, by which the triple creative fire is manifest. The fruit of the tree is the subsequent development, the harvest accruing from the activity of the Divine Life within the matter of the universe, and particularly the fruits of the great Monadic pilgrimage of forthgoing and return.

Adam represents both humanity, the Monad, and the first physical humans on Earth, who were androgynous. Adam and Eve as separated entities represent the later stage of humanity as Monad-Ego clothed in male and female physical personalities. They are personifications of the human race after its division into men and women. Before this takes place, complete innocence or creative inactivity exists. After the separation, procreation begins. Knowledge is gradually gained from this. Evolution and experience bring that knowledge and its resultant power to the highest fruition, so that humankind ultimately becomes a god. Therefore the serpent truthfully said: ". . . in the day ye eat thereof, then your eyes shall be opened, and ye shall be as gods, knowing good and evil." (Gen. 3:5)

The price to be paid for the development of this deific power is heavy indeed. The Souls of humans are encased in matter and they temporarily become prey to the delusion of self-separated individuality, to sex, and to the dangers resulting from sexual abuse. Self-degraded as a result, humanity (Adam and Eve) is allegorically described as being condemned by God and driven out of Eden.

The Flood and the Tower

6

Introduction: Noah and the Ark

Genesis 6–9

The population of the Earth began to grow, and these people were living wickedly. Beings of spirit took human women as wives—"when the sons of God came in unto the daughters of men, and they bare children to them." Great evil and violence spread over all the Earth, and God saw this and was saddened—even to the point of regretting having made man and woman.

But one man, Noah, found grace in the eyes of the Lord because of his virtue. God told him that "all flesh, wherein is the breath of life . . . and every thing that is in the earth" was to be destroyed because of its corruption. The plans for a great ship—the ark—were given to Noah by God, and he was instructed in the making of it. For God said, "behold I, even I, do bring a flood of waters upon the earth, to destroy all flesh. . . ." God then made a covenant with Noah, telling him that his wife, his sons, Shem, Ham and Japheth, and two of every living creature would be spared in the ark. As a token of his convenat, God set a bow in the cloud. And because Noah was righteous, he did all that God commanded him.

Chapters Six to Nine of Genesis reveals a more marked merging of the cosmogonical with the historical. The engulfing of universes and their several component Solar Systems within the waters of space at the end of every Manvantara, major and minor, and the successive floods by which portions of the Earth have been overwhelmed are

51

allegorically merged in the account of the Flood (see Gen. 7:10). While the historicity of stories of local floods is not here discounted, the deluge described in Chapters Six through Eight of Genesis is also able to be interpreted as connoting the periods of relative quiescence of the objective universe which intervene between those of creative activity.

As a permutation of Yahweh, Noah—considered macrocosmically —represents the masculine creative potency. His presence within the ark—the feminine aspect—indicates that creative union of which all things are the products. Noah may also be regarded as a personification of *Chokmah,* one of the ten Sephiroth, together with its associated hierarchy of archangelic and angelic Hosts included in the kabbalistic tree of life. In one aspect this member of the Elohim is associated with the closing phases of Manvantara, the task being to sum up and sublimate into the highest spiritual essence all the fruits of the period which is coming to an end. The Monads and the essential power, life and consciousness of this epoch are symbolized by the family of Noah and by the pairs of the selected animals and birds. These are preserved within the aura (the ark) of the representative and head of the appropriate order of the Elohim.

In the cosmos as a whole this process of conservation of the seeds of living things throughout Pralaya is said to be carried out by an archangelic member of the inner government of the Solar System. In the case of Chains, Rounds and Globes, however, indications are to be found that this function is performed by a member of the human kingdom of nature who has attained a very lofty superhuman stature. Potentialities and seeds are thus preserved in a sublimated state during the period of Pralaya, in which all forms disintegrate and their substance loses its individualized vibratory frequencies, returning to the quiescent, precreative state symbolized by the waters in flood legends. Pralaya ended, the appropriate member of the Elohim, the seed Manu (Noah), delivers to the corresponding official of the new cycle the preserved seeds of the preceding epoch of which the Manu has been in charge. The great pilgrimage of involution and evolution is then repeated on a higher round of the ascending spiral.

In one sense the rainbow ("bow in the cloud") or covenant with God, as described in Genesis 9:13, symbolizes the office of the Elohim in bridging two epochs or cycles of manifestation. The return from simplicity to multiplicity, from the white light to the spectrum, from the One to the many, is also implied.

The Failure of God?

The suggestion in Genesis 6:5-7 that the Supreme Deity could conceive of an imperfect plan which failed, experience wrath at that failure and then decide to destroy "both man, and beast, and the creeping thing, and the fowls of the air," in its literal reading is surely quite unacceptable. The assertion that God could be guilty of such actions and could be moved to make the later promise not to "curse the ground any more for man's sake" or "again smite any more every thing living" (Gen. 8:21) is either an erroneous attribution to the Deity of conduct of which even humans would not be guilty, or else a deliberately constructed blind for the concealment of an underlying truth.

Such a conclusion is strengthened by the divine proclamation that humanity was created in God's own image (Gen. 1:26,27). It is similarly inconceivable that the conjoined Elohim (wrongly translated as "God") which emerge from and constitute the One Alone, could be capable either of error in the planning and fulfillment of their cosmic functions or of wrath at a failure which was solely attributable to themselves.

In the presence of such affronts to human reason, acceptance of the use of a special category of literature known as the sacred language is surely preferable to total unbelief in such biblical inconsistencies and errors that a literal reading necessitates. This could lead to the consequent rejection of the Bible as a whole, with its affirmation of the existence of a Supreme Being as the directive intelligence in nature. The renowned scientist Albert Einstein evidently felt no need to make this rejection, for he expressed the view that "that deeply emotional conviction of the presence of a superior reasoning power which is revealed in the incomprehensible universe, forms my idea of God." Nevertheless the actions attributed to the Deity in the verses under review certainly are not presented in the guise of a "superior reasoning power."

Esoteric philosophy teaches that the objective universe is ruled by cosmic law and that under this law Pralaya follows Manvantara as inevitably as night follows day, for alternation is a law of manifestation. As already stated, the introduction into an account of cosmogenesis of a capacity for failure and the attribution to the One Law, and to the Elohim who are its agents, of the gross and unphilosophical vice of violent and destructive anger are such notable errors that they must surely be regarded as deliberate blinds. Indeed, the presumedly initiate authors of the inspired portions of Genesis, having already revealed so many sublime truths, would hardly be capable of falling into such a profound mistake. Their complete knowledge, and their skillful use of many components of the entire range of symbols, show them to be highly illumined humans. We may therefore regard as fraudulent interpolations, inaccurate translations or deliberate blinds the suggestion of the visitation of the wrath of God upon Adam and Eve in the Garden of Eden, and later upon humanity and all living creatures of the succeeding — the Noahian — cycle of manifestation.

The "bow in the cloud" — the rainbow displaying the seven colors of the spectrum — underscores this interpretation; for the illuminated clouds may be taken to represent the root substance into which the positive, creative potency descends, changing it from precosmic, virgin (white) matter into its seven gradations of density, thereby preparing it to serve as the field of evolution for the seven kingdoms of nature. The analogy of the rainbow, produced by the splitting up of white light into the seven colors of the spectrum, aptly presents this idea. In addition, the stretching of a bow across the heavens represents the linking together or bridging of successive cycles, an interpretation seemingly indicated by God's description of the bow as a "covenant." Furthermore, the speech of God to Noah, giving comfort and command, may refer to the uttered creative Voice — the formation of the universe by sound — implied by the Logos doctrine. This doctrine asserts that the universe is first conceived in divine thought, which is the governing power in creation. The creative Word expressive of the idea is then "spoken" and the previously quiescent seeds of living things germinate and appear from within the ocean of space, the great deep.

If the account of the Flood is applied to the physical evolution of humanity on Earth, Noah represents the Manu of one of the seven Root Races, an official in the hierarchy of the Adepts who is largely responsible for the evolution of a Root Race with its seven sub-races. A further function of this official is to select certain of the more advanced members of the Race under his or her direction who are to be employed as the physical progenitors of its successor. They are then segregated, and their descendants in due course are inspired to emigrate to the country chosen to be the birthplace of a new Race. [In theosophical thought, the seven Root Races represent stages in the development of human consciousness in interaction with the material plane.]

"The Waters Prevailed Exceedingly upon the Earth" – Gen. 7:19

According to esoteric philosophy the Flood, its various symbolic meanings apart, was an historical fact. The continent of Atlantis and millions of the bodies of its inhabitants, human and subhuman, are said to have been drowned in four great floods [see Powell's *The Solar System,* Scott-Elliot's *Legends of Atlantis and Lost Lemuria,* and Preston's *The Earth and Its Cycles.*] Thus, historically regarded, the Flood recorded in Genesis was the fourth and culminating cataclysm. The psychical and spiritual Souls of the Atlanteans were saved by this catastrophe from the deeper degradation into which, as practitioners of sorcery and black magic, they were in great danger of sinking. Indeed, very large numbers of the Atlantean people did fall into those errors. These are taken by some students of the esoteric arts to be the wickedness erroneously referred to as provoking the wrath of God. Members of the esoteric hierarchy of Adepts on Earth are, however, no more capable of wrath than are the Elohim of the universe. Danger to the evolving Souls of humans arising from imperfect control of their personalities, which were engaging in deeply degrading black magical practices, alone necessitated esoteric intervention by the Adept hierarchy of this planet.

In terms of the human sevenfold constitution with successive reincarnations (see Hodson, *Reincarnation, Fact or Fallacy?*), the ark itself may be interpreted as the Auric Envelope (the edge and sum total of the substance of the seven human bodies, physical and superphysical, and their subtle radiations) and more especially the radiance of the body of light referred to as the *Augoeides* (Gr.), the Robe of Glory (Gnostic) and the Causal Body. This particular vehicle of consciousness both contains and preserves the fruits harvested from each life cycle or incarnation. In addition, it functions as a vesture for the threefold spiritual Self of humans – divine Will, Wisdom and Intelligence. The inhabitants of the ark, human and subhuman, typify both the fruits of the evolutionary process and the indwelling triune Spirit, and the three stories refer to the three levels of divine consciousness of the triple Self.

The Flood Narrative as Allegory of the Human Life Cycle

The student of symbology must ever be on guard against reading into an allegory and its component symbols more than was originally intended or may be justly attributed. However, descriptions of levels and conditions of human consciousness after the death of the body, with which event the physical part of the life cycle of a person is ended, may possibly be discerned in the Flood narrative. Esoteric science teaches that, having lost its physical instrument by death, the inner Self is thereafter conscious in the emotional world for a time, during which karma generated at that level may be precipitated. This phase is followed by the detachment and disintegration of the substance of the desire nature, after which the Ego is aware in the mental principle. This period is a heaven-like state of happiness due to the inability to experience desire. In esoteric philosophy human suffering is said to be caused by desire or, in the words of the Buddha, "craving." The cessation of human sorrow can only be achieved by the cessation of desire. Behind desire, however, is the delusion of self-separateness, from which desire itself arises. The period of happiness eventually draws to a close, with the Soul then being clothed in its vesture of light, the Causal Body. This is the storehouse of the capacities attained during the life cycle just closed and for the development and expression of the faculty of abstract thought. (See Hodson, *Through the Gateway of Death.*)

The Flood story is an apt allegorical description of this human experience. Water, for example, is used as a symbol of both primordial substance or space and the emotional life of humans. The deluge itself might thus be interpreted as the "precipitation" upon the individual, during the first postmortem period, of the adversities that were generated during the preceding life. Thus applied to procedures and human experiences immediately after the death of one physical body and before rebirth into its successor, the cessation of the rain would symbolize entry into the mental phase of the life after death. The summit of Mount Ararat would represent the purely spiritual condition of egoic consciousness into which the reincarnating ray of the inner Self then withdraws. Emergence onto level ground after descent from the summit represents birth in a new form, with the rainbow as the egoic bridge or link between two lives. The Causal Body, which is the vehicle of the Ego, is iridescent with all the colors of the spectrum and, being immortal, is also the promise of assurance of safe passage from one cycle to the next. This vesture is therefore also well described as God's convenant with humanity, since it constitutes the essential link between the spiritual, immortal Self and the more material and decisively mortal personality.

7

Wickedness and Grace

This sixth chapter of Genesis is one of the most wonderful in the Old Testament. It is a profound esoteric allegory with references to communion and union between "the sons of God and the daughters of men." As previously mentioned, the wickedness of early humanity and the occurrence of a flood are historically correct. According to esoteric ethnology, during the Atlantean or Fourth Race period sin did indeed fall upon the Earth. The Atlanteans were guilty of most grievous wickedness—sorcery and other gross forms of the misuse of psychic forces—the only remedy for which was the destruction of their physical bodies. This was brought about by four floods, the last of which finally engulfed the Atlantean continent. Certain mountain ranges and peaks have, however, remained above the waters, as evidenced by the various archipelagoes and islands of the Atlantic Ocean.

The Establishment of a New Root Race

Before the great floods began, the Manu (a creator, preserver and fashioner who presides over a Manvantara), personified by Noah, began to draw together those tribes and individuals who were to be the progenitors of the next Root Race. They were taken to places of safety, one of which was in Arabia and another on the shores of the then existing Gobi Sea. There, through hundreds of thousands of years, symbolized by the period within the Ark, the Race with its inherent faculties—represented by the human, animal and bird dwellers in the

Ark—underwent specialized development. Then at the appropriate time, the descendants of these specially selected people were liberated from their Arabian and Central Asian homes and charged with the task of settling and populating the chosen countries with the newly established types. Thus arose the first beginnings of the sub-races of the Fifth Root Race. These are, according to esoteric science, some of the chief historical events recorded partly in plain language and partly in allegory in the sixth chapter of Genesis.

> And it came to pass, when men began to multiply on the face of the
> earth, and daughters were born unto them,
> That the sons of God saw the daughters of men that they were fair;
> and they took them wives of all which they chose. *(Gen. 6:1–2)*

In the microcosmic reading the "sons of God" are the human Monads, while the "daughters of men" represent the personal consciousness of late Third and early Fourth Root Races. Up to that time humanity as a whole had been unillumined by any spiritual awareness, being conscious only at psychophysical levels. At the stage of evolution which had then been reached, a further development occurred which consisted of a descent of Monadic influence. In this sense the Monads ("the sons of God") "married" the personalities ("the daughters of men") and the product was mental and later egoic consciousness. Thus the triplicity of Monad-Ego-personality was completed, the flesh having then become the vehicle of the Spirit.

In another possible interpretation the sons of God are the angelic teachers of the first wholly physical humans with bony structure (the third group of humans numerically). In yet another view they are the Pitris (highly evolved, incorporeal, spiritual Beings) or ancestors, advanced products of preceding Schemes of evolution who, together with the Elohim, constructed the forms of superphysical nature. These Beings fashioned the first gigantic physical bodies and inducted human consciousness into them.

> And the Lord said, My spirit shall not always strive with man, for
> that he also is flesh: yet his days shall be an hundred and twenty
> years. *(Gen. 6:3)*

The threefold nature of humans, and the ultimate subservience of the material nature to the spiritual Self are indirectly indicated in this verse. The stated life period of one hundred and twenty years might indicate that early physical humans lived to that age. By numerical integration the number one hundred and twenty becomes three, and this may also imply the first establishment in humans of physical, emotional and mental vehicles of consciousness through which the Monadic ray, itself triple, could be expressed.

> There were giants in these days; and also after that, when the sons
> of God came in unto the daughters of men and they bare children
> to them, the same became mighty men which were of old, men
> of renown. *(Gen. 6:4)*

In this verse the mystical and the historical are interwoven. Mystically, the Monad-Egos ("the sons of God") mingled with the personalities ("the daughters of men"), which means that they found growing expression in and through them. Historically, the physical bodies of primitive humans were gigantic, being at least twice the size of those of Fifth Race (the current) humans. In addition, the Adept tutors of these people lived physically among them and directed them. These were the renowned divine teachers and kings of prehistoric periods, giants of intellectual and spiritual power.

The Wickedness of the World

> And God saw that the wickedness of man was great in the earth, and
> that every imagination of the thought of his heart was only evil
> continually.
> And it repented the Lord that he had made man on earth, and it
> grieved him at his heart.
> And the Lord said, I will destroy man whom I have created from the
> face of the earth; both man, and beast, and the creeping thing, and
> the fowls of the air; for it repenteth me that I have made them.
> *(Gen. 6:5–7)*

As previously discussed, the process of the incarnation of purely spiritual and immortal Monads—themselves ever unstained and unstainable—into mortal, material, physical personalities involves a measure of temporary degradation for the manifested Monads. The reference to the great "wickedness of man" is thus allegorical, being actually descriptive of the inevitable staining of pure Spirit by the intimate contact (marriage) of Monads ("sons of God") with the desire-charged matter of human physical bodies ("daughters of men"). The sin referred to is also descriptive of certain experiences associated with the human exercise of generative powers.

An allegorical interpretation is further supported by the fact that, as has been previously stated, no sin whatever is involved in the ordinary exercise by humans of the procreative power. In its literal sense, the idea is entirely unacceptable that the Creator of those human beings, who exercised a power with which they had been divinely endowed, would find them guilty of wickedness. The further statement that this completely innocent action evoked the wrath of God, and led to the act of total destruction with the exception of the inhabitants of the Ark, is also an affront to the intellect. If the God of Genesis implies the Supreme Deity, the one conceiver, fashioner, preserver and transformer of universes as a whole, then this God must be assumed to be endowed with the attribute of omniscience. This power would include complete foreknowledge—even in transcendence of the restrictions of time—so that in the consciousness of such a Being full awareness of the total created product from beginning to end must be presumed to have been present. If this is true, then from the outset God would have been fully aware of every forthcoming event and, in consequence, could in no sense have been surprised or aggrieved by any action of the children created in the image of God. Once again, therefore, acceptance of the literal reading of this, as of so many other passages, becomes an impossibility.

The statement that God repented of having created humanity must either be rejected or regarded as a blind to enveil knowledge of the deeply esoteric process of involution, partly described in allegory by the Christ in the parable of the Prodigal Son (Luke 15). The descent of the ray of the human Monad from the realm of pure Spirit through the intervening planes into physical incarnation is also implied. The stories of the salvation of Noah and his family, of the raising of Joseph from the pit (Gen. 37), his ultimate attainment of high office under Pharaoh (Gen. 41), of the liberation by Moses of the Israelites from bondage in Egypt (Ex. 14), of their eventual arrival under Joshua at the Promised Land (Josh. 3) and of the spiritual salvation of all humanity by the Redeemer—all these both veil and reveal the process of evolution, or the returning ascent of the Monadic ray to the purely spiritual state.

God, whether as Law or as the source, emanator and director of the creative impulse in nature, neither rejoices nor repents. Completely impersonal, the creative power and its archangelic and angelic Intelligences (Elohim) skillfully operate the vast cosmic machinery throughout alternating Manvantaras and Pralayas, the former with their innumerable subcycles of forthgoing and return. As suggested above, the attribution of human limitation to the Deity is to be regarded as either complete error or part of the veil of allegory which must be drawn aside if the concealed spiritual verities are to become known, just as the veil of matter must similarly be removed from the eyes and minds of people if full realization of spiritual truth is to be attained.

Grace in the Eyes of the Lord

But Noah found grace in the eyes of the Lord.
These are the generations of Noah: Noah was a just man and perfect
    in his generations, and Noah walked with God.
And Noah begat three sons, Shem, Ham, and Japheth. *(Gen. 6:8–10)*

In one meaning as we have seen, Noah is a personification of the holder of an office (Manu) in the spiritual government of Solar Systems, Chains, Rounds, Planets and Races. Noah in particular represents the root and seed Manus, whose vocation it is to absorb and preserve within their auras (arks) during Pralayas (flood) the seeds of living things and the Monads of humans. These they deliver to their successors at the opening of the next Manvantara (postdiluvian dispensation).

In the mystical interpretation Noah represents the Monad-illumined Ego which, though limited and even stained in its mortal manifestation in the physical body, nevertheless in its own essential nature remains unstainable and unstained. Thus "Noah found grace in the eyes of the Lord" and "was a just man and perfect in his generations, and Noah walked with God." In this interior sense the term "God" refers to the human Monad, of which the Ego is product and with which it is ever at one. The three sons of Noah personify the human mental, emotional and physical bodies; their wives represent the expressed powers and attributes — in Sanskrit, *shaktis*. Noah and his family thus stand for the whole nature of humanity.

The earth also was corrupt before God, and the earth was filled with
    violence.
And God looked upon the earth, and, behold, it was corrupt; for all
    flesh had corrupted his way upon the earth.
And God said unto Noah, The end of all flesh is come before me;
    for the earth is filled with violence through them; and, behold, I
    will destroy them with the earth. *(Gen. 6:11–13)*

Historically these verses refer to the degradation or corruption into which the people of the early Fourth Root Race fell. The maximum materialism which occurs during all fourth-phase manifestations, when compared with the spirituality typical of both earlier and later epochs, is also indicated. The fourth phase of a sevenfold cycle of forthgoing and return represents both the deepest level of descent and the beginning of ascent (see Volume I, Part 3). It is marked by the maximum degradation of Spirit produced by embodiment in densest matter, and of life and consciousness by incarnation in mortal vehicles. According to esoteric philosophy the corruption of the Atlantean (Fourth Root Race) people was an historical fact, as also was the destruction by drowning of great numbers of physical bodies. The flood legends of the scriptures of other ancient civilizations are also partly based upon these events.

The Ark as a Symbol

Make thee an ark of gopher wood; rooms shalt thou make in the ark, and shall pitch it within and without with pitch.

And this is the fashion which thou shalt make it of: The length of the ark shall be three hundred cubits, the breadth of it fifty cubits, and the height of it thirty cubits.

A window shalt thou make to the ark, and in a cubit shalt thou finish it above; and the door of the ark shalt thou set in the side thereof; with lower, second, and third stories shalt thou make it. *(Gen. 6:14–16)*

Regarded as a symbol, the ark is able to be interpreted numerous ways. In general, it is any vehicle of consciousness, whether of cosmos, Solar System, Sun, Planet, Race or individual. The arks and ships of the allegorical language employed by the initiates of the Mystery Schools of early civilizations all refer to containing vehicles of consciousness, of whatever dimensions and at whatever level, including cosmic matter when formed into universes, and also the Spiritual or Causal Body of humans, their Auric Envelope, the animal and human wombs, the enclosing membrane of a cell and the shell of an atom.

The outer hull of the ark is the "Ring-pass-not" (the outermost edge or limit of the system marked out by the Logos) of universes, the Auric Envelope of humans and the skin of the physical body. The inner lining, symbolized by pitch, is the hardened, protective substance which forms at the edge of the sphere of manifestation, enclosing the creative forces with their distinctive frequencies of oscillation. The pitch keeps out water; so do these vibrating energies render impossible any intrusion by forces and Intelligences foreign to those within from the sea of space outside. The division of Noah's ark into rooms describes the establishment of the various planes of nature in the cosmos, the vehicles of consciousness in humans, the constituent parts of the embryo and the cell, and the differently charged particles of the atom.

The Dimensions of the Ark

The number of cubits in each direction, namely three hundred in length, fifty in breadth and thirty in height, can be regarded as referring to cycles and phases of development. In this sense the three hundred cubits in length may indicate the plant kingdom of nature, for that number reduced becomes three. Plants are triune in nature, consisting of three principles — the physical form, the vital force and the dawning sensitivity or feeling. The stated breadth of fifty cubits, which by reduction is five, refers to the animal kingdom in which exists the potential development of a fifth principle, the higher *Manas* (mind), which will bestow separated individuality or Egohood. The thirty cubits in height is similarly triune and thus designates the human kingdom. While including all preceding development, humans are in two senses threefold beings; for the inner Self is triple, a trinity in the likeness of its Creator, while the total person, as distinct from the members of all the subhuman kingdoms, consists of highest Spirit (Monad) and lowest matter (physical body) united by intellect.

Noah (the Monad-Ego), his wife (the Causal Body), and Shem, Ham and Japheth (the three vehicles of the personality — mental, emotional and physical) personify the component principles of humans. The ark as symbol, with its carefully indicated dimensions, structure and inhabitants, thus accurately represents humanity at its present evolutionary position on this planet. The Flood narrative is also of universal significance; for it applies equally to the planet Earth, to its Fourth Root Race, and to the Fourth Round of the Fourth Chain of our Planetary Scheme. Since it portrays a basic creative principle, the allegory must apply to all Schemes, Solar Systems and cosmoi.

The Window and Door as Symbol

The window of the ark, placed in its upper portion, points to the fact that the human faculty of abstract thought, which is a function of the Ego in the Causal Body (the ark), constitutes a window or opening to metaphysical states of consciousness. In the physical body the "window" is the anterior fontanelle (the opening in the top of the human skull which closes during development), and in the etheric and superphysical bodies it represents the *Brahmarandhra* (crown) chakra or force center.

The oft-used symbol of the door can be interpreted in at least two ways. In one it represents the possibility of an entrance into the mind of power, light and inspiration from supramental levels. In this sense the door symbolizes a means of access for spiritualizing influences through the abstract to the concrete mind. Such influences are sometimes in their turn personified by a great teacher. Jesus would appear to use the symbol in this sense in his words: "I am the door: by me if any man enter in, he shall be saved, and shall go in and out, and find pasture" (John 10:9). In another meaning the door is a symbol of the possibility of an entrance into the mind of certain forces and predilections from lower levels, particularly those of the emotional and purely physical parts of human nature.

In verses eighteen through twenty-one, God establishes a covenant with Noah and instructs him to gather his family, all living creatures, and all food that is eaten into the ark. Despite their brevity, these verses describe a long continued processes of evolution in which the four kingdoms of nature had become established on the Earth. By the time the present Fourth Chain had been reached, adequate vehicles of consciousness (arks) for each kingdom had been developed. As has been previously discussed, in the interpretation of Noah as Manu, the Flood refers to the period between cycles of manifestation.

Mount Ararat—Symbol of the Evolutionary Heights

> The fountains also of the deep and the windows of heaven were stopped, and the rain from heaven was restrained;
> And the waters returned from off the earth continually: and after the end of the hundred and fifty days the waters were abated.
> And the ark rested in the seventh month, on the seventeenth day of the month, upon the mountains of Ararat. *(Gen. 8:2–4)*

In Chapter Eight of Genesis the Flood passes, and the ark comes to rest upon the mountains of Ararat. Noah's entire story indicates the more advanced phases of the spiritual evolution of humanity to be entered upon during later periods, and with the greatest skill the accounts of the development of the Fifth Root Race and the advanced phases are successfully intermingled in it. In this latter interpretation — the spiritual evolution of humanity — the process is described of the transmutation of the baser human attributes (the animals) into the fine gold of the noble qualities of the human higher Self (Noah and his family in the Ark). This was accompanied by the sublimation of the force behind the grosser, animal passions from its physical (the surface of the Earth,) to its mental and spiritual expressions (Mt. Ararat).

The Ark, as symbol of the vehicle of the human Spirit, the Causal Body, is rightly described as having been built by Noah (the Ego) under the direction of the Lord (the Monad). By means of both natural evolution and deliberate self-quickening on "the way of holiness" (Isa. 35:8), the power, the capacities and the attributes of the lower, mortal human were being raised or sublimated to spiritual levels of expression. Simply put, human consciousness — which until then had been largely limited to the physical world — was being elevated towards the egoic level.

The Window, the Raven and the Dove

> And it came to pass at the end of forty days, that Noah opened the window of the ark which he had made:
> And he sent forth a raven, which went forth to and fro, until the waters were dried up from off the earth.
> Also he sent forth a dove from him, to see if the waters were abated from off the face of the ground. *(Gen. 8:6–8)*

The existence of the window in the Ark from which the raven (the formal intellect) and the dove (the intuition) went forth portrays the fact that the spiritual Self or Ego of humans in its turn is open to supramental states of consciousness (the upper air). The window itself indicates that the Ego in the Causal Body always has a means of access to the more lofty spiritual levels of awareness.

The failure of the raven to return indicates that the concrete mind alone cannot receive and reveal full spiritual illumination. This interpretation is supported by the return of the dove with the olive leaf, indicating that the intuition is able to convey illumination because of its oneness with universal life, typified by the olive tree from which the leaf had been plucked. Flight through the air also aptly portrays by allegory the supramental realms from which the intuition flashes into the otherwise darkened mind. The element of air is frequently used in the sacred language of symbols to represent the level of consciousness in which the intuitive faculty inheres and from which it is derived. A similar use of the dove to symbolize spiritual influences and states of awareness is found in the description of the baptism of Jesus in Jordan as given in the three synoptic Gospels (Matthew, Mark and Luke). It is recorded that "the heavens were opened unto him, and he saw the Spirit of God descending like a dove, and lighting upon him" (Matt. 3:16).

The Universality of the Flood Legend

The Flood legend also appears in the Assyrian Tablets, the Hindu scriptures, Greek mythology and the Troano Manuscript of the Mayans. The Chaldeo-Babylonian Tablets describe a flood as having lasted for "six days and nights, [during which] the wind, deluge and storms overwhelmed [the Earth]. On the seventh day in the course was calmed the storm and all the deluge which had destroyed like an earthquake, quieted. The sea he caused to dry, and the wind and deluge ended."

A Hindu version of the flood legend is found in the Mahabharata, the Puranas and the Brahmanas. Vaivasvata, the Hindu Noah, saved a little fish which proved to be an avatar of Vishnu, the second aspect of the *Trimurti* or triune Godhead. The fish warned him that the globe was about to be submerged and that all that inhabited it would perish. It ordered Vaivasvata to construct a vessel in which he was to embark with his family. The ship was made ready and Vaivasvata entered it with his family, and also with pairs of all animals and the seeds of plants; then the rain began to fall. The fish, now gigantic and having developed a horn to which the Manu tied the ship, guided it through the raging elements, and when they calmed landed it on the summit of the Himalayas.

In Greek mythology Zeus had resolved to destroy humankind which had become degenerate. Deucalion, the Greek Noah, and his wife, Pyrrha, were the only mortals to be saved on account of their piety. He built a ship in which he and his wife floated to safety during the nine days of flood that destroyed all the other inhabitants of Hellas. At last the ship rested on Mount Parnassus in Phocis. Thereafter, by very strange magical actions, the human race was restored.

The Troana Manuscript appears to have been written about 2,500 years ago among the Mayans of Yucatan and was translated by Le Plongeon. It gives the following description of the submergence of a continent in the Atlantic, presumably the Poseidonis referred to by Plato:

> In the year of 6 Kan, on the 11th Muluc in the Zac, there occurred terrible earthquakes, which continued without interruption until the 13th Chuen. The country of the hills was covered by mud, the land of Mu was sacrificed; being twice upheaved it suddenly disappeared during the night, the basin being continually shaken by volcanic forces. Being confined, these caused the land to sink and to rise several times and in various places. At last the surface gave way and ten countries were torn asunder and scattered. Unable to stand the force of the convulsions, they sank with 64,000,000 of their inhabitants 8,060 years before the writing of this book.

The Book of Chilam Balam is a later find of an ancient Mayan manuscript discovered by A. M. Bolic. In it a flood is referred to — "and then in one watery blow, came the waters . . . the sky fell down and the dry land sank."

Flood narratives, in addition to their historical bases, are also able to be interpreted in a manner similar to the biblical account of the Noachian deluge. As previously advanced, the uniformity and universality of these and many other legends, myths and allegories of ancient peoples that are still preserved may be regarded as indicating both a single source of all of them and a similar system of symbology. Esoteric philosophy affirms that source to be the hierarchy of Adept sages, still existent on Earth, the "just men made perfect" (Heb. 12:23 and 1 Cor 2:6). The similarity of the symbols employed to denote the same ideas is explained by the use of the language of allegory and symbol in which world scriptures and mythologies have been written.

8

The Tower of Babel

Genesis 11

At this time in history all of the people on Earth spoke one language. They journeyed eastward until they came to a plain in the land of Shinar, and the people decided to dwell there. On this plain a city made of bricks and clay was begun, with a tower whose zenith would reach to the heavens.

God observed their labors on the city and the tower, and declared that this project was only the beginning—that now nothing the people could imagine would be impossible for them. Remarking that they were all united by one speech, God gave the people different languages.

Unable to understand each other any longer, they abandoned the city and scattered over the face of the Earth. The name of this city became Babel, meaning confusion, because it was there that God confounded the people in their prideful goals.

Escape from Suffering

In the Hindu scripture *Yogavasishta*, a celebrated Vedic sage states:

As the source of all waters is the ocean, so the idea "I am this" and "this is mine" is the cause of all our suffering. The thought of the ego is the cause of our fatal bondage. He gets bound himself who imagines a limit within his Self which is immeasurable and infinite. We are deluded and undergo terrible experiences of the world, because we feel ourselves as different or separate from Brahman, in spite of having our being in the ocean of Brahman. Trust in perishable things is known to be the source of numberless troubles. The individual becomes liberated when he gives up the attributes of mind and acquires the attributes of Brahman. The individual becomes liberated when he perceives without distinction the Self in all beings and all beings in the Self. (Adapted by B. L. Atreya in *Yogavasishta and Modern Thought.*)

In *Reign of Religion in Contemporary Philosophy,* S. Radhakrishnan writes:

So long as we feel ourselves to have individualities of our own, we will be beset with conflicts and contradiction, pain and pleasure, but when once we disinterestedly give ourselves up to the Whole, there is an end to all discord. . . . We can never completely break the shell of egoism and attain the infinite if we remain in the finite universe, giving a substantial existence to our own individual self. The release from this world of trouble, risk and adventure can be had only by losing the separate self.

In *Book of Meditations,* James Allen states:

Seeking to save his personal life, man forfeits the greater impersonal life of truth; clinging to the perishable, he is shut out from the knowledge of the Eternal. . . . Love of self shuts men out from Truth, and seeking their own personal happiness they lose the deeper purer and more abiding bliss. . . . He who has yielded up that self, that personality that most men love, and to which they cling with such fierce tenacity, has left behind him all perplexity, and has entered into a simplicity so profoundly simple as to be looked upon by the world, involved as it is in a network of error, as foolishness.

The spirit of man is inseparable from the Infinite, and can be satisfied with nothing short of the Infinite, and the burden of pain will continue to weigh upon man's heart, and the shadows of sorrow to darken his pathway until ceasing from wanderings in the dream-world of matter, he comes back to his home in the reality of the Eternal. As the smallest drop of water detached from the ocean contains all the qualities of the ocean, so man, detached in consciousness from the Infinite, contains within himself its likeness; and as the drop of water must, by the law of nature, ultimately find its way back to the ocean and lose itself in its silent depth, so each man, by the unfailing law of his nature, at last returns to his source, and loses himself in the heart of the Infinite.

The story of the Tower of Babel in Chapter Eleven of Genesis has both exoteric and esoteric interpretations. To the student of esoteric wisdom, the suggestion in this story that God, in order to restrict its power, deliberately cast humanity into confusion by breaking their unity and destroying their common language is not plausible. The Supreme Deity could not be responsible for the subsequent sorrows of "the sons of Noah"—the whole of humanity—that arose from this action.

In one possible interpretation, however, the narrative may be read as an allegory describing normal processes of evolution. The use of the term "the Lord" in the account ("And the Lord came down to see the city and the tower, which the children of men builded" Gen. 11-5) should be understood as the creative and evolutionary impulses and the laws governing their manifestations in nature and in humanity. A full knowledge of the existence of this irresistible, propellant power and of the laws under which it finds expression in all kingdoms of nature, including the human, would bestow very great theurgic and hypnotic powers upon its possessor. Evil-minded people—as history has shown—grasping at this knowledge and not hesitating to misuse it unscrupulously and to divert nature's purposes to their own personal ends, could corrupt the character of individuals—and even of nations. Under such almost demoniacal misuse of power bestowing knowledge, people who have previously been reasonably harmonious members of the family of nations can temporarily be changed into active and cruel enemies of humanity, as is demonstrated by wars of aggression. For example, the evils of the Nazi regime—the oblivious national acclaim for its leader and his immediate associates, the embarkation upon an unprovoked war of aggression on a vast scale, the extermination of some six million Jews and the horrors of the Nazi concentration camps—are examples of the danger resulting from the possession of even a modicum of misused esoteric knowledge. With such events frequently recorded in history and still occurring in living history, the veiling of esoteric knowledge in the language of allegory and symbol by the authors of the scriptures and mythologies of ancient peoples is more than justified.

An Unveiling of the Allegory

How then should the story of the Tower of Babel be interpreted? It may be regarded as descriptive of an epoch in the history of humanity as individuals and as a people. The allegory also may have a cosmic interpretation. Pre-Babel or primitive humanity may have been largely motivated by a tribal consciousness, their actions being principally guided by collective instinct. Post-Babel humanity, on the other hand, had begun to develop the mind. As cognition later entered in, displacing instinct by reason, individuality began to be born. The Tower of Babel is thus a symbol of the natural evolutionary ascent from the first purely physical people, through the development of instinctual and emotional states of consciousness, and on to the capacity for free personal choice based upon the conscious exercise of the intellect. The subsequent sorrows of humanity are traceable to the misuse for gain, often at the cost of others, of this power of self-centered thought and action. In eastern philosophy, as the quotations at the opening of this chapter indicate, such individualistic attitude of mind is called "the heresy of separateness."

The city of Babel with its tower is aptly described as unfinished ("So the Lord scattered them abroad from thence upon the face of all the earth; and they left off to build the city" – Gen. 11:8) because human evolution was at that time, and still is, incomplete. The construction of the symbolic tower will, however, be continued by the Sixth and Seventh Root Races, which will develop the capacity to use intuitive perception and the spiritually inspired and reinforced power of the will. This latter is to the greatest and most Godlike attainment of humanity; for, recognizing the identity of its own interior Spirit-essence with that of the Deity, humankind will share in increasing degrees in the divine omnipotence. This will be the pinnacle of the as yet unfinished Tower of Babel.

The Bricks

The tower is thus both a symbol and a chart of the evolution of human consciousness. Its foundations are rooted deep in the earth and represent the androgynous Adam, the symbol of the first truly physical humans which existed on Earth and evolved through some millions of years in a state of both mental and desire-free torpor (Adam's sleep). The later appearance of Eve beside Adam, or of males and females with a self-conscious experience of the emotion of sexual desire and its resultant gratification, represents the first layer of bricks above the ground. This desire, as was suggested earlier, is portrayed in the temptation of Eve in the Garden of Eden by the serpent (symbol of the serpent fire or universal, creative life-force), while Adam's response is allegorically indicated by the actions of receiving and sharing the fruit of the tree of knowledge of good and evil.

The Clay

The clay of which the bricks were made is a symbol of primordial substance, and the sun which dried and baked the bricks represents creative Spirit which fructifies matter and on the involutionary journey of forthgoing produces forms according to their archetypes. Gradually, on the downward arc, these creative ideas are projected from Universal Mind to become manifest as physical forms. Symbolically, the clay is hardened and the bricks are baked. Eventually the different species developed, to culminate in the emergence of humanity. Slowly, as the Third Race was followed by the Fourth, the great tower or symbol of the new Race arose. Since this progress occurred in humanity and was the result of human experience and effort, the narrative correctly states that the Tower of Babel was built by humans.

The Development of Individuality

The allegory is carried no further than the discontinuance of the building of the city and its tower and the scattering of the people "upon the face of all the earth." This progressive change from pre-Babel instinctual, tribal unity into post-Babel individualism and consequent separation was not the result of action by a personal Deity but came about through the natural development of the human mind. The seeds of disunity, divided activity and competitiveness then germinated and began to produce their first fruits. The unifying, cohesive influence of the collective instinct, which had until now held the people together in families and tribes, began to lose its hold.

A spirit of enquiry and a search for knowledge also became evident, and these led individuals and groups to explore the Earth and gradually to emigrate from their original centers of civilization. Through vast ages, as the analytical and separative attributes of the mind developed, differences of language and custom accentuated a growing diversity. This culminated in the production of the entirely distinct races and nations characteristic of humanity at the present time.

The change from unity to diversity was thus inevitable—indeed completely necessary for the evolution of humanity. Despite its grievous results destined to endure far into the Fifth Root Race (the present time), this was an essential phase in the process of the unfoldment of human life and consciousness. It might even be said that nature demanded this diversity as the price of the triumph to follow and the crown to be won. The triumph will consist of a conscious, self-chosen return to unification, and the crown will be the realization of the unity of the life within all the diversities of form.

From Matter to Spirit, from Earth to Heaven

Macrocosmically, the incarnation of the one life into many forms and the expression of the one creative idea through its innumerable manifestations in nature are allegorically described by the story. From this cosmic point of view the building of the Tower of Babel might symbolize entry on the pathway of return from matter to Spirit, or from Earth to Heaven. The unfinished state indicates a continuing process as yet incomplete, while the limitless regions of the sky above suggest an infinity of potential attainment.

The whole story of the city and Tower of Babel may be said to portray progression by the one life from unity (pre-Babel and Babel— Gen. 11:1) through diversity (post-Babel—Gen. 11:7-8) towards unity again. It is thus entirely symbolic and is one of the many flawless jewels of wisdom which are scattered in prodigal abundance throughout the pages of the Bible.

An indirect reference to the sacred language of the Mystery Schools may possibly be perceived, the significance of which was—and still is—the same for all peoples. In the distant past this cryptic tongue was employed universally as the literary vehicle for esoteric knowledge. Later the primeval wisdom religion and its hierogrammatic language were forgotten by the masses, who had become restricted to the several tongues of the different nations of the world.

The Generations of Shem

Although verses ten to thirty-two of Chapter Eleven of Genesis are largely genealogical, they also serve to indicate the general expansion and growing diversity of early peoples, and particularly of the Semitic. They close with the introduction of those two momentous figures, Terah and his son Abram, whose deeply allegorical adventures begin in Chapter Twelve of Genesis. Historically Abram represents the father and leader of the Israelites, and his experiences are those of one selected branch, the Palestinian.

PART THREE

The Life of Joseph as a Mystery Drama

9

Introduction: The Story of Joseph

Genesis 37

Joseph was Jacob's favorite son, the son of his old age. To show him his immense love, he made Joseph a coat of many colors. Because of this favoritism Joseph's brothers hated him bitterly. This hatred only increased when Joseph told his father and brothers of two dreams that he had dreamt. In the first, sheaves of wheat that the brothers were gathering bowed down to his sheaf; in the second, the sun, moon and eleven stars bowed down to him. Although his brothers were jealous, Joseph's father kept his son's dreams in mind.

One day Jacob sent Joseph on an errand to see his brothers, who were tending the flocks. Out of envy the brothers planned to kill Joseph. But Reuben, more virtuous than the rest, persuaded them to throw him in a pit instead, intending to rescue him later. While Reuben was away, the remaining brothers sold Joseph to a passing caravan as a slave. They then took Joseph's beautiful coat of many colors and dipped it in the blood of a goat to deceive their father into believing Joseph had been killed by a wild animal.

Jacob went into deep mourning at the loss of his beloved son. In the meantime, Joseph was sold as a slave to Potiphar, captain of Pharaoh's guard in Egypt.

Joseph may be regarded from three points of view — as a personification of the conscious life of a universe (macrocosm), as the highly evolved spiritual Soul or immortal Ego of humans (microcosm), and as an initiate of the greater Mysteries (see also Volume I, Part Five).

A Macrocosmic Interpretation:
Joseph as the Indwelling Life

At the formation of a new universe its divine architect first marks or circumscribes the area in the virginal, unparticled, precosmic space in which the universe is to appear. This Supreme Deity then projects an atom-forming energy which differentiates the enclosed matter from undifferentiated space. This process is carried out by the Holy Spirit, the third aspect of the Trinity, the creative mind, which is the source and director of the atom-forming electrical energies.

From the same divine Source—the threefold, active Deity—the all-preserving and vitalizing life-force of the second aspect enters the prepared universal field. This outpoured life of God is personified by Joseph. It enters the newly projected universe in its most spiritualized, tenuous condition (conception), gradually becomes more fully incarnate (Joseph's birth), and later is imprisoned (his adulthood) in matter of gradually deepening density (Joseph is lowered into the pit). This process of forthgoing thus culminates in incarnation in solid substance—earth and all that is of the earth, including the densest, hardest metals and jewels, an imprisonment indeed.

Joseph personifies the forthgoing life of God, and the authors of the Pentateuch (the first five books of the Old Testament) recount the sending forth of Joseph by his father, Jacob, into the field as an allegory of entry into a region of creative activity. Out in the field Joseph is rightly wearing a coat of many colors; for when the one life becomes manifested in innumerable forms its white light is broken up into the many hues of the spectrum. Shelley expresses this idea in his poem "Adonais": "Life, like a dome of many-coloured glass, Stains the white radiance of Eternity." Unity has become displaced by diversity. As the path of forthgoing is entered upon, the one becomes the many, a fundamental fact which is allegorically portrayed by the action of Joseph's father, Jacob, in robing his son in a coat of many colors (Gen. 37:3).

The descent of the life of the Logos from the highest spiritual level to the densest material encasement is typified by Joseph's departure from home. Its embodiment in the myriad forms of nature, super-physical and physical, is assisted by ministers of the Supreme Deity, first fruits of preceding universes (Elohim), who fulfill a major role during the forthgoing of the one life into matter (Joseph goes out into the field and later is lowered into the pit). Joseph's older brothers personify these high Intelligences, themselves manifesting in the superphysical realms of nature and dwelling amidst the life of the cosmos and its associated forces. Appropriately, Joseph's brothers carry out their function from above the pit and so, Elohim-like, do not themselves go down into it.

These same procedures are allegorically described in the parable of the Prodigal Son (see Volume I), in which corresponding cosmogonical procedures are revealed. In that story the elder son is stated to be jealous of his younger brother. Similarly the brothers of Joseph are presented as being envious of the youngest member of the family. This may legitimately be regarded as a deliberate blind used in order to conceal, and yet reveal, power-bestowing knowledge concerning the mystery of forthgoing, the descent of the Divine Life and of human Monads into the tomb of matter, and also of the divine Intelligences associated with that descent. The action of the brothers in forcibly lowering Joseph into a pit after they had taken off his coat of many colors does, however, aptly portray by allegory the function of the order of Intelligences involved in the forthgoing or involution of life. The revelation particularly applies to those members of that order who bring about the manifestation of life at the densest physical level (the pit). One of the aspects of Satan is a symbolic personification of these Beings who thus imprison life in matter, sometimes referred to as the Satanic Hierarchy.

James Stephens, the Irish poet, expresses this profoundly esoteric idea in his poem "Fullness of Time":

> On a rusty iron throne,
> Past the furthest star of space,
> I saw Satan sit alone,
> Old and haggard was his face;
> For his work was done, and he
> Rested in eternity.
>
> And to him from out the sun
> Came his father and his friend,
> Saying—Now the work is done
> Enmity is at an end—
> And He guided Satan to
> Paradises that He knew.
>
> Gabriel, without a frown;
> Uriel, without a spear;
> Raphael, came singing down,
> Welcoming their ancient peer;
> And they seated him beside
> One who had been crucified.

THE DIVINE LIFE AS THE PRODIGAL SO

THE MACROCOSMIC CYCLE

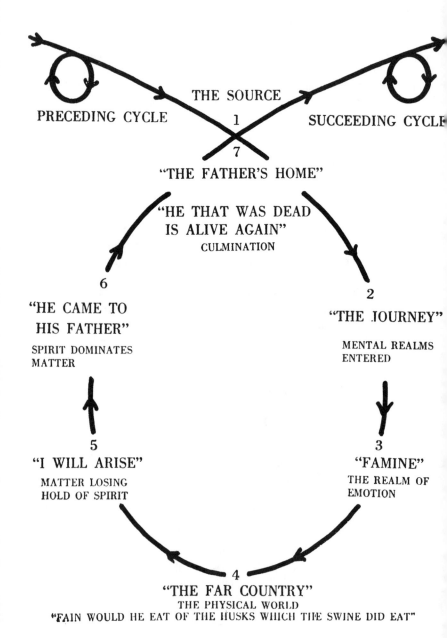

THE SOURCE
1
7
"THE FATHER'S HOME"

PRECEDING CYCLE

SUCCEEDING CYCLE

"HE THAT WAS DEAD
IS ALIVE AGAIN"
CULMINATION

6
"HE CAME TO
HIS FATHER"
SPIRIT DOMINATES
MATTER

2
"THE JOURNEY"
MENTAL REALMS
ENTERED

5
"I WILL ARISE"
MATTER LOSING
HOLD OF SPIRIT

3
"FAMINE"
THE REALM OF
EMOTION

4
"THE FAR COUNTRY"
THE PHYSICAL WORLD
"FAIN WOULD HE EAT OF THE HUSKS WHICH THE SWINE DID EAT"

THE HUMAN SPIRIT AS THE PRODIGAL SON

THE MICROCOSMIC CYCLE

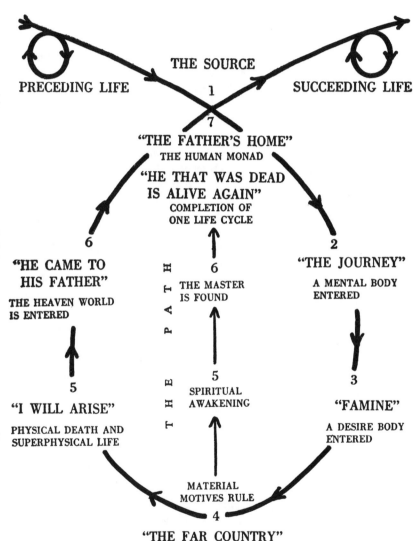

Life incarnate in substance inevitably becomes stained with the taint of matter. In the animal and human kingdoms, sensation and sense-pleasure entrap the pure spirituality of the emergent life – restricting and degrading it by materialization. This is portrayed by Joseph's brothers dipping his coat in animal blood before sending it back to their father with the untrue story of his beloved son's death. If accepted literally this is a very unpleasant episode. Thus interpreted, however, it proves to be a revelation of a spiritual law.

In the sacred language the final stage of the path of forthgoing is frequently described as the death and burial of a savior, hero or heroine, just as entry upon the path of return is portrayed by a resurrection and ascension. Up to this point the story of Joseph may be read as an allegory describing the forthgoing of the Divine Life into a universe in order that its substance and forms might be vitalized, ensouled and preserved. God is said to die in order that the universe may live. Christ, as the one life, is crucified and buried in the rock tomb. St. John the Divine refers to Christ as "the Lamb slain from the foundation of the world" (Rev. 13:8).

In the cosmic interpretation the merchants who raised Joseph from the pit and sold Joseph into slavery (Gen. 37:28) in their turn represent a group of spiritual Intelligences, members of which participate in and assist the evolution of life following its involution, in this manner performing a spiritualizing function. This is in opposition to that of their "brothers" (Pitris), who are concerned with the downward arc. These two orders of archangels and angels are sometimes portrayed as being at war (one interpretation of the "war in Heaven") or as being redemptive and satanic respectively. The truth, carefully veiled in the allegorical method of revelation, is that the function of each order is equally important.

A Microcosmic Interpretation:
Joseph as Personification of the Human Divine Spirit

The Ageless Wisdom teaches that human as Monad, in the innermost essence of being, is pure Spirit, indestructible, eternal, a spark within the one undying fire which is God. This primordial seed of Deity contains in various degrees of latency all the powers of the parent Godhead, which one day will become fully manifest ("Ye shall be perfect, even as your Father which is in heaven is perfect" [Matt. 5:48, RV]). In the sacred language the divine aspect of human nature is generally personified by the Supreme Deity who inspires saviors and prophets.

In order that the seedlike powers innate in the Monad may germinate and develop, a ray is projected from it into evolutionary fields—universes, superphysical and physical. This ray in due course becomes expressed as an immortal, unfolding individuality, a spiritual Soul, a human Ego, which thereafter unfolds its Monadic powers to the degree of adeptship or perfected humanity, "the measure of the stature of the fulness of Christ" (Eph. 4:13).

In this microcosmic interpretation the Ego is personified by Joseph, the Monadic ray by his father, Jacob, and the Monad itself by God, who inspires both. The ray shining forth into the denser fields of matter is dramatically portrayed by Joseph's departure from home, the loss of his coat of many colors (his aura, which becomes invisible at the physical level) and his imprisonment in the pit. This action also symbolically describes the descent of the immortal Ego into human birth.

These procedures are variously represented in the sacred language as murders, dismemberments, entombments and burials. Since, however, the human inner Self is immortal, all such symbolical descents and deaths are followed by ascents and resurrections. Major and minor cycles of manifestation—whether cosmic or human—are, as above stated, portrayed by these forthgoings and returns, descents and ascents, burials and resurrections.

In the human interpretation of great allegorical dramas, various people personify qualities of character, powers, faculties, weaknesses and defects. These last two are sometimes symbolized by sickness, blindness, sleep and death. The twelve children of Jacob typify, for example, zodiacal attributes present in humans from the beginning and ultimately to be fully developed—their father himself having described them in such terms (Gen. 49).

When recovery from adversities is said to be miraculously brought about by an inspired person, an evolutionary phase is being described in which limitations are outgrown. This is achieved by virtue of an awakened and active divine power within the previously unillumined personality. The brothers of Joseph display these defects and are made to feel envy and even hatred towards Joseph. They rob him of his coat, for example, and deceive their father by returning it to him bloodstained.

In terms of the sacred language, these brothers microcosmically represent the material encasements of the Soul—the mental, emotional, vital and physical bodies with their limitations and shortcomings. They also personify tendencies which materialize bodily consciousness and diminish the degree of the light, power and spirituality of the Monad-Ego manifesting in the personal nature. They display undesirable qualities of character, and thus metaphorically imprison the Soul in a tomb or pit.

An Initiatory Interpretation:
Joseph as Candidate for Initiation and as Initiate

The unfoldment of the human Monad from the prosaic human to the superhuman may be delayed, may proceed normally, or may be hastened. Delay arises from deliberate selfishness and self-materialization in thought, motive and mode of life. Since the evolution of germinal Monadic powers from latency to increasing potency inevitably occurs throughout Manvantara, this process may be regarded as the normal procedure. Hastening, however, is achieved by self-spiritualization and by service to others. The impulse to embark upon self-quickening, or to tread the initiatory path, arises within a neophyte when the inner Self has reached a certain degree of development. This is evidenced by the responsiveness and ultimate surrender of the outer personality to purely spiritual influences. The decision to find and tread "the way of holiness" (Isa. 35:8) is thus perfectly natural, because it is inwardly inspired.

As a youth Joseph typifies a spiritual neophyte, while his adventures, including his disasters and triumphs, allegorically portray difficulties encountered and successes achieved by those who enter in at "the strait gate" (Matt. 7:13) and tread the narrow way. The tests, ordeals, victories and rapid unfoldment of many faculties and powers are also described allegorically in the narrative. Progressive stages in the story of the life of a savior portray expansions of consciousness associated with passage through the five great initiations, culminating in Adeptship at the fifth (see Volume I, Part Five).

This method of revelation of the inner life of those who tread the ancient Way is also exemplified by the action of placing Joseph in a dark pit, or out of the sight of normal passersby. Reference is thus made to rites of initiation in ancient times in which, in secret halls of initiation, candidates were deprived of physical consciousness and laid either upon a cross or in a sarcophagus within a temple or crypt. The candidate was literally in the dark—physically unconscious—

having been plunged into an initiatory trance. Three days and three nights then passed, and during this period the spiritual Self entered into full realization of oneness with the Divine Life within all nature, knowing itself to be identical with that life. At the end of this period the Ego reentered the body, which then awakened to the light of day. Thus Joseph is raised from the dark pit and restored to the blessing of light. As a result of this experience the initiate was as one reborn, renewed, and is sometimes referred to as being born again or twice born. In allegorical literature all nativities of saviors, heroines, and heroes can be interpreted in a similar manner.

The resistance of the substances of which the human mental, emotional and physical bodies are built, and of the involving (the opposite polarity of evolving) consciousness within those substances, the despiritualizing effects of undesirable habits and the difficulties of adverse karma—all these create obstacles and cause sufferings on the path of swift unfoldment which, in consequence, is sometimes referred to as "the Way of the Cross." In the Joseph story these adverse influences are portrayed by his attempted seduction by Potiphar's wife and by the several misfortunes which followed. Joseph's interpretation of dreams, his rise to power as Grand Vizier of Egypt and his death in great honor—all these portray degrees of development, powers attained, and the initiate's final triumph at becoming an Adept.

10

An Allegory of the Law of Cycles

The story of Joseph, who is presented as a historical character, is—along with other narratives in the Pentateuch—an allegory descriptive of the law of cycles, one major cycle being composed of almost innumerable minor ones. The major cycle of the outpouring of creative life, the emergence of creative officials, the building of the cosmos, its densification, and the entry of the indwelling life into the deepest depths are all revealed in that part of the story which states that Joseph was out in the field with his brothers. This culminates in the supposedly enforced descent of Joseph into the pit. Incarceration in a pit which had been dug down into the earth—as also the entombment of Christ "in a sepulchre which was hewn out of a rock" (Mark 15:46)—may be taken as indicating that in the process of involution the emanated Monad-bearing life wave had reached the deepest level of embodiment in solid physical substance, the mineral kingdom of the Earth itself.

The ultimate victory of Spirit over matter, of life over form, is allegorically described in the account of Joseph's rescue from the pit and his later high attainment. The phenomena accompanying both interior unfoldment and outer development of cosmoi and humanity leading to the close of a cycle are also portrayed in the closing portion of the story. In conformity with the unchanging rule, plans are made at the close of one cycle for the opening of its successor, the officials for which are also chosen. This chronicle applies to cosmoi, Solar Systems, Planets, kingdoms of nature and human Monads, and also to the cycles of the successive reincarnations of the individual spiritual Soul. This remarkable allegory is conceived and related with such skill that it is equally applicable to, and a revelation of, the principles governing the processes of involution and evolution in all degrees of magnitude. Experiences and attainments of those initiates who tread the path of deliberately hastened evolution to perfected humanity, their passage through the grades of the lesser and the greater Mysteries, and the temptations, tests and ordeals to which aspirants are submitted are also described in the story of Joseph, with its macrocosmic, microcosmic and initiatory interpretations.

The Characters as Logoi and as Human Monads

An elucidation of the story from these points of view requires a preliminary examination of each of the characters. Jacob, the patriarch, for example, represents both the creative Intelligence or Logos of a larger cycle and also the human Monad. In the first example his cycle is drawing to a close and his successor, Joseph, has been produced, equipped with a coat of many colors and introduced into the evolutionary field. Joseph's marriage to Asenath, the daughter of Potipherah (Gen. 41:45), is interpreted as an indication that he was an initiate of the Egyptian Mysteries (SD, Vol. 5, p. 266). In some Jewish allegories the Logos is personified by a farmer, and frequently he was portrayed as a keeper of flocks. This choice was doubtless influenced by the fact that many of the patriarchs were indeed wandering herdsmen and sheep breeders, the wealth of the tribes consisting for the most part of their herds and flocks. If this temporal fact is given a spiritual significance, then the symbology is remarkably apt. A Hebrew patriarch is invested with the powers received from his predecessor, while the places and fields in the allegories represent the material universe. The various kinds of flocks are the Monads of angels and of people which have to be sent out into the field, shepherded, and brought to maturity. The members of the family of the patriarch and those of the tribe, namely the shepherds and their wives and children, are seen as the directive spiritual Intelligences, the Sephiroth and their subordinates.

Creative and evolutionary laws are revealed by means of minor allegories supposedly descriptive of the activities, experiences and adventures of these people. In these stories one particular boy is generally chosen as the favorite son, who despite the enmity of jealous brothers proves to be the lawful successor. At the death of the father this son inherits the flocks, riches and tribal responsibilities, and his life history continues the revelation. Each of the patriarchs therefore personifies the Logos of a system of whatever magnitude, and also represents the human Monad. In the former case—as Logos—its inherited possessions are the seeds of life delivered to it by its predecessor, while the additions which it is able to make represent the fruits of its own evolutionary Scheme.

Applied to the Monad, the "inheritance" (because the Monad is a seed of its parent—the Logos—and therefore contains all parental characteristics and all the divine powers in a latent state) is descriptive of innate powers, and the additions represent the gradual evolution of faculties which are the harvest of the successive lives as a reincarnating Ego. The elders of the family may be regarded as those Dhyan Chohans or Monads which reached the greatest evolutionary heights in the preceding Scheme and, in consequence, undertake the creative responsibilities and offices in its successor. In the Monadic interpretation these elders and workers in the fields are those egoic qualities developed in earlier cycles which form the powers and the characteristics of the individuality. Wives, universally interpreted, represent the ensouling, creatively responsive life which is the Soul of matter, and also matter itself. The female members of the patriarchs' families typify the vehicles of the Monad, especially the Causal Body and the Auric Envelope. In the initiatory reading, women generally personify both the wisdom of the sanctuaries, the Gnosis, Theosophia, and the sanctuaries themselves.

Like his father, Joseph may be regarded as representing both the divine principle in a universe and the Spirit-essence or human Monad. Since he follows his father Jacob as the principal character in the story, he may be interpreted as the personification of the Logos of a new Solar System or of any of its subcycles. Joseph's story, thus read, is that of the transference of the center of creative activity from one Manvantara to the next within the Maha-Manvantara partly described in the Pentateuch. Joseph—as Logos—is also the involving and evolving one life itself. His story is an allegory of the experiences of that life from its initial manifestation in matter and form (birth and descent into the pit—involution), through periods of increasing importance (rescue and governorship—evolution), to full expression (feeding the nations), followed by his death (end of Manvantara). Joseph is also the sun from dawn (birth) to meridian (rulership in Egypt), and on to setting (death). Uniting these into a single concept, we may say that Joseph typifies the solar Logos, whose involution culminates in entombment in the mineral kingdom (descent into the pit). This is followed by evolution (deliverance, slavery, and later success in Egypt), all this being allegorically described with great skill. Ultimate full self-manifestation throughout the Solar System and full fruition at Manvantara's close are indicated by the wealth and power which Joseph attains.

Jacob, father of Joseph, represents the Logos of the preceding Solar System, while Joseph himself portrays the human Monad which comes forth from the parent Source endowed with the parental qualities (brothers and one sister). The involution and evolution of the Monadic ray through the seven planes and kingdoms of nature to individual Egohood is described in the narrative of the early period of Joseph's life. The coat of many colors provided by his father is the aura as a whole, with special reference to the Augoeides (the Causal Body). In this microcosmic view physical incarnation is represented by the descent into the pit and the time spent there. Death is portrayed by elevation from the pit. Passage through the underworld (the astral plane entered after death)—the region of desire—is indicated by the period of slavery, the imprisonment, and the enticements of the wife of Potiphar (Gen. 39). Ascension beyond the realm of desire and the casting off of the desire body, followed by entry into the world of heaven (Mental and Higher Mental Planes), are portrayed both by favors received by Joseph from Pharaoh and by his continually increasing prestige and power (Gen. 41). The withdrawal of all the fruits of the life cycle into the higher Self, and the inception of a new incarnation are allegorically described by the events of the closing years, particularly the feeding of Joseph's family (Gen. 43). The new incarnation itself is represented by Benjamin, in whose sack of corn is placed a silver cup, symbol of egoic power, life and consciousness (Gen. 44:12).

Joseph as Initiate

The entry of the Monad-Ego upon the path of Holiness is also portrayed in the life story of Joseph. The tests and trials of an initiate (false accusation and imprisonment), the growing wisdom, the advancement, the favors of the land of Egypt and its Pharaoh—these indicate the procedures of initiation into and through the lesser and greater Mysteries. The services rendered by Joseph and his death refer to ascension or Adeptship (see Volume I, Chapter 14). Every initiate enacts—at first only figuratively (in the lesser Mysteries) and eventually fully (in the greater Mysteries)—the cycle of manifestation of the solar Logos and of the human Monad. The initiate thoroughly identifies with both of these, and even adopts the name and the persona of the Deity during this ritual [see Hodson, *Light of the Sanctuary: The Occult Diary of Geoffrey Hodson* and Volume I for more information about this ritual]. Thus the story of Joseph, one of the most remarkable allegories ever written, is also the story of the one life in both its universal and its individual or Monadic self-manifestations.

Despite its richness of content, the revelation of hidden wisdom is achieved with remarkable economy. Only the bare essentials survived the pruning process to which the narrative apparently was submitted. Councils of initiates were presumably responsible for the original documents, which contained the best of the biblical allegories. Very close supervision was evidently given, with the result that even the distortions of successions of translators have not been able to completely destroy the story with its esoteric meaning. Joseph, then, is the Word made flesh (John 1:14), the manifested Deity, and the ruler of the universe in all of its manifestations, as the dreams (obviously zodiacal) of the sheaves and of the heavenly bodies clearly indicate.

Biblical narratives into which the (supposedly) supernatural intrudes—and, without explanation, is blended with natural or physical events—are to be regarded by students of symbolism as having special significance; for in them, revelation by allegory is associated with historical events. When such intrusions are absent, history is for the most part being related. Esoteric wisdom is, however, not very far away. The Old Testament abounds with illustrations of this. For example, the seven-branched candlestick (the Menorah—Ex. 25:31–40) of the Holy of Holies in the Jewish temple partly represents this sevenfold esoteric wisdom, which, like its symbol, is also a unity. All septenates in nature, including the seven Chains, Rounds, Globes, Root Races and sub-races of a single Globe in one Planetary Scheme, the seven Sephiroth and the seven sacred Planets with their presiding regents, are symbolized by the shape, the knops, the decorations and the lights of the seven-branched candlestick. As these seven lights shone in the darkness to illumine the altar, so the secret wisdom shines through this Sanctuary-inspired Jewish history to illumine responsive minds. The mission of the Jews and the purpose of the erudite and initiated authors of the Bible were, I propose, to preserve, to enunciate and to deliver to humanity this wisdom of the Chaldeo-Hebrew Sanctuaries.

> And Jacob dwelt in the land wherein his father was a stranger in the land of Canaan. *(Gen. 37:1)*

In this verse the authors of Genesis make it clear that a new cycle opened with the birth of Joseph, the cycle of Jacob thus drawing to a close. Jacob's successor had been born and was later to be taken into the new field, of which Egypt is the topographical symbol, there to continue the great succession. In the same way Jacob himself had moved from Mamre to Canaan, a land in which his father had been a stranger.

> These are the generations of Jacob. Joseph being seventeen years old, was feeding the flock with his brethren; and the lad was with the sons of Bilhah, and with the sons of Zilpah, his father's wives, and Joseph brought unto his father their evil report. *(Gen. 37:2)*

The age of Joseph — seventeen — is deliberately introduced here. The numbers 7 and 1 each refer to generative activity, for 7 indicates the close of a minor cycle and 1 the opening of its successor. By reduction the number 8 is gained, representing the cancellation or equalization of debts — the balancing of karma. The action of destiny and its agents, as well as the summation into unity and the absorption by the inner Self of the fruits of preceding cycles, are also denoted by the number 8.

Jacob, the father, who loved ten of his sons less than the eleventh, Joseph, and who had yet another and still younger son named Benjamin, here is a symbol of the Logos or incarnate Intelligence of a universe. As earlier suggested, the twelve sons each represent one of the signs of the zodiac, meaning powers, attributes and capacities present within the incarnate Deity, gradually to be developed in humanity. While elder sons represent those attributes of earlier times and cycles already well unfolded but not completely developed, in the younger sons these powers are as yet only partially awakened. They are therefore temporarily of greater importance or more loved, in the sense of being in receipt of special care. Interpreted in this way, the story of Joseph is an allegory of the development from within the Logos (Jacob) of the Joseph-like powers. Since this development was the immediate task, the greatest attention was being bestowed upon that attribute. In this sense "Israel loved Joseph more than all his children" (Gen. 37:3).

Joseph's Coat of Many Colors

Since under the Law of Correspondences (the mutual resonance between the many apparently separate parts of the universe and corresponding parts of the human constitution) a correlation exists between numbers and colors, the coat (previous lives Joseph received from his father) may be a symbolic representation of the possession of faculties (fruits of preceding cycles). In the Augoeides — the body of light — in which these faculties are established and upon which they are impressed as vibratory capabilities, each developed capacity is indicated in terms of color. Therefore, the shining human Augoeides is the true coat of many colors. Every human being is accordingly enrobed in such a coat, in the sense that it is the parent Monad whose light shines through both the inner and the outer person. Furthermore, it is Monadic power which makes possible the response of the human Ego to the experiences of life as a result of which faculties are developed. The personal, mortal nature is similarly lighted and colored, the various hues representing temperament, qualities, capacities and faculties of both the immortal Self and the mortal vehicles. The mental and emotional bodies of the human adult thus shine with many Egoic and personal hues, but these are physically invisible except to those whose inner eyes are opened. The Ego is personified by Jacob, who gave the coat to his son (the new personality).

In addition to the interpretation already given, the provision of a coat of many colors for Joseph indicates that this special attention caused the associated attributes to shine out, each in its own particular hue, in the aura of the unfolding Logos, and therefore in the auras of those representative existences in the evolutionary field in whom the powers were being expressed. This verse, then, refers to the temporary accentuation of a special group of qualities by an evolving being, whether Logos or Manu of a major cycle, or human Monad or Ego, because for the time being attention upon these qualities is being especially concentrated.

In all interpretations the septenary principle is also indicated by the presence of the seven colors of the spectrum. The Monad, or father, is the source of the light, and the faculties developed from life's experiences are represented by the colors. Some of the coloration in the Augoeides, however, also portrays certain potential and active qualities in the Monad, as well as the fundamental temperament or Ray. [See Hodson, *The Seven Human Temperaments* for more information about these Rays.] In the mystical sense Joseph is the Monad-Ego bringing illumination and grace to the personality. Every human being is Joseph-like, robed in a coat of many colors. This is the human aura with its many hues, each expressive of a developed power and a quality of character.

The symbolism of the coat is carried even further. The colored auric forces are only visible superphysically, these becoming lost to view when the Soul becomes incarnate in a physical body. Symbolically, Joseph as the conjoined mind, emotions and body of one human incarnation is "robbed" of his coat of many colors. Their frequencies of scintillation are too rapid for usual physical perception, but not for the clairvoyant. Allegorically, Joseph loses his coat, the visible aura, when he is lowered into the pit—or incarnated in the physical body.

Microcosmically, the field in which Joseph was feeding his father's flock represents those planes of nature in which the higher Self is to be born (lowered) and is to become increasingly active. The descent into a physical body is thus described, and the brothers who bring it about are those Pitris and Devas responsible for the furthering of progress on the downward arc of an Ego going "down" into incarnation. These exalted Beings are of course not really enemies of the pilgrim Soul, though the descent into the depths of matter does for the time being bring about a serious deprivation and limitation of Egoic freedom.

Joseph—the Divine Life—Becomes Incarnate in Matter

Macrocosmically interpreted, Joseph is the Logos of the new cycle. He has been handed—by his predecessor and in the esoteric sense progenitor or father—the powers and the seeds of living beings, which are the fruits of the previous cycle—also symbolized by the coat of many colors. In the aura of the Logos-to-be all these shine as the solar spectrum at the physical level, and superphysically as the typical colors of the various fundamental forces, frequencies of vibration, planes of nature and their indwelling major Intelligences. They constitute the ineffable radiance, the shining aura, or biblically, the "coat of many colors" of the Logos of a universe.

The story of the supposed antagonism of the elder brothers, their hostility, their actions in stealing Joseph's coat and in lowering him into the pit and all that followed (Gen. 37:23-33) may be regarded as a veil concealing a deeply esoteric revelation. This concerns the process of the descent of the Divine Life into the depths of matter, the process being assisted by certain more highly evolved (elder) Intelligences, personified by Joseph's brothers who were made responsible for lowering him into the pit. Just as such incarceration would be a severe restriction upon Joseph's movements, and the elder brothers who bring it about are presented in the allegory as enemies, in like manner matter appears to restrict—to be hostile to—Spirit.

These previously mentioned Intelligences, variously named the Satanic Hierarchies and the Inverse Sephiras, participate and assist in the penetration of the abyss of space by the creative Spirit, which means the entry of cosmic electricity—life itself—into the limitations of the vast electrical machine which is a universe. Indirectly their actions bring about the partial limitation of the normally universal awareness of the first Logos to the locally focused state. This materializing action is as essential to the full and complete manifestation of Spirit in matter as is the apparently opposite assistance given on the path of return when the embodied Spirit gradually frees itself from the imprisonment temporarily imposed upon it by matter. These seemingly adverse and beneficent functions are not regarded by the philosopher as either evil or good, since both are but parts of an inevitable, impersonal procedure of forthgoing and return.

In order to bring this profoundly metaphysical and power-bestowing knowledge within reach of the uninstructed, and to conceal it against premature discovery and misuse, the two processes have always been represented in the symbolic language of all cultures as being Satanic and redemptive, evil and good, respectively. Typhon, Ahriman, the Asuras, the Titans and Satan are all allegorically presented in world scriptures and mythologies as monstrous embodiments of evil, or the Devil, and so the opposite of good, or God. The dark Beings are no more evil than the fulcrum which offers the necessary resistance to the lever; for, not unlike the fulcrum, they perform a function essential to the material expression of energy.

Joseph's hostile elder brothers personify these supposedly evil agencies, being in fact none other than certain of the Sephiroth (Inverse Sephiras). In esoteric philosophy these are referred to as the "first fruits" of preceding cycles, and therefore as elders from the point of view of the present cycle (of return). Such officials undertake the task of assisting the descent into matter of the triune Spirit-Life-Consciousness, as a result of which this triplicity becomes self-manifest in the field, which is the area between the center and the circumference of a universe.

The powers of darkness are represented by those human beings who turn and distort the forces of nature, who resist evolutionary progress, who seek the will of the individual self against the will of the universe. These are the true enemies of humanity and they definitely exist on Earth. There are certain hallmarks by which evil people, their movements, organizations and actions may be unfailingly known. Among these are monstrous selfishness, egotism, pride, demoniacal ruthlessness, cruelty and intolerance. Behind and within all this exists a continuing egotistical desire to dominate the mind and the life of others; for the unfailing mark of these enemies of human happiness is fanatical egotism and the denial of the all-essential freedom of thought and life. The human agents of darkness vary in evolutionary stature from the cruel, lustful, selfish barbarian (whether considered civilized or not) up to the highly intellectual person who works for self, either openly or secretly behind a veil.

The world's allegorical dramas, when interpreted according to the symbolic language, may reveal the powers, processes and events of the first half of the great cycle of forthgoing, during which a universe is produced and all that it contains is brought to the highest degree of development. The prenatal period of each human birth is a repetition in miniature of this major procedure. Humans in the microcosm continually reenact major macrocosmic processes. By so doing they in turn bring their own innate powers into expression, and finally to perfection.

In addition, as we have already seen, Joseph is a symbol of the Logos of the succeeding cycle. He is preparing for the activities of his office during the period when his predecessor, Jacob, is approaching the end of his cycle. The suggestion of jealousy in the fourth verse

("And when his brethren saw that their father loved him more than all his brethren, they hated him, and could not speak peaceably unto him"—Gen. 37:4) is of course a blind, though not without significance as has already been shown.

Joseph's Dream of the Corn and Wheat

Although doubts may be felt concerning Joseph's wisdom in relating his two dreams to his brothers (Gen. 37:5–11), they both offer opportunities for interpretation in accordance with the view now being presented—namely that Joseph personifies the successor to his father, Jacob. The increasing importance and ascendancy of the Godhead of the new cycle and the representative of zodiacal powers are perfectly portrayed in this allegorical dream. The period in the life cycle of forthgoing and return, indicated in the dream, is that of the harvesting of its fruits, the close of the preceding cycle being also clearly implied. The analogy of farming is particularly appropriate; for involution may aptly be likened to planting, and evolution to growth and ripening. The process of storing the fruits of the dual process and using them as food and as seed for later cycles corresponds to the harvesting and the preserving of the ripened corn. This, together with the bound sheaves in the field, refers to that closing phase or arc in the cycle at which form, symbolized by root and straw, was being disintegrated. The indwelling life had unfolded further capacities (the grain) through experience in form, and these were being garnered. The ripened seed of the corn plant thus represents acquired characteristics and powers sublimated to their finest essence, thereafter to be retained partly as food (acquired knowledge) and partly as seed for new plantings and harvestings (innate faculties to be manifested and further developed in later incarnations). This is equally applicable to the macrocosm, where ripened and harvested corn is a symbol of the powers developed by the Logos in the universe. In their turn these are similarly retained and used (planted) in the succeeding cycle.

Ripened grain is thus a very interesting emblem of those powers which the Monad-Ego has developed in a single life cycle or incarnation and has stored in the Causal Body. The death of the physical body and the later casting off of the astral and mental bodies (*kama-manasic* vestures) are represented by the reaping and subsequent dissolution of root and straw. The winnowing of the grain from the enclosing membrane or chaff corresponds to the withdrawal of the Ego, with its developed powers, from the last vestiges of the disintegrating personality. This occurs at the conclusion of the intermediate period between two Earth lives that follows the separation of the Ego from the lower, mortal principles, which then disintegrates. This period is called *Devachan,* meaning literally "home of the gods," and refers also to a state of consciousness in which the fruits of good deeds performed during the preceding Earth life are fully enjoyed. Thereafter, a new cycle opens for both macrocosm and microcosm, since a new physical incarnation also begins for the Monad-Ego.

Thus the time period of Joseph's dream corresponds to that of ripened corn and harvesting, or the closing phases of a life cycle. This also implies the near approach of the opening of its successor. In biblical terms the Israel cycle is closing and the Joseph cycle is about to begin, the Logos of that cycle being represented by Joseph. The powers harvested from the past and preserved (like seeds in a granary) are depicted by the sheaf of Joseph, each grain of which may be thought of as a Monad of the macrocosm and a potential power in the microcosm.

Clearly the Logos of a new system is young only in relation to that system, itself newborn. Actually this Logos is the most highly evolved Being of the preceding system — its first fruits. In the dream, therefore, though Joseph is the youngest of the brothers his sheaf remains upright, while those of his older brothers make obeisance to it; for the brothers, in the macrocosmic sense, are the assistant *Cosmocratores* or the Dhyan Chohans, the sephirothal manifestation of powers and attributes of the solar Logos itself.

The dream of Joseph becomes a symbolical dramatization of universal processes and procedures. It also portrays the Logos-to-be absorbed in contemplation of the numerical principles and laws by which it first "dreams," or mentally conceives, the future universe which it will later project as an external expression in time and space. A hint of this occurs in Lewis Carroll's book *Through the Looking Glass and What Alice Found There* — a highly, if unconsciously, allegorical work. For example, in the incident of the finding of the dreaming and snoring Red King by Alice, Tweedledum and Tweedledee, Alice would represent the Ego and the twins the higher and lower Mind with whom she dances, debates, and visits the Red King. In the King's presence she is told by them that she, like themselves, is not real but "only a thing in his dream." This is a parallel to the eastern (Vedantic) doctrine of *Maya,* in which only the changeless and eternal Principle is real. All that changes, meaning the manifested universe and its contents, is from this point of view Maya—an illusion or dream. The divine dreamer—the Red King in the book—is also thought of as the Logos in rapt contemplation—the *Maha-Yogi* whose creative ideas are the archetypes according to which all forms are molded, in this sense being only dreams.

At this point one wonders why the oldest son or brother does not become the Logos of the new cycle, since presumably he would personify the most highly developed product, or son. Remember, however, that in a Solar System there are many offices as well as many Dhyan Chohanic fruits. The line of succession to each office is carefully preserved, each being occupied by a member of the Sephiroth according to predominant attributes. These differing offices and functions in the externalization of divine thought, or production of an objective universe, are well presented and explained in the kabblistic tree of life with its ten Sephiras, each an agent for the outpoured divine life.

In the manner of Joseph, the chosen Logos is then born or deeply incarnated, in one sense imprisoned (lowered into the pit) within the matter of the Solar System, this being the Divine Immanence. Thus clothed, the Logos is a new creation. Its manifestation is symbolized by a Nativity and the Logos is portrayed as a little child. In one sense, full spiritual freedom has been surrendered by that voluntary birth. Although while in the highest consciousness and being—transcendence—the Logos is still free, nevertheless it is bound in material manifestation within the limits of its Solar System. Similarly the human Monad-Ego is transcendent in relation to its mortal personality, while during incarnation it is partially bound within the imprisonment of the physical body.

The Dhyan Chohans, however, are not all similarly restricted. The offices held by the majority of them are fulfilled at lofty spiritual levels alone, where life and consciousness, though circumscribed, are not wholly limited as is the case at the physical level. These officials are not therefore, born. All this is brilliantly shown in Joseph's dream of his upright sheaf to which those of his older brothers make obeisance. Again, in order that these profound truths may be veiled from the profane, the purely human attribute of capacity for jealousy and hatred is drawn as a cover or blind over the revelation.

Joseph's Dream of Celestial Bodies

In Joseph's second dream, the macrocosmic principles of creation are deliberately indicated. Human beings are eliminated from the allegory, the brothers being represented by the sun, moon and eleven stars. The sun is the Logos, the moon is the matter of the universe, and the eleven stars are zodiacal Powers and Intelligences, twelve in all when conjoined with the sun.

In the microcosmic interpretation the sun is the individual *Atma,* the Monad in manifestation both as an Ego and as a personality. The moon is the individual *Prakriti,* the Monad-illumined and thus specialized substance of all the vehicles, and particularly of those of mortals in any one incarnation; for the moon is the planet of generation, death and disintegration. This substance of which the superphysical and physical bodies are built corresponds universally to the matter of the planes of nature and to the sheaths of differing degrees of density in which the one life is clothed.

The stars correspond to the intelligent life essence of each of the human bodies or principles. However, it was not the physical celestial bodies which made obeisance in the dream but rather their informing Intelligences, whose collaboration was obtained. The life essence of each of the human bodies is vibrationally attuned to the informing Spirit or Dhyan Chohan of one of the stars. These vibrate in unison — interaction is continually occurring.

Normally the interior, zodiacal qualities in humans and the external influences of the twelve signs are beyond human control. When the later stages of evolution are entered upon, however, the Monad assumes increasing control of planetary, stellar and zodiacal attributes and influences on the one hand, and of their effects upon the various spiritual vehicles on the other. Ultimately they are completely mastered, and it is this state which is mirrored in the two dreams of Joseph.

This chapter of Genesis and these verses can be regarded as typical examples of the revelation and yet concealment of potentially power-bestowing knowledge. As above interpreted, the dream refers to the kabbalistic doctrine that the whole universe with all its parts, from the highest plane down to physical nature, is interlocked, interwoven to make a single whole — one body, one organism, one power, one life, one consciousness, all cyclically evolving under one law. The organs or parts of this body — the macrocosm, although apparently separated in space and plane of manifestation — are in fact harmoniously interrelated, intercommunicative, and continually interactive. The human being who discovers this truth could enter the power aspect of the universe and tap any one of these forces. This person would then become endowed with almost irresistible influence both over nature and over the rest of humanity. A similar allegory is the story of Joshua making the sun and the moon stand still (Josh. 10:12–14).

Returning to Chapter Thirty-Seven of Genesis, Joseph personifies the forthgoing ray of the Monad (Atma) nearing Adeptship, and is therefore capable of controlling the manifestation in him of the solar and lunar forces. This achieved, the mind of the initiate is both perpetually illumined (it is always day) and able to overcome all adverse attributes (enemies) previously present in his or her human nature.

In the story of Joseph this whole incident happens in a dream, thus implying a supramundane state of awareness. Acting consciously in his immortal Selfhood, Joseph, typical of all initiates, brings his vehicles, their powers and their attributes under the direction of his will. These are represented by his brothers who, correctly in one sense, resent the idea of being placed in a subordinate position. The father, or Monad, however, comprehends the dream or "observed the saying" (Gen. 37:11).

An Allegory of Emanation

Verses twelve through thirty-six of Chapter Thirty-Seven of Genesis offer a study of the life of Joseph as an allegorical description of the emanation of creative and formative power, life and Intelligence (Logos), and of the shaping of universes with all which they produce. (See also the discussion of cosmogenesis in Volume I, pp 120–122 and in Chapter 12.) As Joseph is lowered into a pit deep in the earth, so these Logoic attributes become embodied, "lowered," "imprisoned," "buried" in densest matter. This descent is followed by an ascent out of the depths towards the spiritual heights, a procedure which is also symbolically portrayed in the life story of Joseph by his liberation from the pit and transportation to Egypt. All of this wisdom of the ages concerning the creation and perfecting of universes is perceivable in the closing chapters of Genesis.

The first "Being" to emerge from infinity to finiteness is the Supreme Emanator, personified in this allegory by Israel in conscious unity with the Lord God (Gen. 28:13–15). From this concentration of the irresistible, outpoured, creative power a more individual manifestation emerges. This "Being" is to perform the function of an active Logos throughout the life-period (Manvantara) of the universe-to-be. Personified by Joseph, who was sent out by his father into the field, the Logos — Joseph-like — goes out into the "field" — the area of Self-manifestation and evolution.

The hostility projected by the brothers is a cleverly constructed and very effective blind for the collaboration between the Logos and its "Hosts," the archangel and angel hierarchies associated with the whole vast enterprise of the emanation, fashioning and evolution of a universe. These are jealous, hostile and actively destructive only in the sense that their task is to "allure," "induct," "imprison" and "enchain" (allegorically) the logoic life and its Source. All that is described in the above verses of Chapter Thirty-seven is able to be interpreted in this manner.

One of the methods used by writers of the sacred language is to conceal and yet reveal a profound and normally secret, power-bestowing knowledge by describing it in reverse. In these instances the characters in the stories will be made to act in enmity to the heroine or hero, to be directly hostile and to plot — and even achieve in some measure — her or his downfall even if, as in Joseph's case, this proved to be only temporary. They really are personifying agencies active in the formation of universes and planets and in the generative processes in the organic kingdoms of physical nature. Thus, though made to appear evil, these agencies (Elohim) are actually beneficent. The murderous intentions of Joseph's brothers towards him, for example, and the way in which these intentions were actively expressed, constitute an allegory of the very opposite relationship between the Logos and the cosmic genetic agencies. This relationship is of course entirely collaborative. This method of writing may be discerned in many of the myths and scriptures of ancient peoples in which great material powers are made to be at war with whichever character in the story is personifying the Logos. This hostility is only apparent, and the way in which it is described is a cover or blind for the real revelation.

This obscuration is used because powers and procedures are being revealed in which a developed will can control human minds for better or for worse. The need for secrecy is especially necessary in descriptions of emanative and formative processes. Another reason for the original secrecy is that in ancient times this deeply esoteric knowledge was imparted under a vow of silence to initiated members of the temples of the greater Mysteries. Times change, however, and the esotericism of one age becomes the exoteric knowledge of a successor. Hence it is permissible in this time to openly refer to certain but not all ideas which originally were wrapped in the profoundest secrecy. The real revelation, however, is not of ideas stated in words but rather in the direct experience itself—in this case to actually see the Elohim at work.

Joseph—Personification of the Eternal Wisdom

A further possible interpretation of the great allegories is founded upon the application of the first of the four keys [see Volume I, Chapter 7], namely that all the recorded and supposedly external historical events also occur interiorly. All happens within every individual, each event being descriptive of a human subjective experience, whether advancing by the normal evolutionary method or achieving hastened unfoldment by treading the way of holiness. The latter choice is made after the spiritual Self has begun to illumine the person, who in eventual response seeks and finds spiritual wisdom and a temple of the Mysteries in which successive initiations are conferred. This is one possible interpretation of the life of Joseph.

Patriarchs, heroes and heroines are regarded in this interpretation as personifications of the Eternal Wisdom, the Gnosis itself. Their adventures, trials and triumphs portray the process of bringing illumination to the human mind, collective and individual. From this point of view Joseph typifies the Eternal Wisdom. His birth portrays its first perception by recipient human minds, and his coat of many colors the effect upon it of analysis, *ahamkara* (the illusion of self as a self-separate existence in contrast to the reality of the universal One Self), modification and limitation.

The hatred and jealousy of Joseph's brothers allegorically describe the resistance of the mind, the emotions, and the general attitude of the personality to the reception of spiritual illumination. They also describe the implications of its application to life—notably to established habits, many of which must go. The mortal or lower self at first tends to resent the implied ascendancy which the higher Self will gradually assume. The ultimate and inevitable complete domination of the outer by the inner Self is instinctively foreseen and resisted. Eventually the personal will must be surrendered. The natural, selfish, worldly outlook (the brothers) – now on its deathbed – calls into action a self-saving instinct to prevent, or at any rate to stave off, the day of triumph. The brothers plot the death of Joseph (the influence of spiritual wisdom in worldly life), as did King Kamsa that of Krishna and King Herod that of Jesus. They seek to destroy the influence of the dawning idealism, to bury truth deep in the matter of mind, brain and material pursuits. Symbolically, Joseph is forcibly lowered into the pit.

Failing in their impious design, the brothers commercialize esoteric wisdom. Joseph is sold into slavery, as spiritual knowledge is so constantly sold for material gain. Nevertheless the power of the awakening spiritual Self proves to be irresistible. The Eternal Wisdom inevitably triumphs, as did Jesus in driving the moneychangers out of the temple (Matt 21:12). The slavery and imprisonment are, however, temporary (Joseph is raised from the pit). Governorship over the whole of human nature (Egypt) is attained and the nations (the human race) and the family (the individual vehicles of the initiate) are fed from an abundance which exists amidst the famine-stricken condition (unillumined state) of the rest of humankind.

Moreover, the divine power and light are handed on, as the story later reveals. Benjamin receives, hidden in his cornsack, a silver cup (Gen. 44:2) – symbol of the higher Mind receptive of the hidden truth. Each Adept who passes beyond humanity hands on her or his wisdom to a chosen but natural human successor, training and aiding the person to the rapid fulfillment of human destiny in the attainment of perfection. Benjamin is a permutation of the beloved disciple, Ananda or John, upon whom the teacher bestows a special love.

Joseph as Initiate in the Greater Mysteries

As a description of the Mysteries, the life story of Joseph allegorically portrays the progress of the candidate through the degrees of a sacred rite. Birth represents passage through the first great initiation. The mother personifies the Mysteries themselves, while the father represents the hierophant. The elder brothers are the officiants and other members of the temple. The two dreams describe the effects upon consciousness of the initiations into the second and third degrees.

The bowing of the brothers' sheaves to that of Joseph signifies that development and attainment by the candidate as a result of which spiritual and esoteric progress is both won and acclaimed. The existence of the sheaves themselves indicates that it was harvest time, which in its turn refers to the gathering into a synthesis of all the developed powers and fruits of preceding incarnations. In the symbolism of the Mysteries corn represents both richness of attainment and the achievement of the required standard of a particular degree.

Similarly the sun, the moon and the stars which in the second dream make obeisance to the dreamer represent the solar, planetary and zodiacal attainments required for admittance into the third degree. While the sheaves of the earlier dream for the most part indicate the harvested fruits of successive lives as a mortal, the heavenly bodies of the later one refer to the newly awakened cosmic powers of the higher Self. Their obeisance indicates that they have been mastered and that their powers are now consciously wielded by the inner will of the candidate's (Joseph's) essential Self, the true dreamer of the wondrous dream.

11

Joseph in Egypt

Genesis 39

Joseph was now a slave in Egypt, and he was delivered into the hands of Potiphar, captain of Pharaoh's guard. But God was with Joseph, causing all that he did to prosper. This did not go unnoticed by Joseph's master, Potiphar, who soon put him in charge of his whole household.

Joseph was a handsome man, and his master's wife began begging him to sleep with her. But because Joseph was a virtuous man, he turned away her advances. One day, however, when they were alone in the house, she came to Joseph, caught him by his clothing, and again insisted that he sleep with her. In alarm Joseph fled from the house, leaving his tunic in her hand. Later in the day she made the accusation to Potiphar that Joseph had tried to rape her, and in rage Potiphar had Joseph thrown into prison. But even in the dungeons God was with Joseph, again causing all that he did to prosper.

Although Egyptian monuments, literature and history give little support for the incidents narrated in this and the following chapters of Genesis, their historical probability is not denied. The story of Joseph, however, includes so much supernatural intervention that it offers a fruitful field for the student of symbology.

This chapter of Genesis allegorically describes the beginning of entry upon the pathway of return and the varied resistances to the ascent of Spirit offered by matter. In the human interpretation, Joseph as the inner Self in a new physical body grows up towards adolescence, as the action of Potiphar's wife—introducing the sexual motif—indicates. Nevertheless, the imprisonment which follows portrays the still potent influence of matter over Spirit and of the physical body over the human soul. The subsequent release from prison and the rise to power refer to later stages of the great journey, while the wise and beneficent actions—and especially the eventual death in honor—refer to the triumphant return of life to its source towards the end of Manvantara. The entry of the Israelites into Egypt, their bondage to the Egyptians and their subsequent deliverance all portray the same process in nature, as do so many other scriptural and mythological narratives.

The Narrow Way

The possibility that a person may forestall nature, may hasten deliverance from the bondage of the flesh and attain to liberation or salvation in advance of fellow humans is also indicated in the story of Joseph. Again the meanings of certain symbols in the narrative are reversed.

Egypt was a center of the spiritual life at that time, and its temples, their sanctuaries and their halls of initiation into the lesser and the greater Mysteries offered the necessary assistance to treading the spiritual path. Joseph's successful resistance of the temptations associated with sexual desire (Potiphar's wife), his undeserved imprisonment, his deliverance as a result of the exercise of an esoteric power (interpretation of dreams) and his subsequent rise to the chief position in the kingdom all allegorically portray passage through the initiatory tests and rites and the attainment of the accompanying expansions of consciousness. These culminate in the attainment of Adeptship, generally portrayed by a figurative death and resurrection, meaning the transcendence of all limitation imposed by matter during evolution through the human kingdom of nature.

Then follows entry into the superhuman kingdom, with conscious absorption into the life and spirit of the universe, though mysteriously without the total loss of identity. This is the salvation of Christianity, *moksha* or liberation of Hinduism and Nirvana of Buddhism. When this state is attained during the present period of human occupation of the planet, enforced self-spiritualization is implied. The same process is referred to by Jesus as entering in at the strait gate and treading the narrow way (Matt. 7:13,14). Isaiah refers to the pathway of hastened attainment as "the way of holiness" (Isa. 35:8).

As has been noted earlier, this relatively secret or esoteric life has been followed by a small number of spiritually awakening and awakened human beings from the earliest period of the human occupation of Earth. Guidance by a master upon this secret pathway, descriptions of experiences through which the soul passes, the tests, ordeals and triumphs of the candidate—all these run like a silver thread, now hidden, now revealed, which is woven into the tapestry of the scriptures and mythologies of ancient peoples. The great figures—heroines and heroes, prophets, apostles and saviors—all represent successful followers of the ancient way who have arrived at various stages of attainment. The story of their lives is extremely instructive for those who can pierce the veil of allegory and symbol beneath which the secrets of esoteric science, discipleship and initiation are concealed.

Joseph in Slavery

The first verse of Chapter Thirty-Nine of Genesis tells of the capture of Joseph, his journey to Egypt and his purchase by Potiphar, an officer of Pharaoh and captain of his guard. Here the story of the early stages of the ascent of life from the mineral kingdom may be allegorically referred to, since Potiphar's name means "gift of the risen one." This is supported by the statement that Joseph, though still a captive and a slave, is granted a measure of freedom, being brought to and placed in the service of Potiphar, a wise and discerning man.

Joseph Finds Grace in His Master's Eyes

The statement that "the Lord was with Joseph" in verse two does not so much indicate that the Logos of the Solar System had singled him out for personal favors, as that the Lord within him—his own divine Self—was beginning increasingly to direct his motives and life and inwardly to enlighten him. Each character in the story represents a part and a power of the human constitution. In this reading of the story the Lord is the divine Monad, itself a ray of the Supreme Deity, the one eternal light. Potiphar stands for the mind and his wife for the emotions, while their house refers to awareness in the physical body.

Joseph, when helpless in the pit into which his brothers had lowered him and so shut out from the light of day, portrays that stage of human evolution at which there is no spiritual awareness during waking consciousness. His inner Self had not yet begun to endow him with the degree of illumination which later enabled him to interpret dreams and wisely to foresee and prepare against a famine. Nevertheless, his earlier history, and especially his own dreams, indicate that egoically he was unusually advanced, being of considerable evolutionary stature. Thus for him Egypt does not represent bondage to sensual and material existence, which is the usual interpretation—as in the case of the Israelite nation as a whole, for example. Rather Egypt for Joseph was a center of the ancient Mysteries where the great initiations were conferred.

Every candidate for initiation must prove herself or himself by passing successfully through certain temptations, and through tests of preparedness and capacity. These also are described in allegory in Joseph's experiences in Egypt.

In the various aspects of human nature, personified by the characters in inspired allegories, Joseph represents the highly evolved, illumined Ego, the unfolding, immortal Being. Throughout his whole nature, mental, emotional and physical, this dweller in the innermost displays wisdom and self-command. Symbolically, Joseph finds favor in the eyes of Potiphar and is recognized as being divinely inspired.

Joseph's overseership of the house and affairs of Potiphar (v. 5) indicates domination of the more earthly part of human nature by the indwelling spiritual Self. As noted above, Joseph, the Ego, had become sufficiently involved to be in charge of his outer nature—his mind, emotion and body (Potiphar's house and fields). Potiphar's trust in Joseph, and the fact that he left the whole management of his affairs in Joseph's hands, describes that state at which the physical nature has, in its turn, been surrendered to idealism and direction by the inner Self. This surrender, implying detachment, dispassion and personal disinterestedness, is one of the marks of the highly evolved person and a sure sign that they are approaching readiness for initiation and the expansions of consciousness which this will produce.

Acceptance of a candidate by those who are already initiated and passage through a ceremony of consecration can occur only as a recognition of spiritual unfoldment. The immortal Self is visible to the hierophant and his or her officers, and must display those powers and qualities which are characteristic of humans at the required evolutionary stage of development. The essence of initiation, therefore, is not passage through a rite and receipt of a degree, although these are important, but rather the achievement of a certain stage of unfoldment. In this the aspirant is not entirely alone—assistance in the development of wisdom, comprehension and faculties is always available. In addition, guidance in bringing the fruits of such progress to bear upon and be expressed through the outer person in the waking hours is both needed and received. The initiatory rite, with its descent of power, definitely assists in this procedure. The touch of the wand of power—the thyrsus in the hand of the hierophant—upon the crown of the head of the candidate opens up the channels of communication between the inner and the outer selves of the initiate. These consist of whirling funnels of force in the etheric and superphysical bodies, and of organs in the physical brain which become intensely vivified by the descent of the hierophantic power. Thereafter, the initiate has access to her or his own living Self, which in its turn can also illumine and inspire the initiate in daily life. The narrative indicates that Joseph, "a goodly person, and well favored" (v. 6), was approaching readiness for the receipt of this spiritual and esoteric assistance.

The Attempted Seduction of Joseph

Every candidate for initiation must have reached a sufficient degree of self-command to be able to resist desire and the temptations of the flesh. This attainment has been gradual, but is frequently represented in allegories of initiation by a single incident descriptive of resistance to temptation to indulge, sometimes illicitly, in the pleasures of sense and sex. Potiphar's wife is made to play the role of temptress.

In other allegorical versions of this theme the would-be seducer may be male, and even a deity. Thus Apollo pursued Daphne, and Zeus had intercourse with various nymphs and young women. The story of the attempted seduction of Joseph by Potiphar's wife is not only an incident which may actually have occurred, it is also a symbolical description both of human victory over desire and of an actual test of readiness for initiation.

Joseph's refusal of the attempted seduction by Potiphar's wife (v. 8 & 9) gives a major key to the mystery of sex transmutation. This consisted of the application of reason—the powers of the mind—to the dangerous situation. In his case reason was stronger than either temptation or any desire that Joseph may have experienced. The responsibilities of office and the call of duty were given as reasons for refusal to respond to the invitation.

In verse ten the ordeal is made to continue in preparation for initiation, and the temptation is repeated until victory is attained. In Joseph's case only sternness of will, an appeal to reason and complete devotion to duty—the threefold secret of success—were evoked.

While the literal reading of the account of the woman's catching or holding Joseph's garment may seem natural under the circumstances, the language of symbols is also employed; for a garment is used in that language to represent a vehicle of consciousness and also a covering—even an encrustation affecting the mind. Nakedness, on the other hand, implies freedom from such limitations, the faithful exposure of intellect to Spirit and an unclouded expression of the spiritual through the human nature of the subject of a narrative. All occurs within one person, and in this case Joseph rose above the distracting and distorting influences brought to bear upon him. Symbolically, a garment was left behind.

The Accusation of Joseph

A lying accusation, apparently supported by evidence, is brought by Potiphar's wife against Joseph (v. 13–18). The treacherous nature of certain aspects of human emotions is portrayed here. An apparently inescapable experience, source of suffering and test, must necessarily be passed through by Joseph, as also by every candidate for initiation, especially those who during the time of their trial remain in the material world. Even in ordinary life unsatisfied desire, envy, jealousy, hatred, and fear that position and power may be lost can evoke in certain people the worst of human attributes. Those susceptible to these temptations turn against and betray friends, teachers and leaders. For example, Peter denied the Christ; Judas betrayed him.

The Imprisonment of Joseph

As the mind can and frequently does inhibit the illuminating functions of the intuition, resulting in imprisoning consciousness, so Potiphar—representing the mind when a victim of delusion born of deceit—temporarily imprisoned Joseph, the illumined spiritual Self. All allegorical dramas are enacted within one person, who represents both an individual and a Race. The various characters personify attributes of that person—qualities, powers, weaknesses and vehicles of consciousness, whether habitual or just beginning to appear.

Joseph is portrayed as a wise and mature person, indicating a highly developed mind possessed by a highly evolved representative of humanity. Potiphar also represents the mind, but at a lower level of evolution. As a result he fell prey to the treacherous and untrue accusations of his wife (desire), and imprisoned his previously trusted officer, Joseph (the illumined mind). The narrative is thus carried beyond the realm of mere emotion into that of the mind, the limitations of which are displayed. The psychological revelations are quite profound, as in so many scriptural narratives in which the language of symbols is employed.

Verse twenty-one states that even in prison, Joseph still had grace in the eyes of God. This reveals that he is too highly evolved to be seriously incommoded by the imprisonment, and his intuitive powers and gift of interpretation are not affected.

> And the keeper of the prison committed to Joseph's hand all the prisoners that were in the prison; and whatsoever they did there, he was the doer of it.
> The keeper of the prison looked not to any thing that was under his hand; because the Lord was with him, and that which he did, the Lord was with him, and that which he did, the Lord made it to prosper. *(Gen. 39:22-23)*

These verses show how the prison represents both the substance of the human mental body—mind-stuff—and those attributes of the mind which, misused, prevent its illumination by direct perception or intuition. Prisoners themselves personify those people who have become restricted in this way. The whole prison, together with its keepers and its inmates, aptly portrays the temporary limiting effects —particularly on those people of a wholly materialistic and individualistic mentality—produced upon human consciousness by incarnation in a mortal personality. Joseph, said to be favored by God, is the illumined spiritual Self of a highly evolved person, and therefore is never entirely subject to the above-mentioned hindrances. These last two verses of the chapter indicate that this degree of evolutionary stature had been attained by Joseph. The statement that all that was accomplished in the prison was done by him may be interpreted as meaning that his inner Self was in complete command of the outer self. The keeper's apparent neglect of his office and the relegation of his duties to Joseph would seem to support these interpretations.

It is notable that although Potiphar's wife, by a false accusation, was the cause of Joseph's imprisonment, she is nevertheless not mentioned again in the narrative. The initiated inner Self can neither be successfully lured nor in any way affected by desire. The last verse of the chapter indicates that the innermost Self, the Monad (the Lord), could and did empower and inspire the immortal Soul (Joseph).

Joseph Interprets His Fellow Prisoners' Dream

Genesis 40

Pharaoh's butler and baker eventually fell out of his favor and were imprisoned with Joseph, where he attended to them both. One night they both dreamt, and Joseph saw that the dreams troubled them. With the power of God in him he interpreted these dreams.

The butler dreamt of a vine with three branches that budded, blossomed and brought forth grapes. He then took these grapes, pressed their juice into Pharaoh's cup and placed the cup in his hand. Joseph's interpretation was that in three days Pharaoh would restore him to his position — that all would be as before. Joseph then asked the butler to mention his unjust imprisonment to Pharaoh.

The baker told Joseph that in his dream he saw three baskets on his head. The top basket contained baked goods, but the birds were eating them. Joseph gave the baker this interpretation — in three days the baker would be beheaded and hanged, and the birds would eat his flesh.

These prophesies were fulfilled in full. But the butler forgot about Joseph.

The purely secular interpretation of the butler's dream given by Joseph by no means exhausts the spiritual possibilities. Whether these were in the authors' minds cannot be determined. The symbology and allegory, however, suggest veiled instruction concerning profound truths.

The vine with three branches, for example, may be regarded as a symbol of the vital energy by which the universe is sustained, and of the power or thrust of Spirit which is responsible for the evolution of life and form. This is the mysterious, inexhaustible power ceaselessly at work within a universe from the first moment of its emanation from the Absolute, throughout its objective existence, and up to its final withdrawal back into its Source. It is, in fact, that invisible and intangible quality which is called "life." The tree of life in the Garden of Eden, the sephirothal tree of Kabbalism and the vine, as indeed all fruit-bearing trees, are used as symbols of this hidden force in nature. Thus, apart from the divinatory interpretation given to the butler by Joseph, the dream was also a revelation of deep universal significance. The spiritual life-force or great breath is actively expressed in three ways or as three currents of power. In the dream symbolism these are represented by the three branches of the vine, and in world religions by the three persons of the blessed Trinity. This latter has lead to excessively anthropomorphic concepts of the threefold divine manifestation.

In the dream the vine budded and brought forth blossoms, followed by ripened grapes. Here in symbol is portrayed the unfolding and evolutionary processes inherent throughout all nature, and this is the spiritual interpretation of the dream—namely that nothing throughout the universe is static (the vine budded), that innate powers unfold from within (fruit was produced) and that forms improve their capacity to express those powers as a result of the evolutionary process (the fruit ripened).

The initiates of the sanctuaries of the ancient Mysteries were taught the fact of evolution, even though this was not discovered by western science until modern times. In reality it was a rediscovery. Although Darwin limited his concept of evolution to the development of forms, since they were all that he was able to observe, nevertheless he partially revealed a profound truth—the parallel unfoldment of life and development of form. The choice of fruit-bearing trees and phases of their life as symbols of evolution is exceedingly apt, for as mentioned previously in Chapter 5, fruit trees display in their forms and natural processes deep spiritual truths.

In addition to the interpretation of the butler's dream given by Joseph, the symbol of the cup may also refer to a localization of a universal principle such as the material form of a solar system, and also to the vehicle or body in which the inner human Spirit abides— the vesture of light, the Gnostic Robe of Glory, the Causal Body. The Pharaoh's or king's cup, filled with grape juice and placed in Pharaoh's hand by the dreamer, symbolizes that of the universal. The initiate whose experiences are being described by means of allegory has come to know completely that divine Spirit and life which is the true Self, and also that it is identical with the Spirit and life of the universe as a whole (Pharaoh's cup is full of wine). The same interpretation may be applied to all cups and chalices used as symbols in the sacred language.

Since the evolutionary impetus of the universe (the vine and its products) is the subject of the dream, and service to the Pharaoh constitutes the culminating action of the dreamer, the attainment of freedom is implied. Liberation has been gained from the shackles of desire and from all bodily limitations, symbolized by the prison and its head keeper. The illusion of self-separateness (a prison indeed) has also been transcended. This allows the butler's dream to be interpreted as a description of the expansion of consciousness which the initiate has attained, the familiar symbols of grape, wine and drinking cup being employed.

Since the facts of the unfoldment of Monads, whether human or of the universe, and the development of forms were in those days part of the secret teachings of initiation, it may be that the two dreams recorded in this chapter of Genesis are veiled references to experiences passed through by Joseph during his own initiation. All the incidents leading to Joseph's imprisonment, his remarkable freedom and prestige while there, his fellow prisoners' dreams, their interpretation and his subsequent liberation may be regarded as having happened to one person. Although this may well have been a Hebrew initiate, perhaps Joseph himself, the interpreted events may also refer to every initiate, since all who win admission to the greater Mysteries pass through similar experiences and receive similar revelations. This view is to some extent supported in Genesis 40:13 by the mention of the three days which were to elapse before the butler was to be freed and restored to his office. In ancient rituals, the period required for the expansions of consciousness produced by initiation was three days and three nights, during which time the body lay entranced, sometimes supine upon a cross and sometimes in a tomb.

The spiritual Soul—the immortal part of humans—was thus freed from the heavy limitations of bodily encasement and elevated for three days and nights into spiritual awareness, after which it returned to the body. Possibly with similar intention, Jonah was made to spend three days and three nights in the interior of a large fish, and Jesus was buried for the same period of time, after having informed his disciples that he would pass through a comparable experience to that of Jonah (Matt. 12:40). Conscious absorption into the all-pervading life principle of the universe, with realization of complete identity with that life, formed part of the mystic effect of the rite of initiation. Knowledge of certain fundamental laws and facts of nature—divine and human—was also bestowed. After awakening, the candidate was instructed physically and verbally in the secret knowledge that pertained to the degree which had just been attained [see Volume I, Chapter 15].

When an illumined initiate wrote of these experiences, whether voluntarily or under instructions, he or she would perforce include in whatever was written only veiled references to their experiences and knowledge. Instructed in the sacred language invented and used by predecessors, they would use historical metaphor to relate much of what had been passed through and learned. As Hebrew Kabbalists affirm (in *The Zohar* and other kabbalistic works), the authors of the Pentateuch may be presumed to have followed this practice, using Jewish history as a basis for their revelations. Studied from this point of view, the butler's dream is an excellent example of an allegory which reveals in symbol the universal process of evolution.

> But think on me when it shall be well with thee, and shew kindness, I pray thee, unto me, and make mention of me unto Pharaoh, and bring me out of this house.
> For indeed I was stolen away out of the land of the Hebrews; and here also have I done nothing that they should put me into the dungeon.
> *(Gen. 40:14–15)*

Joseph's asking of the butler to mention his unjust imprisonment to Pharaoh hardly rings true and may perhaps be regarded as a deliberate inconsistency. It does not seem reasonable that Joseph, the acting keeper of the prison who enjoyed superior prestige and was also a consulted seer, should seek favors from one of the other prisoners who was only a domestic servant. It is distinctly stated that "the Lord was with Joseph" (Gen. 39:21), and he would therefore have no need to ask a butler to ingratiate him with the Pharaoh. This verse suggests that an undermeaning should be sought, not only to the particular occasion recounted but also to the whole narrative.

The Seven Principles of Humanity
Portrayed During Joseph's Imprisonment

A key to the interpretation of the imprisonment of Joseph and all that befell him consists of the fact that the seven principles of humanity are introduced into the story under the guise of people and powers. The chief baker represents the vital or nutrifying principle (the etheric double) in the physical body, and even the physical body itself. The butler personifies the emotional nature with its access to the intuitive faculty, as evidenced by his remarkable dream of the life processes in nature. The mind is portrayed by the keeper of the prison, whose power is delegated to Joseph in the sense that the illumined Ego inspires the otherwise materialistic mind. The prison itself is the material world and the prisoners the human personality, composed of the three main vehicles—physical, emotional and mental. Joseph is the initiated spiritual Self attaining to freedom in the limitations of the outer self, particularly those of the mind (is released from prison). Note that Joseph frees himself not by either subterfuge or force, but solely by virtue of his own character and the exercise of his special capacities. Indeed, he submits almost passively on the outer plane, while at the same time bringing the intuitive and interpretative powers of the higher Self to bear upon the problem, thereby winning both freedom and honor.

The intuition is not personified, but portrayed as a power to interpret dreams. This means not only dreams as night visions, but especially the dream which is material life itself, including the illusion of self-separate existence distinct from all other selves. To the illumined inner Self physical life is as a dream, spiritual awareness being the true waking state. Joseph, having evolved to the stage where he knew this, is correctly portrayed as a seer and an interpreter of dreams. The God who inspired Joseph is his own purely spiritual Self, the dweller in the innermost, the Monad-Atma, the true "Father in heaven."

1. The Physical Body . . . . the prison.
2. The Etheric Double . . . . the baker.
3. The Emotional Nature . . . . the butler.
4. The Mental Body (Manas II) . . . . the keeper of the prison.

5. The Ego in the Causal Body . . . . Joseph.
   (Manas I)
6. The Intuitional Body (Buddhi) . . . . . . Joseph as interpreter.
7. The Spiritual Body (Monad-Atma) . . the Lord God.

Joseph's plea to the butler to intercede on his behalf for the good graces of Pharaoh indicates the necessity for the establishment of harmonious relationships between the inner, immortal and the outer, mortal self. This, therefore, is sought rather than demanded or obtained by force. It is not an inconsistency, but a reference to the best method of obtaining cooperation between the various parts of human nature. Resistances are overcome by a process of harmonization rather than by the exercise of power in their suppression. Transmutation, and not repression, is the ideal way of changing such enemies into friends from the point of view of subduing undesired attributes. A similar allegory in Greek legend is that of Jason, leader of the Argonauts, who subdued the two serpents guarding the Golden Fleece, not by the aid of the might of Hercules, but through the mediation of Orpheus and the charm of his music.

Joseph's words in verse fifteen, if lifted out of the immediate time, describe the descent of the Monad into matter. This is also indicated by his being lowered into the pit. In both cases the enforced imprisonment of the divine in a physical body is allegorically portrayed, together with the resultant hardships and limitations experienced, particularly on the downward arc and at the turning point of the cycle. (See diagrams of the microcosmic and macrocosmic interpretations of the life cycle portrayed in the parable of the Prodigal Son, pp. 80–81.)

The Dreams' Symbols Compared

The dreams of the butler and the baker both have the number three in common. They differ, however, in the nature of the substance specified, in Joseph's interpretations of the dreams and in their outcome. In the butler's case the triple substance was a fruitful vine, a natural, growing, living plant and, moreover, a source of sustenance. Divination apart, this represents the triune Deity in nature and in humanity, the power, life and consciousness of macrocosm and microcosm. As earlier suggested, the vine is a symbol of the vitalizing and sustaining life-force. The ripened grape and its juice typify that life coming to fruition, reaching maturity in both universe and illumined humanity. To dream of a vine with three branches which brought forth ripe grapes was to know by direct experience the triple spiritual powers within nature and humanity, and particularly in the dreamer himself.

In the baker's dream the substance (bakemeats) was not a natural but an artificially prepared food. Baskets are also the products of human hands, even though woven from the dried stems of plants. The suggestion is therefore less of living than of dead material, and Joseph accordingly interpreted the dream as a prophecy of death. The baker, he said, would be killed in three days.

While not wanting to read more into the symbols of the cup and the baskets than is reasonably permissible, nevertheless the distinction between the substance from which the cup and baskets had been constructed may indicate a difference in both state of consciousness and position in evolution. A cup, being formed of solid matter, has permanence and does not permit the escape of its contents through the sides. A basket, on the other hand, is not long lasting and is not a closed container. The bakemeats are lost, however, having been taken by the birds of the air.

The three baskets and their contents, humanly prepared, may refer to the three mortal bodies of mind, emotion and flesh. These, being basketlike and subject to time and change, can neither comprehend nor retain divine power and wisdom in their purest state. Joseph's divinatory interpretation was consonant with this idea, in that to him the three baskets meant three days (v. 18), at the end of which death would come to the baker. This, of course, proved to be true.

The two dreams may also be deemed significant as allegorical portrayals of the principle of the reflection of the triple Deity in both the matter of the universe and the human constitution. The cup represents the containing vehicle for the higher triplicity, and the baskets the receptacles for the lower, or their reflection. In philosophic thought the former is regarded as "the real" (the infinite) and the latter as "the unreal" (the finite).

To dream of a cup (the immortal Self) portrays freedom; to dream of a basket (the mortal self) indicates imprisonment. It should always be remembered that all the people in such metaphorical narratives personify parts of the constitution and qualities of the character of one person, and that the events allegorically describe experiences through which that person passes [see Volume I, Chapter 7, the Second Key]. Thus the butler, like the other people in the story, personifies an attribute of Joseph's own mind.

> Yet did not the chief butler remember Joseph, but forgat him. *(Gen. 40:23)*

A characteristic quality of human nature is portrayed in this verse. If the butler is regarded as depicting certain undesirable attributes, notably those of self-seeking and selfishness, then—so far as personal service is concerned—the tendency to neglect or even forget a benefactor would be in character. His dream had been interpreted, his mind had been put at rest about it, and he had regained both his freedom and his former position. Apparently afterwards he ceased to trouble himself about the fellow prisoner who had asked him to intercede with Pharaoh on his behalf, for according to the story the butler went free and Joseph remained in prison. Nevertheless, as the next chapter of Genesis shows, the imprisonment was not to last much longer. The forgetfulness and perfidy of the butler could not cause Joseph to be imprisoned for a greater period than his destiny and his capacities permitted.

An Eastern saying states that "the mind is the great slayer of the real." [See Blavatsky's *The Voice of the Silence,* Fragment I.] Joseph, though he had advanced along the way of holiness and had passed through the gateway of initiation, had not quite outgrown those mental tendencies which are portrayed by the action of the butler in failing to respond to Joseph's request to "make mention of me to Pharaoh, and bring me out of this house" (v. 14). In this part of the narrative of Joseph's life guidance is offered, not only in the moral but also in the esoteric sense; for although the mind is essential in humans for information gathering, it nevertheless remains the great enemy, even up to the threshold of salvation or Adeptship. The concrete or lower mentality is not only the slayer of the real, but also the potential prison of the higher, interpretative intellect and of the intuition and its fruits. The individualistic as well as the overcritical and argumentative tendencies of the human mind must eventually be outgrown or superseded, and thereafter it ceases to be a limitation—having been changed into an illumined instrument in the service of the liberated inner Self.

Genesis 41

A couple of years later Pharaoh dreamt two notable dreams. In the first he saw seven fat cows come out of the Nile followed by seven emaciated cows. As he watched, the thin cows ate the fat ones. In the second dream Pharaoh beheld seven plump ears of grain ("corn") and seven blighted ears growing on a stalk, and the diseased ears swallowed up the healthy ears of grain.

The dreams troubled Pharaoh greatly. His magicians, however, were unable to interpret these dreams. Pharaoh's butler finally remembered Joseph, that he could interpret dreams, and he brought this to Pharaoh's attention. Joseph then gave the following interpretation to the dreams: The seven fat cows and the seven plump ears of grain represented the same thing—seven years of abundance. However, these seven years would be followed by seven years of great famine, represented by the emaciated cows and the blighted grain. Joseph advised Pharaoh to store all excess food during the good years against the years of famine.

At the telling of this, Pharaoh recognized in Joseph the spirit of God. He then gave Joseph many boons: He made Joseph second only to him over all of Egypt; he bestowed upon him his ring, robed him in fine linen and put a gold chain around his neck. Potipherah's (the priest of On's) daughter, Asenath, was made his wife, and two sons were born of her during the plenteous years. It was put in Joseph's charge to gather all of the excess food during the seven years of plenty.

As predicted, the seven bounteous years were followed by seven of famine. Joseph stored up the grain against the years of tribulation, and when they arrived all the people came to Joseph for the much-needed grain.

The Dreams of Pharaoh

Several well-known symbols are employed in the verses which portray the two dreams of Pharaoh. Among them are a dreaming king and his dreams; a river and its meadows; kine (cows) and corn; fatness and leanness; and the predatory devouring of the fat cows by the lean ones and of the full ears of corn by the thin ones. Moreover, the description of events which could not possibly have occurred draws the attention of the reader to an undermeaning. Cows, whether fat or lean, do not eat each other, since they are herbivorous. Cornstalks do not feed upon each other, but instead upon their natural food. Even though these things happened in a dream, in which all things can seem possible, many of the events in dreams are themselves symbolic and therefore worthy of serious consideration.

The setting of the three dream episodes – those of the butler, of the baker and of Pharaoh – and the effect of their interpretations upon Joseph should also be noted. His esoteric perceptions enabled him to make these interpretations, if only from one point of view – the divinatory or physically prophetic. The result was his liberation from prison and his advancement under Pharaoh to the highest position in the land. Strangely enough it was not as ruler of Egypt, but as an interpreter of dreams that Joseph won his freedom and his elevation to so high a rank.

If the whole story of Joseph is given a mystical meaning, then as has already been suggested, his going forth into the field and his enforced descent into the pit describes the path of forthgoing from a purely spiritual into a densely material condition, and refers both to the outpouring of the Divine Life into a universe and the descent of the human spiritual Self into physical birth. Similarly the raising of Joseph from the pit, his liberation from prison and his appointment as "ruler over all the land of Egypt" (Gen. 41:40–44) portray the returning arc of the great journey of life and the progress of the spiritual Self to deliverance, perfection, "the measure of the stature of the fulness of Christ" (Eph. 4:13).

"Entering the Stream"

The introduction of accounts of the supernatural and the impossible (as in Pharaoh's dream where cows eat cows) and of divine intervention not only suggests a deeply symbolic meaning but also describes the path of hastened unfoldment and the experiences of those who tread that path. From this point of view the dreams are revelations of the spiritual wisdom attained by mystics and of the expansions of consciousness produced by passage through the great initiations.

This view is supported by the introduction of the symbol of the river into the first verse of Chapter Forty-One. A reference to the river or ever-flowing stream of the outpoured life of the Logos can be discerned here, and also to direct experience of unity with that life, referred to in esoteric terminology as "entering the stream."

Pharaoh, however, did not himself go into the river but remained standing upon its bank. He was on the verge, as it were, of embarking upon a further evolutionary phase, but had not yet done so. One of the various functions of the preparations for initiation and of the rite itself is to bring this about. The touch of the thyrsus upon the head of the candidate opens up and sets in operation the channels of communication between the Ego and the physical brain. Before this can happen, however, both the inner and outer Selves must have attained a certain level of evolution. The description of the dream begins, therefore, with the statement that Pharaoh stood by the river, meaning that he was almost ready for initiation or "to enter the stream."

As has so often occurred, esoteric knowledge reaching those unable to understand its hidden significance can become merely superstition. In India, for example, very large numbers of people bathe in sacred rivers and other waters, believing that a purification, a blessing and ultimate salvation will be the results. Admittedly, strong faith, even when founded on a misinterpretation of the effects of ceremonial, can produce potent results. Some benefit may therefore accrue to those who in all sincerity perform sacred rites. Belief that the continuance of indulgences and evil practices is permissible so long as bathing or other ritual is continued is, however, one of the harmful aspects of such blind faith. Theological dogmas affirming the possibility of escape from the educative operation of the law of cause and effect, and the forgiveness of sins without the restitution and proper resolve not to sin again, are regarded in esoteric philosophy as being potentially harmful. No intermediary—such as a Divine Savior—and no action of bathing in sacred waters can possibly preserve a willful culprit from the effects, interior and external, of deliberate wickedness.

Nevertheless, when a person becomes a candidate for initiation and stands upon the brink of "the stream," ready to enter it, almost incalculable blessings may be received. These are, however, not to be regarded as unearned spiritual riches or grace, since all of them have been won earlier either in the same life or in preceding incarnations.

The Symbolism of Cows and Corn

These blessings may be symbolized by the cows which are made to emerge from the river in Pharaoh's dream. In many world scriptures cows are used as symbols for divine fertility, reproductive capacity and boundless supply. Oxen add the quality of service, while bulls accentuate that of masculine virility and creative capacity. Both are seen as manifestations of those God-like attributes in both nature and humanity. The uninitiated, ignorant of these inner meanings, worship the outer form—an all too common example of the degeneration of sublime truth into superstition. The wise, on the other hand, recognize the aptness of the symbology and revere the divine power which it represents. They see in such living creatures manifestations of that power.

The introduction of the number seven into the dream suggests a numerical significance. Macrocosmically, this is a ruling number referring to the levels of density of matter of which the universe consists—the so-called planes of nature—and also to the divine consciousness, presence and orders of Intelligences associated with each of such planes—the sephirothal tree. Similarly, the microcosm, the seven human vehicles of action and awareness at those levels, evolutionary progression and accompanying experiences are all indicated by this number. It also denotes a major change in both universal and human history and affairs. A sevenfold cycle has been completed and its successor is about to open.

Corn has from time immemorial been used as a symbol for the fertility of nature in its aspect of all-provider. Ears of corn were introduced into the Eleusinian rites of initiation, for example, and are depicted on the third card (the Empress) of the trumps major of the tarot. They are also referred to in modern freemasonry, where they are given the same significance. The general and more exoteric meaning attributed to ears of corn is that of abundance, while esoterically the all-pervading, divine life-force and its complete availability to universe and humankind are indicated. The masses are unaware of the esoteric meaning, but the initiate learns by direct experience of the unity with that life. Joseph perceived and related the not dissimilar temporal meaning of the symbology and of the number seven. Famine was imminent, supplies were going to be greatly reduced, and it was essential to prepare for this emergency.

Preparation for Initiation

Verses eight through twelve, where Pharaoh futilely tells his dreams to the magicians and the butler remembers Joseph the seer, indicate two states of consciousness—passage through mystical experiences (dreams) and enquiry for enlightenment. These aptly portray the condition of the inner Self of a candidate for initiation. At this stage he or she is already illumined and has begun to convey spiritual light to the outer personality (Pharaoh). Thus the search has begun, and the quest for truth embarked upon. As is not unusual, the needed guidance can come from apparently unexpected sources, such as a butler or even a supposed criminal in prison. In the choice of possible sources of spiritual knowledge, truth and light, the truly questioning mind is unaffected either by convention or by worldly achievements.

This manner of search is exemplified in the following story of St. Christopher. Before St. Christopher was canonized he saw a poor old woman waiting to cross a river—probably symbolic of "the stream" that the successful candidates for initiation enter. Taking her upon his shoulders, he found that she was in reality the Christ-child himself (pure wisdom) in disguise. Together they crossed the river (initiation) and reached the further shore (Adeptship). A similar example can be found in the Nativity of the Christ, which occurred in the humble surroundings of a stable.

Pharaoh's readiness for the direct receipt of truth as an interior experience is affirmed by the fact that in the first dream he was standing on the banks of a river. He awoke, slept again and had a second dream. On awakening, after the magicians had failed to interpret his dreams, he sought for and found the needed guidance from Joseph, who was still a prisoner. The age-old and continuing search for truth wherever it may be found is thus allegorically described.

Pharaoh Summons the Prisoner—Joseph

As a source of inspiration and guidance where spirituality and discernment are concerned, rank and station in the material realm are without significance. Reality is a great leveller, as Diogenes demonstrated to Alexander in Greece, and Joseph to Pharaoh in Egypt. True spirituality is no respecter of persons, and in Joseph Pharaoh found not only an interpreter but one who recognized and affirmed that his interpretations were not the result of any special mental capacities as a human, but of the activity of the divine within him. Thus, even in the historical sense, the account is full of deep meaning.

Mystically interpreted, Pharaoh – the ruling mental power and life of the outer self – turns to the immortal Self, the divine Spirit (Joseph) in search of light and truth, knowing that Spirit alone to be the source of true illumination. The whole person is thus allegorically described as having reached such a stature that prison could no longer keep him or her. Neither mind nor body could inhibit the powers of the immortal Self anymore, because now they are vehicles rather than prison. The fact that the king himself orders the liberation of Joseph and eventually elevates him to a high position in the land indicates not only recognition of this inner power but also complete surrender to it – the all-important factor.

The Dreams Interpreted

In the dream interpretation, Joseph immediately perceives – and so informs Pharaoh – that the number seven and the two main symbols, cows and corn, both have the same meaning. They represent time, each single symbol passing for one year. Joseph also reveals himself not only as an interpreter but also a prophet when he explains that the lean cows and the empty ears of corn represent the coming seven years of famine and warns Pharaoh so that he may prepare against disaster.

> And for that the dream was doubled unto Pharaoh twice; it is because the thing is established by God, and God will shortly bring it to pass. *(Gen. 41:32)*

Joseph offers an explanation of what he calls the doubling of the dream – namely that the two different symbols being used (the cows and the corn) each refer to the same condition of the land of Egypt (the feast being followed by famine). Each of these two was in its turn doubled, in that there were fat and lean kine and good and withered corn. The divinatory interpretation does appear to be somewhat farfetched, and it is not surprising that Pharaoh's magicians failed to suggest even a worldly interpretation of the two dreams – that they foretold oncoming periods of both abundance and famine. This failure of Pharaoh's soothsayers seems somewhat unusual, since the annual inundations of the land by the Nile, upon which prosperity depended, were carefully noted and measured, with records having been kept throughout a considerable number of years. The absence of any historical reference to seven years of famine in Egypt also suggests that the authors intended the whole narrative to be regarded as an allegory with mystical significance.

The interpretation of the dreams as revelations of successive septenary cycles has greater probability than if they were regarded purely as history, particularly as this revelation was part of the then concealed knowledge revealed to initiates in the sanctuary. Even though today the more exoteric portions of the doctrine of the seven-fold manifestation of Deity and of septenary cycles in the life of universes, Races and individuals are publicly taught in philosophic literature, they are still far from being generally known, accepted and understood. The esoteric significance of the number seven and its ramifications has not yet been wholly divulged nor, one may presume, is it likely to be completely revealed before humanity's entry into the intuitive age. Individuals, however, may discern the hidden truth, while initiates like Joseph have progressively received it in the sanctuary.

The dreams of Pharaoh can be considered the mental experiences of one person. Joseph, who interprets them, represents the spiritually illumined inner Self of that same person, while all the other characters in the story of Joseph's life in Egypt are symbolic portrayals of various parts of the sevenfold human constitution at different stages of evolution and undergoing different experiences. The complexity of humanity, especially its sevenfold nature, was well known by the ancient writers, who had been instructed concerning it in the Mystery Schools of their days. Forbidden under vows of silence to reveal it directly, yet desirous of preserving such valuable knowledge, they made it available to humankind in allegorical form in world scriptures.

Joseph's Rise to Power

In the literal reading of verses thirty-three through forty-one, Joseph, having displayed wisdom and foresight in advising Pharaoh to prepare for the famine, gains his confidence and is appointed prime minister. Esoterically, however, the outer self (Pharaoh and his kingdom) surrenders to the immortal, inner Self (Joseph). Thereafter, in both senses, all things work out as Joseph had prophesied and advised. The essential qualities of caution and forethought and the recognition of variability in the affairs of both ordinary and initiated humans are also indicated in the wise advice which Joseph gave and Pharaoh accepted.

> And Pharaoh took off his ring from his hand, and put it upon Joseph's hand, and arrayed him in vestures of fine linen, and put a gold chain about his neck. *(Gen. 41:42)*

The culmination and the harvested fruits of completed cycles (the ring) are referred to in this verse. Macrocosmically, a septenary cycle, represented by the sevens in the dream (Chain, Round, Globe and Race), closes and its successor is about to open (Joseph's new position in the realm). In the microcosmic application of these symbols, humanity attains one of its successive culminations. Spiritualized, it achieves a level of awareness in which realization of oneness and of the law of cycles rejuvenates the mortal personality and renews humanity itself.

Pharaoh's ring placed upon Joseph's hand indicates the capacity to put interior expansions of consciousness and the knowledge gained from them into active operation in the management of life. The ring symbolizes both eternity and eternal cyclic progression. When these are realized, the enlightened one becomes empowered and enthroned. The vestures of fine linen represent the illumined aura, and the gold chain is the symbol of the authority of the inner Self over the outer, with which authority the initiate is vested. In this more esoteric rendering these gifts are not received from without as rewards from a king, but are self-achieved and symbolize the natural results of spiritual and esoteric development. A similar symbology is used in describing the return home of the Prodigal Son [see Volume I, Chapter 12].

> And he made him to ride in the second chariot which he had; and they cried before him, Bow the knee; and he made him ruler over all the land of Egypt. *(Gen. 41:43)*

The language used in describing the triumph of Joseph somewhat suggests passages from rituals of initiation, and enthronement as ruler for a certain period of time in a chair of office in the temple of the Mysteries. Response to the words "Bow the knee" would indicate recognition of authority and the readiness of the other initiates of the temple to obey. The chariot as a whole is a symbol of both victory and a victorious person. The details of the component symbolism can be readily interpreted. For example the horse, being a quadruped, represents the fourfold personal nature. The body of the chariot refers to the vesture of light – the Causal Body, while the rider within typifies the immortal Self after having attained complete command of all vehicles of consciousness and activity. The wheels, being circular and so without end, suggest both the deathlessness achieved by the high initiate and the eternal Principle. The fact that Joseph was given the second chariot indicates that he was not yet an Adept, but was within measurable reach of that exalted state.

> And Pharaoh said unto Joseph, I am Pharaoh, and without thee shall no man lift up his hand or foot in all the land of Egypt.
> And Pharaoh called Joseph's name Zaphnath-pa-a-neah; and he gave him to wife Asenath the daughter of Poti-pherah priest of On. And Joseph went over all the land of Egypt. *(Gen. 41:44–45)*

In these verses the natural actions of a grateful king arise from and are blended with the almost supernatural powers displayed by Joseph after illumination had been attained. The events narrated concerning Joseph's imprisonment, liberation and installation in a high office may well have happened, even though no references to any of them have thus far been discovered in Egyptian historical records. Nevertheless, the introduction into the story of Joseph's supernormal powers of perception as the basis and cause of the king's actions and the use of the symbols which are interpreted above do point to a possible revelation of supramundane ideas, laws and truths.

The contrast between Joseph's immediately preceding status as prisoner and his subsequent condition is marked in this passage. In a brief space of time he is transported from a dungeon into the highest office in the land under Pharaoh, given an official name and a wife and sent on an official journey throughout Egypt. Each successive phase of illumination – each new expansion of consciousness attained by a devotee or initiate – can indeed appear to resemble a passage from darkness to light. This progression continues until the last great secret is discovered and the initiate moves on to the highest possible human development – the attainment of the stature of a perfected human, an ascended Adept. The symbol of the chariot, a vehicle of travel, may refer to Joseph's rapid progression in consciousness and his near approach to that exalted state.

The bestowal of a new name upon a person may refer to changes in the inner nature, phase of development and degree of attainment. Changes of name occur frequently in the Pentateuch and in other esoteric works. Jesus, for example, followed the custom of adept teachers in giving newly accepted disciples a mystic name symbolic of their attaining close relationship with him (Mark 3:17). Marriage, which can change a woman's name, indicates less a physical union in the symbolic language than a conscious blending of the mortal with the immortal parts of human nature, sometimes called the heavenly marriage. This mystical reading is somewhat underscored by the statement that Asenath was the daughter of a priest, who is associated with the mysteries of religion.

The Numbers Seven and Thirty

And Joseph was thirty years old when he stood before Pharaoh king of Egypt. And Joseph went out from the presence of Pharaoh, and went throughout all the land of Egypt. *(Gen. 41:46)*

Just as the number seven connotes the completion of a major cycle of both human and divine manifestation, so the number three indicates a completed minor cycle which is a component of the larger cyclic fulfillment. In one of its many meanings seven is a number connoting completed self-expression of indwelling consciousness and life in a field of evolution. Three, on the other hand, represents rather an interior condition of readiness and ability to embark upon such self-expression. The triad is an essential of self-manifestation, whether human or divine. Mentally, for example, it represents the knower, that which is known and the act of cognition. In a more deeply interior significance it indicates the Self, the not-self and the interactive relationship between them.

The number one alone is unavoidably inoperative. A pair provides the possibility of extension, and a triad is the product of the active relationship of the pair. The addition of zeros to numbers contained in allegories may be either a blind or a suggestion of the level or degree of power. Thus Joseph was thirty when his liberation from the dungeon and his exaltation to high office in Egypt occurred, and Jesus was said to be thirty years old, or nearly so, when his full ministry began. This may be because the tenth triad of years is about to open—an age at which the human divine triplicity finds conditions favorable to bestowal of mystic illumination upon the personality, and upon this happening a high calling is embarked upon. The inner, threefold Self—the true immortal person—is able to convey to the mind-brain the necessary degree of spiritual power and enlightenment which bestows the impulse and capacity for the beginning of both new interior experiences and more effective outer action. Even in normal human life the period of change from the twenties into the thirties can be a time when the highest idealism and the deepest understanding influence both motive and conduct. Maturity follows, deepening experience and adding wisdom to decisions and to the resultant actions.

In the familiar symbol of Solomon's Seal, the upward-pointing equilateral triangle symbolizes the threefold manifestation of Deity. The downward-pointing equilateral triangle of the same size interlaced with it represents the reflection and expression of the higher triad in matter of three degrees of density — the mental, emotional and physical planes. The diagram completes a geometrical portrayal of both the divine triplicity and the human spiritual triad in any field of manifestation. The circle drawn around the figure refers in part to the necessary enclosure of the field of expression and activity, the boundary of awareness, the Ring-pass-not.

These and other applications of numerical symbols are referred to in this verse in the statement that Joseph was thirty years old when he passed through the mystical experiences which led to his highest attainments. It is of interest that another wise and mature Joseph, also the son of a Jacob (Matt 1:16), appears as one of the members of a family triad in the New Testament, namely the foster father of Jesus who entered upon his mission at about the age of thirty.

The Seven Years of Plenty

Three symbols – the number seven, corn and abundance of supply –
are employed in the verses (forty-seven through forty-nine) which
describe the seven bounteous years of harvest. The number seven has
already been interpreted as referring to a completed cycle, a sum-
ming up and carrying over of the fruits which had been harvested
into the succeeding cycle, whether in macrocosm or microcosm. Thus
for seven years Joseph gathered up and preserved the ripened corn
of Egypt, storing it for future need which is referred to as a famine.
Harvested corn is a symbol of the powers and capacities attained at
the close of a cycle, while abundance refers to the fact that these are
plentiful, being the ultimate fruitage gained from the almost infinite
potentialities locked up in the immortal seed of both universe and
humanity from the beginning of the cycle.

In a mystical interpretation corn and bread refer to spiritual and
mental food – consisting of knowledge and understanding of divine
truth. Joseph, typifying the initiate, had become richly endowed with
esoteric and mystical wisdom. The abundance which Egypt enjoyed
during the first period of Joseph's office also typifies this rich endow-
ment, or entry into the fullness of knowledge.

Joseph's Marriage and Children

Forgetfulness of past sorrows and gratitude for fruitfulness and
prosperity are suggested by the fact that Joseph is said to have had
two children (v. 50–52). His marriage to Asenath, the birth of two
sons, and their naming may portray the transference of acquired
wisdom through the mind to the emotional and physical parts (the
two sons) of the outer, mortal personality. Interior illumination is first
experienced by the true human Self, the Spirit indwelling in the immortal vesture of light. The transference of the effects of such exaltations of consciousness to the body and the bodily life must be
systematically brought about by all initiates of the sanctuaries who,
in obedience to the laws governing such attainment (Yoga), deliberately harmonize their mortal nature with the higher, immortal Self.

The seven principles and vehicles, which with the indwelling Spirit
constitute the total human being, are sometimes described in inspired
allegories as members of a family. The parents generally represent

the more spiritual aspects of human nature, while the offspring indicate the mortal vehicles (Soul). The processes of naming, the bestowal of gifts and the later handing on of offices such as patriarch, prophet or judge to the children may refer to the handing on of power both from one cycle to the next and from one incarnation of a human Ego to its successor.

The transference of spiritual power from the Logos of one universe to that of its successor, from one incarnation of a Monad-Ego to the next, and also from the hierophant of a temple of the Mysteries to her or his successor in office concerns the manifestation of spiritual power, wisdom and intelligence and occurs in obedience to a system of unbroken and ordered progression. This is of great significance, if only because it provides assurance of both the eternal existence of the Spirit-Essence of manifested universes and the unfailing, and so utterly to be trusted, Monad. When accepted, the affirmation that in the reality of existence humans are immune from death can provide a spiritual and philosophic Rock of Ages upon which confidence in the assured safety and imperishability of the spiritual Self may be unshakably established. This is affirmed in many world scriptures. For example, in the Bhagavad-Gita, translated by Sir Edwin Arnold in his poem "The Song Celestial," this concept is stated as follows:

> I say to thee weapons reach not the Life;
> Flame burns it not, waters cannot o'erwhelm,
> Nor dry winds wither it. Impenetrable,
> Unentered, unassailed, unharmed, untouched,
>
> Immortal, all-arriving, stable, sure,
> Invisible, ineffable, by word
> And though uncompassed, ever all itself,
> Thus is the Soul declared!

Thus the essential human being is affirmed to be immortal and everlasting—a truth which it is important to remember, especially during the present age of transition characterized by so much destruction and death.

The Seven Years of Famine

The symbology of the number seven and of other numbers in the narrative of the life of Joseph has already been mentioned. Periods of plenty can refer symbolically to ages or epochs of the full manifestation of the divine power, life and consciousness in a universe or any of its components, and can apply to Solar System, Race or nation. The withdrawal of the previously outpoured life, on the other hand, is symbolized by famine. Activity and rest, expression and cessation, and other familiar pairs of opposites are described in the sacred language as alternations of plenty and of famine respectively.

Plenty, mystically interpreted and applied to civilizations, nations and smaller groups as well as to persons, also typifies fullness of spiritual experience as far as the evolutionary attainment permits. Famine, from this point of view, is used to imply limitation—even absence—of interior illumination. Within the major cycles of a nation's inception, rise, attainment of greatest height and gradual decline, minor cycles which repeat those phases can also occur. A study of the history of nations throughout a sufficient period of time leads to the discovery that they have passed through such major and minor cycles. Culture, philosophy and religion can reach their height (plenty) during a minor period, later to be followed by superstition, materialism and concentration upon physical existence and enjoyment (famine). Similarly, people during their lifetime can also experience times of upliftment and aspiration which alternate with conditions of spiritual deadness and of concentration, sometimes enforced, upon the concerns of physical life. Even the greatest mystics who have described their spiritual enlightenment refer to this alternation of periods of interior illumination and mental darkness. Plenty and famine are used in the sacred language as symbols for these two opposing and alternating conditions.

Fields, gardens and vineyards on the one hand and wildernesses and deserts on the other are also used to typify these two states. Even Jesus was conscious of temptation during his forty days in the wilderness (Matt. 4:1–11). The statement in verse fifty-six that there was a famine "over all the face of the earth" cannot be accepted as historically true, even though Egypt and surrounding countries may on occasion have suffered a decline of prosperity and shortages of food. Similarly, while accounts of a great flood—which are to be found in the scriptures of the Hindus, the Babylonians, the Hebrews and the Mayans, as also in Greek mythologies—indicate that the rising of the waters was very widespread, no authentic historical or geological records of a total world inundation exist. The Egyptian records that are available and the writings of contemporary and later historians in other Mediterranean countries do not tell of such a disaster. It is therefore reasonable to assume that, consonant with the method of allegorical writers, psychological and mental states of nations and individuals are being described here.

The highly developed person, particularly the initiate, is forewarned of the possibility of these alternations and is taught how to preserve equanimity during periods of exaltation and depression. In consequence, the initiate is able to establish so firmly a spiritual state (plenty) that the onset of less spiritual conditions of the mind (famine) does not plunge her or him into despair. Joseph, personifying such an informed and trained mystic, was so well supplied with corn that he could feed both his Egyptian subjects and the people of surrounding countries even while, allegorically, famine raged all about him.

12

Joseph Reunited with His Brothers

Genesis 42

Jacob heard that there was "corn in Egypt," and he sent all of his sons, except Benjamin, to purchase some, since famine had also come to the land of Canaan. Benjamin was kept with Jacob in case misfortune happened to the brothers on the journey.

When Joseph's brothers came before him in Egypt, he acted as if he did not know them and accused them of being spies. The brothers pleaded innocence, saying that they came only to buy food and that they had left one brother at home with their father. Joseph then put them to a test—all but one brother was to be put in prison, and that one was to return to Canaan and bring the remaining brother to Joseph. He then put all of the brothers in prison for three days.

On the third day Joseph released all but one of the brothers in order that they could return to Canaan and bring back the youngest; however, Simeon was to remain behind. The brothers admitted to each other at this point that their current tribulation was likely retribution for having sold Joseph into slavery. Reuben exclaimed that the price for the brothers' perfidy was now Simeon.

Joseph had his brothers' bags filled with grain. On the journey home one of the brothers discovered that all of his money had been returned to him, and the brothers became afraid. When they arrived in Canaan the rest of the brothers found that their money too had been returned in the sack of grain.

They informed Jacob of all that had happened in Egypt. Jacob replied that he was already bereaved of his children—for Joseph was dead, Simeon was as good as dead, and now the brothers wanted to endanger Benjamin as well. And Jacob refused to let the brothers return to Egypt with Benjamin.

"There Is Corn in Egypt"

The scene now changes from Joseph's new home in Egypt to the country of his birth. He and his associates are temporarily replaced in the narrative by his father and his brothers. There was famine in the land of Canaan, and the patriarch took steps to replenish the local supplies. The phrase "there is corn in Egypt" has come down to modern days as a saying descriptive of a state of plenty existing amid a surrounding state of want. The step which Jacob took of sending his sons to an available source of food, their journey to Egypt and its favorable results may be interpreted in the same way as have been the alternating conditions of plenty and famine in Egypt and Joseph's foresight and his storage of corn during the good years.

If the narrative of supposed physical events is regarded as also applicable to mental and spiritual levels of consciousness, then the action of Jacob may be interpreted as referring to steps to be taken for the recovery of lost or diminishing spiritual awareness. The land of Canaan in this reading typifies humanity in a condition of partial or complete loss of spirituality. The proper course to be pursued is allegorically indicated, namely to send sons (thoughts) to a source of supply. This source is the human spiritual nature which is always in a state of abundance, being composed of divine powers and attributes. Since the lesser and greater Mysteries were still operative in Egypt at that time, the two statements that there was corn in Egypt and that Jacob sent his sons there for food may be regarded as symbolically appropriate.

Benjamin Is Retained at Home

While Jacob's action in keeping Benjamin at home may be literally read as a simple precaution, it is also descriptive of a quality in human nature which finds expression both in the ordinary affairs of life and in the fulfillment of the conditions necessary for illumination. Humans are prone to offer only an incomplete self-giving and self-surrender in secular and spiritual motives and actions – something is often held back. Symbolically, then, Benjamin is not sent to Egypt. In religious matters especially, and even on the path of discipleship, humans are inclined – not unnaturally – to cling to some specially valued quality or habit. If the narrative is interpreted in this manner, then Joseph, the spiritual Self, sees through the subterfuge and the withholding. He first accuses the brothers of being spies and then demands that Benjamin also be brought into Egypt as proof of their innocence (Genesis 42:14–16).

Joseph Fails to Acknowledge His Brothers

The preceding interpretation is somewhat supported by the statement that Joseph knew his brothers, but they failed to recognize him. Similarly, the human inner Self, as personified by Jacob, knows its vehicles of self-expression and their zodiacal qualities, which are personified by his family (twelve sons). The outer, mortal self does not normally know of the existence of the spiritual Self even though, experiencing a divine discontent (famine) and the inexpressible longing of the inner Self for the infinite (need for spiritual food), it is drawn towards it after a certain phase of evolution has been entered (seeks and finds the path).

This also applies to Joseph and the visiting brothers. They were ten in number, Benjamin remaining at home. The inner Self is whole, integrated, illumined, while the outer self, composed of many qualities and faculties, is divided and can even be at war within itself. Under such conditions people are not perceptive enough in their brain-minds to be aware of their own divine nature, even though it is always present ("And Joseph knew his brethren, but they knew not him" – v. 8). Expressed in another way, the ten brothers were sent by their father to Egypt and came into Joseph's presence. This may be read as a description of that stage of human development at which, the outer self being conscious of the emptiness of life (famine) and yet without a philosophic and spiritual understanding, the search for truth (Egypt and stocks of food) begins.

Joseph Accuses His Brothers of Being Spies

When at last the inner Self becomes strong enough to dominate the outer self, it will brook no denial. All must be surrendered. Allegorically, the unillumined sons of Jacob must be brought into the presence of their illumined brother, Joseph.

A spiritual law is enunciated in this part of the story – that selfless giving brings spiritual enrichment. Human attempts to evade its full provisions are being described in metaphor. Such evasion, being contrary to the law of self-surrender which unyieldingly governs the procedure of hastened illumination, cannot be permitted, and eventually the full surrender of the human to the divine is made. This demand and its eventual complete response are well described in Francis Thompson's poem "The Hound of Heaven," particularly in the following line: "Naked I wait Thy love's uplifted stroke!"

The Brothers Are Arrested

The time period of the arrest—three days—recorded in verse seventeen should be regarded as an instance in which to employ the intuition and apply the keys of interpretation. Symbolic meanings of the number three have already been suggested. For example, it may refer to the triple nature of both the immortal and the mortal self. The immortal self is threefold, being a reproduction and an expression of the triple Godhead, while the mortal nature is composed of mind, emotions and the physical body. The ten brothers, in their turn, represent attributes of the latter, and their imprisonment for three days dictates that the whole of the threefold nature of humanity is involved. Mind, emotion and body must each make a complete surrender, especially of their most valued attribute, which is so often kept back— as indicated by the absence of the youngest son, Benjamin. This interpretation is somewhat supported by the admission recorded in verse twenty-one that the brothers felt a sense of guilt and were therefore ready to make amends. "We are verily guilty concerning our brother. . . ."

Simeon Is Taken as a Hostage

Simeon is forcibly taken as a hostage until the brothers return with Benjamin (v. 24). Even so human nature, still clinging to some treasured possession or indulgence, offers an alternative, something less precious, being as yet unready for full surrender. This interpretation gives a deep psychological insight into the writers of the story of Joseph in Egypt. It particularly concerns the attitude of mind of candidates for spiritual progress through the grades of the Mysteries, especially when confronted with the difficulties, psychological and physical, inseparable from passage through those grades. In this initiatory reading, the term "famine" may be interpreted as a symbolic description of a certain poverty of spiritual wisdom, in contrast to full spiritual awareness as typified by plenty.

Joseph as Personification of a Hierophant of the Mysteries

Spiritual wisdom and knowledge (symbolized by the bags of grain in verse twenty-five) are received by the outer self in the brain-mind from the spiritual Self (personified by Joseph). The immediate need of the aspirant seeking both esoteric progress and interior illumination is thus met from sources in Egypt, which at that time was one of the world's great centers of the ancient Mysteries. The story of Joseph is the story of the Spirit, the Soul and the human body. These episodes also appear to be a description of the progress of the human spiritual Soul upon the path of swift attainment; for the incidents are indeed able to be interpreted as allegories of interior experiences, limitations of development and consequent difficulties encountered by aspirants seeking to tread that path. It should also be remembered that all the main characters in such an allegory represent vehicles of consciousness, powers, attributes and weaknesses of one person — humanity itself.

Joseph, for example, personifies the spiritual Soul at an advanced stage of evolution towards Adeptship. He is therefore able to provide the awakened and seeking personal nature, represented by the brothers who visit him, with needed wisdom (food). As an officiant in a temple of the greater Mysteries, Joseph personifies the hierophant. This view is somewhat supported by the statements that Joseph has symbolic dreams (Gen. 37), resists Potiphar's wife (Gen. 39) and is able to interpret the dreams of Pharaoh's servants (Gen. 40), and later of Pharaoh himself (Gen. 41), and correctly predict the famine. Esoteric tradition draws attention to the fact that Jacob was the name of the father of both the Joseph of this narrative and the Joseph who became the Virgin Mary's husband (Matt. 1:16), suggesting possible similar identity, as of reincarnation of the same spiritual Soul. In an initiatory interpretation the complete episode may be regarded as an allegorical description of preparation for and the conferring of an initiation.

The experience of Simeon, who is held as a hostage and is bound in prison, aptly portrays the limiting effects of incarnation in a physical body (imprisonment) and its unresponsiveness to the inner Self (famine). Benjamin, the youngest son, who is most generously treated by Joseph (Gen. 43), personifies the dawning intuitive faculty, the "little child" state of mind, while the father Jacob, who remains at home, may be looked upon as representing the Monad, the dweller in the innermost. Israel, as a country suffering famine, represents the material state of the person bereft of egoic and Monadic "riches," and Egypt the Causal Body in which the Ego (Joseph) abides and which contains the stored up riches (faculties and capacities) resulting from former lives.

The story itself may be interpreted as an account of the drawing together of the Monad-Ego or spiritual part of an evolved human on the one hand and the personal vehicles on the other, in order that the whole person, immortal and mortal, may participate in the attainment of hastened evolutionary progress. The fruits are additional powers of will, wisdom, realized unity with all that lives, and comprehension of the laws and processes under which the abstract divinity becomes manifest in the concrete forms of nature (corn, money and a silver cup).

Joseph's Brothers—Personifications of the Spiritually Awakened

The spiritual need (famine) had been recognized and acknowledged (journey to Egypt for food). As always occurs when the acknowledgement is genuine—when the cry for wisdom is sincere—a response had been received. Under such conditions the life processes can prove prodigally generous. The hierophant of the temple (Joseph) holds nothing back, not only giving to each aspirant the needed supply of "corn" but also returning the expenses. This unlooked-for benefit can produce wonder and amazement in the mind of the recipient. Rich stores, not only of wisdom and knowledge but sometimes even of wealth, can flow unexpectedly into the possession of the sincere, ardent and selfless aspirant.

The Brothers Return Home to Jacob

The verses that describe the brothers' return to Canaan (twenty-nine through thirty-five) reveal again that they did not recognize Joseph as one of their number—a member of their own family. Changed from the time when they lowered him into the pit, fully grown up and robed in both power and the vestments of power, Joseph was unknown to them. Failure to recognize, followed by recognition, is frequently used in the writings of the sacred language. Mary Magdalene does not at first recognize her master when she meets him in the garden after his Resurrection. When he mentions her name, however, she recognizes him and at once addresses him by the title descriptive of his relationship with her — "Rabboni; which is to say, Master" (John 20:16).

Mystically interpreted, a phase in the development of spiritual awareness is represented here. For some time after the quest for light has begun, the aspirant is unaware of the source of the inspiration by which she or he was inwardly moved. Even when conscious that such a source exists, its real nature is not recognized at first. The interior impulse is sufficiently strong, however, to bring illumination and understanding (corn and money) and to bestow upon the devotee the will to continue the search for light. Again, the two conditions of famine and plenty refer to mental states — the absence and the presence of spiritual understanding and intuitiveness. In due course the cry for light is answered abundantly and famine is replaced by plenty. The grief of Mary Magdalene gives way to happiness upon discovering that the master still lives. The veil falls away from the eyes of the disciples at Emmaus. The "hoodwink" of materialism and mental blindness is removed after initiation.

The two mystical states of failure to recognize and subsequent recognition are also presented by allegories of the arrival of a heroine, hero or savior who, withholding their name, may even forbid attempts to discover it — as in the case of Lohengrin. A warning is given against undue limitation of a universal principle, such as forcing abstract truth to subscribe to a personal outlook. Allegorically, a name is sought but for a time withheld. If the warning is disregarded the illumination may be lost. Symbolically, by her insistence upon knowing his name, Elsa (the concrete mind) loses Lohengrin (the intuition and the wisdom it reveals). Ultimately, however, every idea so revealed receives justice at the court of the intellect.

Jacob Resists Sending Benjamin to Egypt

Resistance to the law of complete surrender by which alone full enlightenment may be gained and a certain mental if not unnatural abstinence are portrayed when Jacob refuses to let Benjamin go to Egypt (v. 36–38). This condition is descriptive of a difficult phase through which every mystic must pass. Obstinacy along with possessive desire can persist as an attribute, and this for a time may hold up the progress of the Soul towards light and truth. The necessity for the sacrifice of what is held most dear causes the Soul to shrink from so great a loss. Eventually, however, as earlier in the case of Abraham and Isaac (Genesis 22), mental readiness is attained and the surrender made. This is followed by the discovery that when the mind has liberated itself from possessiveness, the surrender is not demanded. Instead of a great and dreaded loss, a wondrous gain is experienced. There is always a "ram in the thicket" (Gen. 22:13) to offer up instead.

This principle operates not only in the spiritual life in general, and particularly in the attainment of pure wisdom, but also in the affairs of daily life. Undue possessiveness, jealousy and suspicion always come between those who suffer from them and the happiness which they seek. In these verses Jacob in his old age is made to reveal these limitations and also the operation of this law.

Genesis 43

The famine was severe and Jacob and his family ran out of grain. When Jacob ordered his sons to go to Egypt for more, they reminded him of their last encounter with Joseph. Judah firmly told his father that they would not go unless Benjamin accompanied them. Jacob was distraught over this; however, he devised a plan which he hoped would overcome Joseph's supposed apprehension. He had his sons take back double the money to Egypt, along with small gifts of balm, nuts, honey, spices and myrrh. And he sent Benjamin with them, although it went against his heart.

When the brothers arrived in Egypt, Joseph secretly had a meal prepared for them and summoned them to his house. The brothers were afraid, thinking that he was angry about the matter of the money. When the brothers came to Joseph's house they first told his steward the entire story. The steward, however, put their fears at ease and had their brother Simeon brought to them.

The brothers had prepared the presents, and they brought them to Joseph. Joseph made inquiries about the health of their father; he then turned his attention to Benjamin. Joseph was so moved by his presence that he had to leave the room, lest they see him weeping. Returning, he seated them at the meal according to their age, which amazed the brothers greatly. And in serving the portions he saw that Benjamin was given five times as much as the others.

When Judah states that the brothers will not return to Egypt unless Benjamin is sent with them (v. 3–6), he personifies the very Spirit which inspires an aspirant to seek the inner light. He also represents that intuitive perception which has reached the mind-brain of the outer self, and eventually enabled the person to override and outgrow the limitations of a former, narrower outlook. The phase of unfoldment at which those limitations are transcended has at last been reached and, despite a still-remaining sense of loss, the full surrender is made. Jacob (also called Israel in this narrative) surrenders Benjamin, his youngest and most beloved son. The surrender is not made without difficulty, but it is made. Thereafter, symbolically, famine will be replaced by plenty, and separation from loved ones will lead to joyous reunion.

The Noonday Feast of Reunion

And when Joseph saw Benjamin with them, he said to the ruler of his house, Bring these men home, and slay, and make ready; for these men shall dine with me at noon. *(Gen. 43:16)*

Feasts in the sacred language are descriptive of the interior sense of spiritual replenishment, the fulfilled state and the serene ease which are experienced when mystical unions are achieved. These unions are of varying degree and are entered into progressively as phases of unfoldment are passed through.

The primary union is between the mind-brain of the outer, mortal self and the consciousness of the inner ruler immortal, the spiritual Soul. This is followed by the fusion of the higher intellect with the intuitive principle, in its turn leading to entry into the state of being in which abides the inmost Self, the dweller in the innermost. Each of these experiences is gradual and may appear as if attained through successive minor unifications, bringing great intellectual clarification and illumination — a condition of consciousness often symbolized by feasting [see Volume I, pp. 155–158, and Luke 15:23]. Both of these lead to the greatest of all realizations of unity — that of the human Spirit with the Spirit of the cosmos. Although human-Spirit and God-Spirit have always been one, their unity has not been previously realized. All preceding discoveries of oneness and their accompanying expansions of consciousness are included in this great attainment of freedom from the illusion of being a self-separate individuality. Such an experience is referred to symbolically as a union, reunion, or marriage between actors in the allegorical dramas of which the sacred language is built.

The hour of noon at which Joseph decides that the feast must occur may be regarded as a hint of the presence of an underlying esoteric allusion. The sun represents the highest human principle, the innermost Self, the Monad, while the solar ray of power (Atma) is the very core of human existence. Just as night, sleep, blindness and darkness sometimes symbolize conditions of temporary mental darkness and weakness, so also day describes their opposites — the illumined and empowered state. The hour of high noon is the period and condition of consciousness in which the realization of the Self as divine reaches its greatest height. This is an apt analogy, since the sun exercises its maximum power each day at its zenith. It is at that moment, therefore, that important events are made to happen in inspired allegories. In certain esoteric rituals initiatory rites are said to occur when the sun is at its meridian. Remember that Joshua forced the sun to stand still in the middle of the heavens (Josh. 10:12–14), and with this feat supposedly prolonged the period of daylight. The complete physical impossibility of this does not necessarily indicate ignorance of the heliocentric system, but rather it points to the presence in the text of a spiritual revelation. The initiate brings her or his highest spiritual power (the sun) to a position of complete command over the whole being, and especially the mind, which is thereafter maintained in a state of full illumination (day). In consequence the proclivities of the outer nature are all subdued (the enemy — the Gibeonites in the story of Joshua [Josh. 10] — is defeated). Similarly, in the verses under consideration Joseph is made to order the feast celebrating the family reunion for the hour of noon.

In verses eighteen through twenty-four the brothers are fearful that they will be punished because of the returned money, and they tell their whole story to Joseph's steward. The tortuous nature of these incidents, the alarm experienced by the brothers, their attempts to clear themselves before the steward, his explanation and the reappearance of Simeon as the assurance of their security — all these describe typical activities of the mind, for the mind of the unillumined person is tortuous, indirect, fearful, seeing hostile plots where none exist and constantly desiring self-justification. Illumination is, however, about to be attained. The inner Self (Joseph), robed in light, is about to reveal itself to the outer, mortal person (his brothers) with its many qualities and limitations (each brother). The steward serves as a link between the two, as a bridge between the abstract, prophetic intellect and the more factual, concrete mind, thereby preparing for their blending.

Mental clarification is essential to the attainment of mystic union. When the mind is in doubt, and in addition is afraid, there can be neither clear vision nor profound interior enlightenment. This appears to be recognized by the authors of these passages in Genesis, who introduce the steward as a character in the drama and cause him, as a trusted servant of Joseph, to remove the apprehension of Joseph's brothers and so prepare them for the acceptance of Joseph's generosity. All these procedures describe changes of consciousness occurring within one person—every person, indeed—who is on the threshold of illumination. Understanding of truth, serenity of mind and quietness of heart are essential precursors to illumination and initiation.

> And the man brought the men into Joseph's house, and gave them water, and they washed their feet; and he gave their asses provender. *(Gen. 43:24)*

Biblical references to the washing of feet—as Joseph's brothers engaged in—indicate both the purification of the whole nature and the cleansing of the mind of all impurities or obstructions to the receipt of spiritual illumination. In some cases descriptions of actions involving the feet may be regarded as references to "understanding," and also to the general conduct of life (see Volume 1, Chapter 7 and Gen. 18:4; 24:32; 43:24; 1 Sam. 25:41; Luke 7:38 and 44; John. 13:5–14; 1 Tim. 5:10.) The fact that the asses, normally stubborn quadrupeds, were given provender may be taken to indicate that the fourfold mortal self was mentally satisfied, content, serene.

The Importance of Every Symbol

When Joseph's brothers give him the presents (v. 25–26), again deeply interior states of mind immediately preceding spiritual upliftment are allegorically described. To give presents to an exalted person implies that mental self-surrender which is essential to entry into the mystical state, just as bowing typifies selflessness and humility before one who is immeasurably greater. Pride, it is thus shown, is completely banished, as also are fear and distrust.

If all of these instances merely recount minor actions on the part of the characters in the story, they are hardly worth recording. If, on the other hand, essential conditions for true expansion of consciousness and union with the spiritual Self are being described, then each action, however apparently slight, is full of significance. The whole story becomes a textbook of guidance upon the pathway to the inner light. The symbols used, the arrangement of the actions and the order of events as related are so precisely appropriate as descriptions of states of consciousness passed through by neophytes that a mystical interpretation is justified.

> And he asked them of their welfare, and said, Is your father well, the old man of whom ye spake: Is he yet alive?
> And they answered, Thy servant our father is in good health, he is yet alive. And they bowed down their heads and made obeisance.
> *(Gen. 43:27–28)*

The narrative continues with an allegorical description of the more intimate relationship between the immortal and the mortal selves. Question and answer in the sacred language, and also in esoteric rituals, indicate the close approach and mutual rapport between the two protagonists, particularly when the interchanges are harmonious.

During the feast, Joseph was moved to tears when Benjamin was presented to him (v. 29–34). Mystically these verses indicate that full spiritual awareness, full realization of the divine Self, though imminent, had not yet been achieved. The existence of some barriers is made apparent, since Joseph neither ate at the same table with his brothers nor revealed their true relationship. ("And they set on for him by himself, and for them themselves, and for the Egyptians, which did not eat with him, by themselves. . . ."—v.32.)

The Mystical Identity

The processes of the discovery of the Self, of knowing as a direct interior experience one's true identity, and of attaining unbroken realization of unity are preceded by many years—and even many lives—of gradual preparation and unfoldment. These are marked by increasing manifestations of the powers of the inner Self in the physical body. Genius, leadership and many special faculties indicate approach to the great discovery. Quite often, however, these developments are unconscious and unexplained manifestations of the light and power of the spiritual Self of the evolved person. The genius rarely knows the true source of her or his powers. The divine influence does descend upon the person, but they know not from where. When at last the true Self reveals itself to the brain-mind, as Joseph later reveals himself to his brothers, fully conscious illumination is attained. The light and fire within are then recognized as divine in origin, and that origin is known as the true Self, the divine spark within.

Benjamin—Dawning Spiritual Intuitiveness

Benjamin, absent at the first meeting between Joseph and some of his brothers, is now present and may be taken to represent the dawning intuitive sense which is already beginning to illumine the formal mind. From the point of view of the inner Self (Joseph), this is the most valuable part of the outer personality, even though the intuitive faculty is as at this point potential rather than actual (Benjamin is the youngest son). The fact that Benjamin is born of the same mother as Joseph supports such an interpretation. The two (the inner Self and the intuitive faculty) are closely akin and the intuitive faculty is one of the attributes of the immortal Self. Benjamin therefore receives more than his brothers. The number five is possibly a hint that spiritual intuitiveness is an attribute of the human fifth principle—that of divine wisdom manifest in the inner Self. The other four, beginning with the densest, are the physical, the emotional, the purely mental and the abstract intellect, the Causal Body. The sixth and seventh principles consist of vehicles for the spiritual will and the true dweller in the innermost, which is the Monad. This, however, is but one of many classifications of the seven parts of which every human being consists, and the reference here to the number five may or may not have an esoteric significance.

ALL IS WITHIN

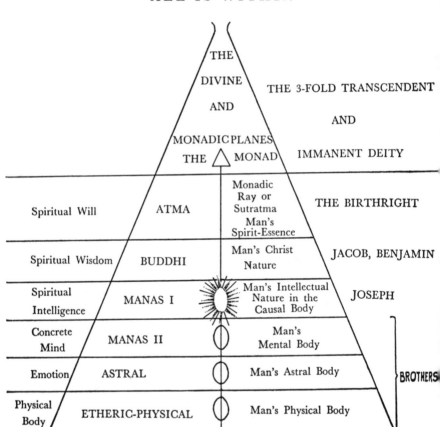

	THE DIVINE AND MONADIC PLANES THE △ MONAD		THE 3-FOLD TRANSCENDENT AND IMMANENT DEITY
Spiritual Will	ATMA	Monadic Ray or Sutratma Man's Spirit-Essence	THE BIRTHRIGHT
Spiritual Wisdom	BUDDHI	Man's Christ Nature	JACOB, BENJAMIN
Spiritual Intelligence	MANAS I	Man's Intellectual Nature in the Causal Body	JOSEPH
Concrete Mind	MANAS II	Man's Mental Body	
Emotion	ASTRAL	Man's Astral Body	BROTHERS
Physical Body	ETHERIC-PHYSICAL	Man's Physical Body	

Genesis 44

After their meal, Joseph commanded his steward to fill his brothers' sacks with grain and to put each man's money in his sack as well. He also told the steward to put Joseph's own silver cup into Benjamin's sack.

Shortly after the brothers left to return to Egypt, Joseph sent the steward to confront them about the supposed theft. They were naturally aghast, swearing that they hadn't taken the cup. They told the steward, "With whomsoever of thy servants it be found, both let him die, and we also will be my lord's bondmen." Of course, a search of the sacks found the cup to be in Benjamin's. In total despair, the brothers ripped their clothing and returned to the city with the steward.

Joseph continued the ruse when his brothers were brought before him. He listened to their excuses, but refused all their offers of slavery except for Benjamin's. At hearing this the brothers were frantic. Judah poured out the entire story of their journey to Joseph, along with their fear that Jacob would die of grief if they returned without Benjamin. Judah then offered to remain as a slave in Benjamin's place.

This account in Genesis can be read literally as a story about the generosity of brotherly love. So many strange actions are ascribed to Joseph in this chapter, however, that it may also be interpreted as possessing underlying meanings. A mystical interpretation applicable to every devotee would indicate a reference to the riches received by the mortal personality (the brothers) when consciously united with the inner, immortal, spiritual Soul (Joseph). Benjamin's sack would then represent both the enclosing aura and, more particularly, the mental body which is the receptacle of spiritual power, life and consciousness. This spiritually nutrifying life force is symbolized by the corn, which is received according to maximum capacity, each brother's sack being filled. Joseph in such a reading represents the conjoined spirit-essence and the abstract intellect within the vesture of light (the Causal Body – Joseph's palace in the city of Egypt where the family meets).

If, however, a rite of initiation performed in a temple of the greater Mysteries is being described by means of allegory and symbol, then Joseph represents the hierophant, his servants become the other officiants in the ceremony, and the corn symbolizes the transferred hierophantic power, wisdom and knowledge. The value of such illumination and the great necessity for it experienced by the candidate are indicated by the famine in the country in which the brothers lived. Symbolically, an unillumined mind and heart are always in a state of "famine," whether aware of it or not. Candidates for initiation, being spiritually awakened and intellectually seeking men and women, experience so pressing a need that their pre-initiation state is comparable to and aptly exemplified by famine. When the condition of a whole nation or of one of its groups (here tribes) is being referred to, it really represents allegorically the actual experience of the initiate.

The Gift of a Silver Cup

The youngest son, in this case Benjamin, generally personifies less a person than the awakening intuitive faculty—the emerging but as yet underdeveloped Christ-nature. Special attention is always given to this newborn, childlike faculty, portrayed in Nativity and post-Nativity narratives in which the babe is said to be visited by angels, shepherds and Magi who offer their gifts. The aid given to these little ones may take the form of white spiritual power which descends into the candidate's aura at the rite of consecration. This added and special gift is aptly symbolized here by a silver cup. Silver, being a white metal, corresponds vibrationally to the Spirit-Essence (Atma) of universe and of humanity. The gift is appropriately cup-shaped to indicate the eucharistic ministrations of every initiate to humankind, as allegorically portrayed by the priestly dispensation of the wine within the chalice at Holy Communion. The symbolism of the Holy Grail offers a further variant of this experience through which every illumined human being passes.

Benjamin thus personifies the dawning Christ-principle, while the filling of his sack with corn and the added gift of the silver cup imply the special assistance given to those who in their gradual evolution have reached the state of readiness for initiation.

> As soon as the morning was light, the men were sent away, they and their asses. *(Gen. 44:3)*

In the sacred language morning and light indicate the attainment of spiritual awareness. Whether referring to Manvantara, national life, or passage through an initiation on the path of Adeptship, light in the above sense has been attained and a new phase entered upon.

Joseph's Strange Conduct toward His Brothers

As in the interpretation of all allegories, each character personifies an aspect of one human being, and all the events and the experiences described occur within the consciousness of that single person. Briefly, Joseph is the higher Self, the brothers as a group personify the outer self, and Benjamin represents the nascent intuitive faculty. The events narrated in verses four through thirty-four, where the brothers are accused by Joseph of stealing the cup and Judah offers to be enslaved for Benjamin, describe interior changes and psychological reactions of each and every human being at certain phases of their evolution. The wrongful accusations which followed Joseph's beneficence are all descriptive of those changes of mind, such as doubt, to which every one is submitted who has decided to hasten their progress on the path and has been especially assisted to do so. The circumstances of life, precipitations of karma and other experiences—all these can cause a devotee or an initiate temporarily to doubt the reality of her or his mystical experiences. This is sometimes described as being in a wilderness or desert.

The illogical and very unkind conduct of Joseph towards his errant brothers is unacceptable to the reasoning mind. Furthermore, it is contrary to the character of Joseph, whether the passage is read literally or interpreted metaphorically. This behavior presages a hidden meaning in the verses. The unaccountable and dishonest behavior of Joseph towards his brothers may perhaps be read as a description of those temporary lapses from the spiritual ideal to which even the most promising aspirants are subject. Both guidance concerning and warning against this possibility may be gained from these verses.

Not only is the physical body subject to the law of alternations and cycles, and not only is a certain repetitiveness discernible in personal and human history, but the psychological and intellectual experiences of humanity are also subject to these phenomena. Even Jesus experienced the states of consciousness symbolized by a wilderness and by the darkness in Gethsemane. He, prototype of every successful aspirant and initiate, shrank from accepting the oncoming sorrow which he so clearly foresaw. Nevertheless he persisted and so succeeded where many others have failed.

The pathway of discipleship and initiation is littered with the remains of those who having traveled it—perhaps to the limit of their power—were thus unsuccessful. This defeat is temporary, however, since it is only the mortal personality which is involved. It was the immortal Self which set forth upon the great quest and inspired its bodily personality to do the same. For this reason the failure is not final, and is applicable only to the particular incarnation in which it occurs. Indeed, a recovery may be made later in that same life, but if this does not happen the great endeavor will most surely be undertaken in a later incarnation.

The strange withdrawal of the awakening power, life and light of the inner Self occurs for various reasons, among them the operation of the law of cycles referred to above. Astrological progressions month by month, and year by year, and even day by day distinctly portray the fluctuations, under the law, in the relationship between the inner and the outer self. The position of the sun relevant to the moon, together with the aspects assumed by other planets as shown in the progressed horoscope, provides an example of these fluctuations. This information can also be useful in its assurance that the changes are only temporary.

Experiences being passed through in the depths of a human being may be considered in this light, and their effects upon the outer person evaluated accordingly. The above interpretation of the remaining verses of this chapter may, in consequence, be useful to spiritually awakening aspirants, along with other accounts of similar adverse changes in the lives of heroines, heroes and saviors recorded in the mythologies and scriptures of ancient peoples. Just as the ebb and flow of ocean tides are characterized by wavelike motions, so until Adeptship or "the further shore" is reached the life of the spiritual neophyte must also be subject to wavelike alternations of lofty exaltations (crests) and of withdrawals of spiritual inspiration (troughs). This must be so, since the undulatory life processes are totally impersonal. Only when a human being has completely realized identity with the inherent life of the Solar System, at Adeptship or its near approach, does this alternation cease so far as consciousness is concerned.

If a moral may be drawn from the strange conduct of Joseph in this chapter, and from similar actions by the central figures in allegorical dramas, then it would be that all aspirants to hastened unfoldment should always hold steadfastly to the ideal and continue on the path, however dark the heavens may appear to be, however dry the

surrounding countryside, and however the whole enterprise may seem
to have lost its appeal. These times of spiritual aridity, moreover,
are really periods when certain capacities in the life of every human
being rising towards greatness are developed, which would otherwise
remain dormant. To keep on despite every obstacle, whether arising
from difficult circumstances in the outer life or from interior conflicts, is no doubt the message of such stories as this one (see Matt.
4:1–11 and Matt. 26:42).

Genesis 45

*When Joseph heard that his father was unable to bear yet another
loss, he could no longer control his feelings and he wept openly in
front of his brothers. With only the brothers present he finally said
to them, "I am your brother Joseph whom you sold into slavery." This
revelation troubled the brothers greatly. He told the brothers not to
be harsh with themselves, saying, "God sent me before you to preserve
your lives."*

*Joseph then related that there were still five years of famine re-
maining, and he ordered them to go back to Canaan and bring their
father, families and herds to Egypt. When Pharaoh heard that Joseph's
brothers were in Egypt, he repeated Joseph's order and promised them
the best of all the land in Egypt. So Joseph sent them homeward with
wagons full of provisions, and to Benjamin he gave three-hundred pieces
of silver and five sets of expensive clothing.*

*So the brothers returned to Canaan and told their father all that
had happened. At first he couldn't believe their story. But when they
told him everything that Joseph had said, and when he saw the wagons
of provisions, Jacob took heart, saying, "Joseph is indeed alive; I shall
go and see him before I die."*

Joseph Restores Unity within His Family

This chapter, with its dramatic reversal of Joseph's conduct towards
his brothers and his self-revelation to them, allows for a deeply spiritual interpretation. The apparently sudden change from an official
to a fraternal relationship may be interpreted as part of an allegory
descriptive of a profound spiritual experience.

As if under an inner compulsion, the spiritual Self (Joseph) reveals itself to the mortal self (the brothers as a multiple symbol) while it is wide awake and fully aware of itself and its surroundings (Joseph's house in Egypt). Since the unillumined person would gain little from descriptions of such spiritual expansions and their physical realization, they are revealed by the authors of Genesis by means of an allegory of the union of those who have long been separated (Joseph's absence in Egypt). Frequently in world mythologies and scriptures hero and heroine meet and are united — members of families or tribes who have long been separated are brought together. Travelers, voyagers and adventurers come home at last. Ulysses returns to Ithaca and Penelope, and Persephone is restored by Hermes to her mother's arms. The Israelites reach the promised land (Josh. 3:17; 5:6), and the prodigal son is reunited with his family (Luke 15:11–32). Generally prizes are won, presents are given and feasts are celebrated by the various characters in the great allegorical dramas. Such narratives may be regarded either as history blended with fable or as parables descriptive of mystical attainments and experiences which reveal hidden laws and processes of nature and the innate powers and destiny of humanity. Thus the self-revelation of Joseph to his brothers as described in this chapter may be regarded as an allegory of regained mystical experience and of entry into the inner realms of nature and into the state of consciousness in which the human spiritual Self abides. When such self-revelations and reunions occur in the sacred language after accounts of stress and demands for great effort they are illustrative of the process of "taking the kingdom of heaven by force" (Matt.11:12).

The obstacles which temporarily prevent return, such as the hesitation, delays and subterfuges sometimes included in these allegories, all describe difficulties in the attainment of self-discovery following full surrender to the Divine. Thus in conformity with this method of writing, Joseph is described as delaying the revelation of himself to his brothers. Similarly Ulysses, who has encountered many grave difficulties throughout his long voyage, enters his home in disguise and overpowers enemies within the home (the suitors) before disclosing his true identity. His wife, Penelope, who has been embarrassed by the suitors and troubled by the absence and delayed return of her husband, resorts to the subterfuge of weaving a tapestry by day and undoing it at night, because its completion means that she will have to make a choice between them.

The book of Exodus, discussed in Part Four, similarly uses as allegories incidents such as the hardening of Pharaoh's heart and his breaking of his promises to let the Israelites depart. These are less historical narratives than descriptions of mystical states of consciousness and the difficulties met with in the process of attaining them. As recorded in the New Testament, the exceedingly painful journey of Jesus from the hall of judgment to Golgotha, his scourging, his forcible crowning with thorns and the Crucifixion itself have similar interpretations. All these may be regarded as symbolic of the mystical "wounds"—mental, psychical and physical—which every aspirant suffers when treading "the way of holiness" (Isa. 35:8), the way of the Cross—meaning the path of illumination and initiation.

The incidents of this chapter can also be interpreted as being descriptive of psychospiritual experiences and changes which precede the mystic's full realization of her or his true identity. In the life of every mystic—as also of every esotericist who is fortunate enough to receive the assistance made available in the instructions and ceremonies of the greater Mysteries—a time comes when the great interior illumination is attained. This is a twofold process. First, the initiate knows herself or himself to be completely distinct from body, emotions and mind, these being mortal. The initiate recognizes her or his immortality, immunity from death. The second revelation is that their Spirit is a ray of the Godhead and forever and inseparably united with its Source. These two discoveries are later followed by a third, in which duality vanishes. The spark then knows itself one with the flame, the dewdrop one with the ocean of life, the Monad being identical with the one eternal principle.

Joseph Reveals Himself to His Brothers

Eventually the time of the great revealing arrives. The attraction of the Spirit is experienced by the human material principles, evoking a yearning for the mystic union. Allegorically, Joseph reveals himself to his brothers. While in a literal reading of the first verse it is natural that Joseph would desire privacy for the occasion, it is also true that self-elevation and illumination, being deeply interior, are best entered into in solitude; therefore Joseph causes "every man to go out from me" (v. 1). The audible weeping and the shedding of tears may be taken to be descriptive of the final stress and strain which precede full spiritual attainment. In addition, joy is perceived, for the consummation is drawing near. Then both feeling and thought are given free expression.

When at last Joseph does reveal his identity to his brothers, saying, "I am Joseph," the brothers are troubled. The mystic, even though long prepared by both premonitory experiences and knowledge derived from the writings of others, can suffer some personal stress before finally breaking through into realization of her or his own divine nature and its unity with God.

"I Am Joseph"

The limitations imposed upon the reincarnating human Ego (Joseph) by incarnation in the material vehicles of mind, emotion, vitality and flesh are great indeed. Birth into them is aptly described as the lowering into a pit, the deepest and darkest part of which would correspond to the physical body itself. Even advanced spiritual Souls experience a grave loss of power and means of self-expression when physically embodied during waking hours. Indeed, the conditions of earthly life are so foreign to those of the level of the abstract intelligence at which the inner Self abides that they could be symbolized by residence in an alien land. Enforced rebirth may similarly be regarded as exile. The story of Joseph's brothers lowering him into the pit and later selling him to the merchants has already been interpreted. The Intelligences concerned with all processes of the descent of consciousness into dense, material encasement and its later liberation, macrocosmic and microcosmic, are personified by the brothers and the merchants respectively.

In this later phase of Joseph's story in which the accent is upon self-freeing from the limitations of dense matter and its attributes, Joseph typifies an initiate on the threshold of final liberation. At this stage, an integration of the whole human nature occurs, the differentiation between the inner and the outer (the immortal and the mortal) parts virtually disappearing. Allegorically, Joseph reveals himself to his brothers and begs them to draw very near to him, and an intimate family reunion then occurs.

> Now therefore be not grieved, nor angry with yourselves, that ye sold me hither; for God did send me before you to preserve life. *(Gen. 45:5)*

This verse gives one of the keys to the interpretation of accounts of outgoing and returning journeys, and of advances from lowliness to loftiness. The story of Joseph reveals a sublime purpose, even though giving it only a material significance—namely to supply food in years of famine. The actual purpose of all such cyclic movements is the germination and development of those seedlike powers which have been present, though latent, in the inner Self from the time of humanity's emergence from the divine consciousness.

Famine represents the absence of spiritual impulses, guidance, and light during the earlier phases of human development while incarnated in a physical body. Evolution dispels this, bestowing upon advanced humans deepening realization of spiritual power and increasing facility in its exercise at all levels of self-expression—spiritual, intellectual, cultural and physical. This is symbolized by feeding those who are hungry, giving drink to those who are thirsty, and a change from a condition of famine to that of plenty. Thus Joseph in no way reproaches his brothers, and moreover tells them not to reproach themselves, since a sublime purpose was being fulfilled throughout. Ethical precepts are also presented, namely that one should both forgive one's enemies and not give way unduly to remorse for past mistakes.

Karma Is Fulfilled

> So now it was not you that sent me hither, but God: and he hath made me a father to Pharaoh, and lord of all his house, and a ruler throughout all the land of Egypt. *(Gen. 45:8)*

Allegorically, the brothers performed no evil when they lowered Joseph into the earth and sold him; for only by this process was he able to come to the fulfillment of his life and be as a father to a great king of a great land.

Complete integration or unification of the whole nature of the illumined person is brought about once the true Self is revealed. Mutual recognition by the inner Self (Joseph) and the outer personality (the brothers) indicates a complete harmonization of all the aspects of human nature—spiritual, intellectual and physical. Mystical experience of oneness with the Divine brings about an interior harmonization, so that the illumined mystic knows herself or himself to be a whole individual composed of the inner, spiritual will (the Lord), the evolving immortal Self (Joseph), and the mind, emotions and physical body (the brothers).

The past and the present are combined. The fruits of former lives on Earth, and even the memory of those lives, become consciously available to the highly evolved person. As the past is the parent of the present, so do earlier existences in forms together constitute the "father" of the present self. In verses nine through thirteen, Joseph sends for his father. Jacob, the father of Joseph, represents that past and those existences, the products of which must be brought into full consciousness and be made fully available to the present personality. This may be the inner significance of Joseph's insistence that his father be brought to Egypt to live near him and under his protection.

The intimate unification or fusion of all the parts of humanity are described in the verses where Pharaoh instructs Joseph's entire family to move to Egypt (Gen. 45:14–20). The total powers of the present human being and all the products of his or her past have now become both interharmonized and actively available. Metaphorically, there will be safety amidst prevalent famine, and even plenty. This is probably historically accurate, too. A generous king might well wish to reward a prime minister who by an act of foresight had saved him and his people from famine. Here again a moral as well as a mystical meaning is legitimately discerned.

The Rejected Stone Becomes the Chief Cornerstone

In addition to the interpretations of the Joseph allegory already given, a further revelation is made. This concerns a fundamental law governing the spiritual way of life. Under that law the aspirant passes through the apparently unavoidable experience of temporary rejection, and even betrayal. This is, however, followed by a universal, and sometimes triumphant, acceptance and acclaim. The person who is first unwanted eventually becomes recognized as worthy of the highest honor, while their contribution, although considered undesirable and perhaps even scorned up to now, proves to be essential to the further progress of the nation, or of humanity as a whole. Jesus, himself a memorable example of the operation of this law (see Is. 53:3–5; Matt. 67:68; Acts 4:11), proclaimed that "The stone which the builders rejected, the same is become the head of the corner" (Matt. 21:42). Thus, those who are destined to become great because of the qualities of character inherent within them evidently must first experience faithlessness and repudiation by others.

The fact that the marked change from imprisonment and distrust to freedom and the confidence of the Pharaoh was brought about by supernormal means—dreams—strongly suggests a mystical under-meaning. Joseph was freed and achieved advancement not by any physical prowess or the defeat of any enemies, but by virtue of his own inherent wisdom from which he derived the capacity to convincingly interpret dreams and correctly to prophesy the future. This unusual and even unlikely element in the story, together with the fact that Egyptian historical records make no reference to him and his exploits, supports a study of the saga of Joseph less from the historical and more from the mystical point of view. The wholehearted adoption of Joseph's family by Pharaoh, and the extreme generosity indicated in verses seventeen to twenty may also be regarded as giving weight to this view.

The journey to the famine-stricken native land in order to bring the father back to the adoptive land where the brother reigns in power and where food is assured indicates both a movement in consciousness and an evolutionary progression. The whole nature of the mortal self is now guided and illumined by the inner Self. As we have already seen, under that influence complete unification of all aspects of human nature—in modern terms, psychological integration—is sought and eventually achieved. A new cycle in the life of the person who passes through this experience is then entered upon. Spiritual and intellectual "famine" is replaced by sufficiency. Joseph, the long-absent brother, is restored to the family and bestows upon it both protection and riches.

The Symbolism of Numbers, Metals and Change of Clothing

The two gifts to Benjamin—silver and clothing—are given in specific numerical quantities, each of which conveys certain meanings. In ancient literature there are indications of a system which gave numbers their real significance and employed a symbolism which referred to something more than enumeration alone. Numbers can be used as symbols because the universe is established upon a coordinated plan in which quantitative relations are repeated through different states and planes. Number is common to all planes of nature, and thus unites them. By the study of numbers, therefore, one may learn the fundamental laws of the creation, constitution and progressive events in the lives of both universes and humanity; for humanity is a modification of cosmic elements, a concentration of cosmic forces. Every number has a certain power which is not expressed by the figure or symbol employed to denote quantity only. This power rests in an esoteric connection existing between the relations of things and the principles in nature of which they are the expressions [see Volume I, Chapter 9].

A law of correspondences exists under which metals are in mutual resonance or vibratory sympathy with certain parts of the universe and of the human constitution. Iron corresponds to the human emotional nature, the planet Mars and the sign Scorpio; gold to the vital energy, the Sun and Leo; mercury to spiritual wisdom, the planet Mercury and Virgo; lead to the concrete mind, Saturn and Capricorn; tin to the Auric Envelope, Jupiter and Sagittarius; copper to the abstract intellect, Venus and Libra; silver to the spiritual will, Uranus and Aquarius (see Hodson, *Lecture Notes: The School of the Wisdom*).

Three hundred pieces of silver, for example, suggests that the gifts refer to the human higher triad, the threefold spiritual Self, while the metal silver indicates the awakened spiritual will. Thus Joseph's gift of silver to Benjamin indicates not only a transference of a material substance from one person to another, but also that by hierophantic power Benjamin's inner will had become strengthened and more active within the immortal Self which, being threefold, is designated by the number three (three hundred).

Changes of garments indicate expansions of consciousness, new outlooks upon life, newly attained levels of spiritual awareness [see Volume I, Chapter 12]. The fact that Benjamin was given five changes may indicate either that the fifth grade in the Mysteries had been passed through or that the fifth or the human intuitive principle had been awakened into increased activity – or possibly both. In Christian terminology the interior Christ-consciousness has been "born" and unfolded, the Christ or "anointed" state has been entered. In the words of Angelus Silesius:

> Though Christ a thousand times in Bethlehem be born
> And not within thyself, thy self will be forlorn.
> The cross on Golgotha thou lookest to in vain
> Unless, within thyself, it be set up again.

Benjamin personifies the Christ Power and Presence in humankind, and this is why he was favored above his brothers.

Jacob's Journey

The father, Jacob, who has not so far participated in the family journeying and reunion, represents in this phase of Joseph's story the innermost Source (Atma) and the totality in unity of every human being. This abstract human principle is sometimes personified by the Deity and sometimes by a patriarch as head of a tribe or a family. As patriarchs occupy their office for limited periods, at the end of which they pass away and a new leader replaces them, so a succession of manifestations (physical incarnations) of the human Spirit marks its progress to perfection.

The dweller in the innermost remains the same, namely the Monad itself. Evolutionary progression brings out additional powers or newly expressed spiritual faculties, so that the very nature of the person seems to be changed. When this phase of development has reached a certain degree it closes, the father dying and being succeeded by one of his sons.

> And to his father he sent after this manner; ten asses laden with the good things of Egypt, and ten she asses laden with corn and bread and meat for his father by the way. *(Gen. 45:23)*

The number ten—twice used as the number of asses and she-asses laden with corn sent by Joseph to his father—indicates the fulfillment of a period of activity, the completion of a cycle. Ten is the number of totality, a synthesis of all the preceding numbers, a rounding off of a particular cycle.

The journey made by Jacob in Canaan with instructions that he be brought to Egypt under the orders of Joseph and Pharaoh may be regarded as descriptive of the close of one cycle of cosmic, human and initiatory activity (Jacob later dies) and entry upon its successor.

History or Allegory?

Although no historical reference to these events has as yet been found, it is not entirely impossible that they might have occurred. This becomes more doubtful from the biblical statements concerning the important part which Joseph played in the direction, under Pharaoh, of the nation's economy, agriculture, and self-protection against famine. All of these functions would have been sufficiently significant to have been recorded in the contemporary history of Egypt. An allegorical reading is supported not only by their exclusion from the records, but also by the inclusion in the scriptural narrative of so much that is supernatural. Joseph claimed, for example, that God actually sent him to Egypt (Gen. 45:5,7,8,9). It is also recorded that Joseph possessed and exercised mystical powers, such as the interpretation of dreams and the capacity to foresee, and so guard against, an oncoming famine. His father Jacob, in his turn, is said to have been directly instructed by God (Gen. 46:2, 3, 4).

The numbers and other symbols employed, the eagerness of Joseph, the revivification of Jacob, his father, and Jacob's divinely inspired journey into Egypt—all these also suggest a possible revelation of spiritual and esoteric truths, laws and procedures. This is achieved by means of the personification as members of a family of the various human vehicles and powers, and an allegorical description of the expansions of consciousness achieved by advanced humanity. The narrative interpreted in this way reveals one profound truth among many others—that when the aspiring thoughts of the spiritually awakened are turned sincerely and meaningfully toward the Godhead within, the Divine Presence becomes more and more readily accessible to and sheds spiritual grace upon the outer self. The inner Ego—the spiritual Soul, Joseph—then becomes united in full consciousness with the Supreme Deity. Jacob, his father, visits him in Egypt.

13

Jacob's Final Journey

Genesis 46

On their journey to Egypt, Jacob paused at Beer-sheeba in order to offer a sacrifice to God. That night God spoke to him in a vision, telling him not to be afraid to go to Egypt. For God told Jacob, "I will make of thee a great nation." God also related that Joseph would be with him when he died.

So Jacob, his sons and their families (seventy people in all) and their flocks traveled on to Egypt. They soon entered the land of Goshen in Egypt, and father and beloved son had a tearful reunion there. Jacob said that now he could die in peace because he had gazed upon Joseph's face again.

Joseph told his kin that he would inform Pharaoh of their arrival. He advised them that when Pharaoh summoned them, they should tell him that they were herdsmen and shepherds. This way Pharaoh would grant them the borderlands of Goshen, since the Egyptians of the interior loathed herdsmen. In Goshen they could dwell in peace.

The possibility of a mystical interpretation in Chapter Forty-Six is again supported by the inclusion in the narrative of a description of an action of the Supreme Deity. Unless a secret wisdom concerning the relationship between the Deity in a universe and in humanity is being revealed, the affirmation that the Logos of a universe should thus personally direct the travels of the ruling family of an obscure tribe is, at the very least, somewhat unlikely. A mystical interpretation certainly lends greater probability to the story. The divine principle (the Monad referred to as "the Lord God") in a spiritually awakened person empowers the innermost Self to enter into intimate unity with the immortal Self or unfolding spiritual Soul (Joseph), and through that with the mortal personality and all its attributes (the brothers). The ultimate unification of all the elements and characteristics of human nature is really being described here.

The genealogical record set out in verses five to twenty-six of this chapter of Genesis is no doubt of great importance to the Hebrews, but not necessarily to the general reader. The descendants of Israel (Jacob), their wives and their offspring from whom the nation developed are all named and numbered. Again the passages may well be regarded as historical, although an interpretation of the names and numbers by the kabbalistic system strongly suggests the presence of esoteric allusions. In this sense a tribe and a family together constitute a microcosm which humanly represents the macrocosm. Viewed in this way, the leader and his family are used to symbolize creative Intelligences—Elohim—who assist in the fashioning of a universe. The names given, male and female, in both their soniferous and numerical significances point to this revelation. In esoteric philosophy certain words, when sounded in a particular way, are said to be capable of exerting both physical and superphysical influences. These can produce either beneficial or adverse effects upon the person who pronounces them with knowledge, and also upon those who hear the sounds. In Sanskrit such words and the sentences composed of them are said to be mantric, meaning sacred speech as an instrument of thought-power.

The family as a symbol for the Elohim is an interpretation that is supported by the verses which refer to the beginning of the journey. The esoteric interpretation of this passage would seem to be upheld by the further statement that God visited Israel in a dream, and that he advised the journey to Egypt and promised national greatness. As in the emanation of a new universe, the action is divinely initiated, so divine intervention in human affairs is also affirmed.

The descent or approach of the inward Spirit of an illumined person having been allegorically described, the quest carried out by the aspirant and its fulfillment are then referred to. The tender reunion and Joseph's tears upon his father's neck (v. 29) appropriately portray the intimacy and depth of such interior and mystical union.

Genesis 47

*Joseph brought five of his brothers before Pharaoh, and as in-
structed, they told him of their occupation. They also requested that
they be allowed to live in the land of Goshen. Pharaoh gladly granted
their request and even offered to put his own cattle in their charge.*

*Jacob came before Pharaoh and blessed him. When Pharaoh in-
quired as to his age, Jacob replied that he was one hundred and thirty
years old.*

*The famine over Egypt became so severe that the Egyptians even-
tually spent all of their money on grain, until only Pharaoh had money.
Joseph then began to exchange grain for the people's cattle, but by
the end of the year all the cattle belonged to Pharaoh as well. In des-
peration, the people finally sold both their land and themselves to
Pharaoh, so that everything in Egypt belonged to him except the land
of the priests. Joseph then made an arrangement with the Egyptians
that one-fifth of all that they harvested would belong to Pharaoh, and
the people were grateful for this.*

*Jacob and his descendants grew and prospered in the land of
Goshen, and Jacob lived to be one hundred and forty-seven years old.
As the time drew near for him to die, Jacob entreated Joseph to return
his body to Canaan upon his death. And Joseph made an oath to his
father that he would do so.*

Jacob and His Sons Are Welcomed in Egypt

In verses one through seven, Joseph's brothers and his father were
now with him in Egypt. Five brothers were presented to Pharaoh,
welcomed by him, and granted their place and their position in the
land. The complete absence in Egyptian records of any reference to
Joseph and his family may be due to the disturbances caused by the
domination of the Hyksos. However, the greater probability is that
a parable was deliberately created by the inspired authors of the Pentateuch. Viewed in this way, Joseph personifies an initiate who
achieves a complete harmonization of all the parts of his or her nature
—spiritual, intellectual and physical—and also their unification into
one instrument of awareness and action in the service of the Monad.
Jacob and his sons typify these three parts—Jacob is the spiritual ray
(Atma), representative of the Monad; Joseph is the immortal, spiritual
Self approaching Adeptship through the portals of the great initia-

tions; the brothers personify various characteristics of the four component bodies of human beings.

Spiritual Starvation

The famine (v. 4) which afflicted the land of Canaan, and therefore Jacob and his sons who were living there, allegorically portrays the condition of human consciousness which precedes embarkation upon the search for wisdom. The symbols usually employed are famine and hunger, the necessity for physical food being related to a pressing need for philosophic understanding and spiritual nourishment. A state of hunger aptly describes the condition of the human vehicles of consciousness before they are unified, vivified and empowered by the presence, the action and the wisdom of the awakened spiritual Self. Once gathered together and unified, all the parts of a person share in the realization of the indwelling presence of the Divine, which is the true self. Allegorically, famine then ceases and is replaced by both plenty and honor. Thus Jacob and his family were afflicted by famine. In order to relieve it they went to Egypt, a geographical symbol for a place where temples of the Mysteries existed. Arriving there they were supplied with an abundance of food and given their due place in the land. Bondage within Egypt, which happened later in the history, implies the opposite—subservience to the flesh.

The History of the Tribes of Israel

Although the history of the twelve tribes of Israel is recorded in the Bible in Genesis and Exodus, the account is not chronicled in Egyptian history. Note, though, that statues have been discovered with semitic features that were carved during this period of history in Egypt. The narrative is, however, rich with esoteric symbolism.

The land of Egypt, largely because of the presence there of Joseph, proved to be of at least dual significance for the Israelites. On the one hand relief from famine, welcome, and settlement in the country were granted to Jacob and his family. On the other hand, though, during the later period as recorded in the book of Exodus, Egypt became a land of cruel bondage, and even slavery for the Hebrews. As already indicated, mutually opposite experiences offer opportunity for their interpretation from the purely mystical and spiritual points of view.

With the exception of Joseph, Jacob's family may be regarded as personifications of the mortal aspects of every human being, while Joseph symbolizes the human immortal Soul. The family's need represents recognition of lack of knowledge and understanding, while the journey is symbolic of the consequent search for spiritual light and truth.

Light did dawn upon them and truth was discovered by them, as indicated by their receipt of corn, money, a silver cup, security, a country and a home. Mystically interpreted, these imply the attainment of wisdom and knowledge and the resultant intellectual security. The language employed and the recognizable symbols which are included all support this reading, while the total absence of historical records both casts doubt upon the historicity of the record of the events and encourages its study from the symbolic point of view.

Viewed in this manner, the land of Egypt itself may be regarded as a geographical symbol for a state of consciousness in which illumination is attained. The existence of the Egyptian Mysteries, their hierophants and other officiants lends weight to this approach. These beneficent institutions were themselves designed to bring about such spiritual realizations and experiences that would fulfill the intellectual need for understanding of the meaning and purpose of human life.

A Blessing Is Given

In the blessing of Pharaoh by Jacob (v. 10), the search for spiritual light and truth nears its end. The life of the person is now dominated by the inexpressible longing for the infinite, and an acceptable source of knowledge has been found. His or her highly evolved mental principle (Jacob) has itself become illumined (is in Egypt). All tests have been successfully passed, all difficulties overcome, and the aspirant is established in truth (settled in Egypt) and accepted as a member of the spiritual community ("the best of the land" – v. 11).

> And Joseph nourished his father, and his brethren, and all his father's household, with bread, according to their families. *(Gen. 47:12)*

The interpretation earlier offered for the symbol of corn may be also applied to bread, with the added suggestion that by means of contemplation (yeast) knowledge had become both spiritual power and esoteric wisdom. Truth had not only been received, but was so fully assimilated as to bestow spiritual and intellectual faculties born of understanding (eating bread).

The Famine Worsens

The symbol of famine has already been interpreted from both the macrocosmic and the microcosmic points of view. In the latter, the resultant hunger indicates recognition – to the degree of suffering – of the total absence of understanding of the plan, purposes, and objectives of human existence. Every human being who has ever embarked upon a determined search for knowledge has experienced this intellectual famine, the hunger which it causes, and the resultant determination to find out truth for herself or himself. Joseph, having succeeded in this quest, was a fully illumined and highly developed teacher, and was in consequence able effectively to assist those who followed after him (his family) on the pathway to truth.

The deeper aspects of the search for knowledge – as also of knowledge itself – are indicated in verses seventeen through nineteen, where the people of Egypt sell their land to Pharaoh for grain. Famine continues externally even though bread is supplied. The symbol of seed is now introduced into the story (v. 19), and this may be interpreted as implying that the great quest is not for knowledge alone, but for the very source of knowledge. This is divine truth itself as contained in the vastness of the Universal Mind in which all truth perpetually abides, less as concrete and conceptual ideas than as abstract varieties.

The totality of the hunger and the determination to satisfy it are referred to in verses twenty through twenty-three by means of an allegory of national famine. Joseph, as the possessor of both bread and seed, personifies interiorly the power (his office) and the beneficence (generosity) innate in the spiritual aspects of the human constitution – divine will and divine wisdom. Interpreted as a description of the passage of a candidate through the grades of the Mysteries, the narrative shows Joseph as the reigning hierophant who confers successive initiations (bread and seed).

> And it shall come to pass in the increase, that ye shall give the fifth part unto Pharaoh, and four parts shall be your own, for seed of the field, and for your food, and for them of your households, and for food for your little ones.
> And they said, Thou has saved our lives: let us find grace in the sight of my lord, and we will be Pharaoh's servants. *(Gen. 47:24–25)*

Surrender of self-desire, of egotism and of pride of possession as a natural result of the elevation of Spirit is allegorically portrayed by these two verses.

Jacob Prepares to Die

All cycles eventually reach their close, all quests their goal, and all seekers for truth and perfection their greatest fulfillment. Strangely, this is not an extension of personal reign and capacity, but the very opposite. Once the stature of high initiate and Adept has been attained by the traveler on the ancient path to the discovery of truth, all limitations—particularly those based upon the delusion of self-separate existence—are outgrown. This transcendence of self, portrayed in world allegories either as decapitation or premature death, is descriptive of the final stages of human evolution. In many cases this is followed by a supernatural resurrection, implying complete transcendence of the prison or tomb of self-centeredness. Both the death of Jacob and the return of his physical body to the home of his fathers indicate this attainment; for the death of heroes, heroines and saviors is indeed figurative or symbolic, being descriptive only of the death of self and self-interest.

Genesis 48

Some years later Joseph was informed that his father was ill, and he went to Jacob with his two sons, Manasseh and Ephraim. Jacob then related to Joseph his message from God at Luz in Canaan—that he, Israel, would be made a great nation. Jacob adopted these two sons of Joseph as his own and said that they would be equal to their new brothers in their inheritance, but that any future children of Joseph's would be his own.

Israel then asked to see Joseph's two sons, but because of failing eyes at first he was unable to recognize them by sight. He prepared to bless them, crossed his arms and laid his right hand upon Ephraim, the younger brother, and his left upon Manasseh, the elder. When Joseph saw this, he was displeased and told his father that Manasseh was the elder and should therefore get preference in the blessing. Jacob related that he knew this, but nevertheless the younger brother would be greater than the elder; and then he blessed them.

When he finished, Israel said, "Behold, I die: but God shall be with you, and bring you again unto the land of your fathers."

The Transference of Power

This chapter of Genesis describes the procedures involved in the transmission of power and authority from the presiding official of one period to that of its successor. Jacob's choice of the younger son to be greater than the older brothers indicates that such succession is not necessarily dependent upon seniority alone. In the sacred language younger sons are sometimes specially favored, since they personify the latest in time, and therefore the greatest attainment and degree of interior unfoldment. In allegories of the present historical epoch, which is characterized by the development of dual mental powers and their vehicles in humans — the abstract, prophetic intelligence and the concrete, analytical mentality — youngest sons generally refer to the supramental, intuitive faculty.

The symbology of earlier chapters of Genesis describing Joseph's relationship with his brothers supports this reading; for it employs the same device of the choice of the youngest for special favors. Benjamin thus receives the gift of a silver cup in his sack of corn (Gen. 44:12). In this chapter Ephraim is set before Manasseh and Jacob prophesies that this younger son will become greater than Manasseh — that "his seed shall become a multitude of nations." (Gen. 48:19)

Acts of laying on of hands in blessing refer not only to the transmission of spiritual power and authority, but also to a transference of actual physical influence and magnetism which is brought about by direct contact. This is very important, because it ensures that the whole being of the recipient — spiritual, intellectual and physical — receives the transmitted power, life-force and magnetism of the predecessor before the master's retirement or death.

In verses three and four, Jacob tells of his prophetic vision of God on his journey to Egypt — that he, Israel, would be the father of a great nation (Gen. 48:3). The prophecies by God to the Hebrew patriarchs that their nation would greatly increase in numbers and populate much of the Earth, in light of history, may be regarded as of spiritual rather than of material and purely human significance. This view gains support when the Torah is regarded as being far less an account of the creation of the world and of an early period in the history of the Hebrews than an allegorical description of both cosmogenesis and the whole of humanity upon the planet Earth. All nations are involved in the great story, as also is each individual person — whether unenlightened, advanced, initiate or Adept. The succession of peoples, the advent of their leaders, and the formal transference of power from one patriarch to his successor are described in conformity with this view. This reading also shows the Torah as transcending the limitations of time to include the events of a whole world period; for the great story tells not only of the past, but also of the present and the future of the whole human race. This is part of the value of the Hebrew Torah or Law.

In terms of human history, not all of the prophecies of the future greatness and leading world role of the Hebrew peoples have, as yet, been fulfilled. Spiritually, however, and applied to the evolution of the consciousness of humankind, their fulfillment is assured, since the domination and illumination of the lower mortal self by the divine Self are inevitable.

The Messianic Age

The prophecy of God to Jacob at Luz must therefore be read as being founded upon this truth and as a provision of that time on Earth when humanity's purely spiritual powers and qualities shall govern all relationships between individual persons and also between the nations of the world. This, it is suggested, will be the true Messianic Age, international rather than national and the product of the evolutionary progress of humankind. Interpreted in the above light, the supposedly historical people in the great story are also personifications of aspects of human nature. Human powers, qualities and tendencies towards certain forms of conduct, typical of one or the other of the seven parts of the human constitution, are also portrayed by the seven stems of the Menorah. The story is thus universal, although containing elements of the early history of the Israelites which are used as a basis for the allegory.

> And as for me, when I came from Padan, Rachel died by me in the land of Canaan, in the way, when there was but a little way to come unto Ephrath: and I buried her there in the way of Ephrath; the same is Bethlehem. *(Gen. 48:7)*

Even certain of the places said to have been visited by the patriarchs and their families have esoteric and symbolical significance, each being descriptive of an attribute of human nature and of a phase of human evolution. Thus Jacob, when reviewing his own past and telling of the death and burial of his wife Rachel, is also revealing truths of profound significance—universal, planetary, historical, and concerning the unfoldment of the innate powers in each and every human being.

Jacob Bestows a Blessing

> And Joseph took them both, Ephraim in his right hand toward Israel's
> left hand, and Manasseh in his left hand toward Israel's right hand,
> and brought them near unto him. *(Gen. 48:13)*

The eyesight of the retiring patriarch evidently had begun to grow dim, for he failed to recognize his grandsons. This failure signifies that he must transfer his ordained power to his successor, as discussed earlier in the text. The intimacy of this procedure of the transference of power is especially revealed in the thirteenth verse, in which the action becomes almost ceremonial. The contact between the hands is indicative of the component polarities—negative or left and positive or right—of the transmitted power. Israel, as the reigning official, knew well of these polarities, while his son Joseph is made to appear completely ignorant of them. His father is insistent, however, and eventually blesses the sons of Joseph, as well as Joseph himself, in the manner which he knew to be the correct one considering the influences and forces involved. The reference in the sixteenth verse to the angel ("The angel which redeemed me from all evil, bless the lads") may possibly refer to the archangel head of the hierarchy of the Elohim which watched over and evolved side by side not only with the young Hebrew nation, but also with the whole human race upon the planet Earth. The Ageless Wisdom, upon which the authors of the Torah may have been drawing, expounds that each nation is placed in the charge of an exalted member of the angelic hierarchy, and it is not impossible that Jacob was indeed aware of the existence of the guiding angel of the Hebrews (see Hodson, *The Kingdom of the Gods*).

> And he blessed them that day, saying, In thee shall Israel bless, say-
> ing, God make thee as Ephraim and as Manasseh: and he set
> Ephraim before Manasseh.
> And Israel said unto Joseph, Behold, I die: but God shall be with you,
> and bring you again unto the land of your fathers.
> Moreover, I have given to thee one portion above thy brethren, which
> I took out of the hand of the Amorite with my sword and with my
> bow. *(Gen. 48:20–22)*

The immediate transference of power from Jacob to Joseph is described in these verses, with a reference also being made to the destiny of the Hebrews under Joseph's care. Not just one small group of people is involved, dislodged from its tribal home, but the whole of humanity and its history and destiny are included in these closing verses of Chapter Forty-Eight.

A spiritual identity exists between each individual person, her or his nation and humanity as a whole. The Torah is related in such a manner that this identity, this intimacy, oneness and mutuality of the manifesting divine Spirit in all that exists is allegorically revealed in its verses. In consequence, the experiences of one person reflect those of the universe as a whole. The evolutionary progress throughout the ages of that one person is an inseparable and interactive part of the total evolution of the universe. Indeed, macrocosm and microcosm — whatever the dimensions given to these twin existences — are one, as both the most ancient and the more modern seers have proclaimed with one voice.

Genesis 49

Jacob gathered all of his sons to his deathbed: Reuben, Simeon, Levi, Judah, Zebulun, Issachar, Dan, Gad, Asher, Naphtali, Joseph and Benjamin. These comprised the heads of the twelve tribes of Israel, and he gave suitable final blessings or curses to each of them.

And again Israel reminded them that he was to be buried in the land of Canaan, in the cave of the field of Machpelah. It was there that Abraham, Sarah, Isaac, Rebekah, and Leah, Jacob's wife, were buried. And when he had given his final blessings and orders, Jacob died.

The Death and Burial of Jacob

The inclusion of the oration made by the dying Jacob to his sons makes this one of the most remarkable chapters in the Bible, particularly from the esoteric point of view: for in it the unity of the macrocosm and the microcosm is affirmed.

The process of dying at a great age, surrounded by offspring and possessed of wealth, symbolizes the fulfillment of human existence, the completion of the human pilgrimage, the attainment of perfected humanity or Adeptship. This implies freedom from enforced physical rebirth, a last death as a human, the end of an epoch.

Completed interior unfoldment and victory over all human weaknesses are indicated by the security, honor and good position of the family in Goshen. External well-being and wealth are customarily used in the sacred language to connote interior well-being and spiritual fulfillment. Poverty, on the other hand, denotes the absence of developed power, though sometimes it refers only to the absence of personal awareness of them. A person may have material wealth, and even great mental skill and ability, and yet be pitifully poor because of the lack of spiritual idealism, wisdom and understanding. Physical poverty, then, is a symbol for an impoverished psychospiritual state, and material well-being is used to denote its opposite.

Macrocosm and Microcosm United in the Adept

The macrocosm in the esoteric sense is the totality of cosmos, of all existence—physical, superphysical and spiritual. The microcosm, which is the human realm, is a profound and—except to the highest seers—an unfathomable mystery. In terms of inexhaustible power, indwelling life-force and directive intelligence—conceived in terms of force rather than substance—the whole of cosmos is mysteriously present within the human Monad. The zodiac, its component stars and their archangelic regents who are highly evolved Intelligences associated with them (Dhyan Chohans), solar Logoi, Suns and Planets, are not only contained within a person—humans are actually composed of them. Indeed, they form the very fabric of human existence.

The evolution of the human Monad partly consists of the emergence of these inherent macrocosmic presences and powers from the germinal to the active state. The more developed a human being is, the greater the degree in which the potencies and the intelligences associated with the Sun and the twelve zodiacal signs are expressed through her or his seven vehicles. The perfected person is one in whom this process has advanced to such a stage that she or he is no longer human, but superhuman; no longer mortal, but Adept. The macrocosm has then become manifested to such a remarkable degree in the microcosm that in the liberated consciousness of the Adept the two are realized as one.

In this interpretation Jacob dying—to human limitations—typifies the Adept degree of attainment. His sons are his powers, and symbolically and sometimes adversely he describes each of them in terms of zodiacal qualities. When translated into theurgical action, unlimited power resides in this knowledge. Discordant elements of society might prematurely discover a part of it and, not having developed the stability of mind and the moral sense which would ensure its constructive use, they could misuse it, thus bringing injury to themselves and to all those who come within their influence. This information—in both its speculative (as in this book) and its operative senses—is only taught directly, and always in secret, during the great initiations. In fact, one of the reasons for the invention and use of the symbolical language was to record this wisdom, preserve it, and yet make it available to humanity in allegorical and symbolic form.

Pursuant to this method of writing, the twelve sons of Jacob and their offspring—the twelve tribes of Israel—are less physical people than personifications of the Divine Presences and Powers in the cosmos. When Jacob is described as having been gathered unto his people (Gen. 49:29), and his body is said to be buried with those of his predecessors, this allegorically refers to the path of forthgoing and return [see Volume I, Part Three] and the conscious blending of the macrocosm with the microcosm in perfected humanity.

Jacob journeys into Egypt, which was then an active center of both the greater and the lesser Mysteries. In an initiatory reading he receives there the benediction of initiation, develops his inborn powers to full maturity, and reaches Adeptship or "the measure of the stature of the fullness of Christ" (Eph. 4:13). Thereafter he "dies" to the limitations of the human kingdom of nature, and so enters into the freedom of the universe which every liberated person achieves. The authors of the Pentateuch employ the allegory of Jacob's journey to Egypt and of his death and burial in order to describe this mystical experience.

A major cycle is closing and its fruits—the innate powers and qualities unfolded up to that time—are described in Chapter Forty-Nine. Indications concerning the succeeding cycle are also given. The authors of Genesis make use of the necessary recording of an historical event to convey profoundly significant philosophic knowledge drawn from the Ancient Wisdom. This knowledge concerns the numerical classifications into which all orders of creation—kingdoms of nature and human beings, for example—naturally fall. In addition, the doctrine of the interrelationships, and so perpetual interactions, between humanity, universe, planet and cosmos is revealed.

Zodiacal Symbology

The number twelve is applied to these classifications, representing—as it does by addition—the number three, thus referring to the triple nature of the active, creative Logos. History here takes second place, whether it is concerned with tribes, offspring or disciples; for the characteristics of the supposedly historical and physical human beings in the narrative are portrayed in such a manner as to reveal the twelvefold zodiacal correlations between humanity and universe.

In this chapter of Genesis the story of a family and a tribe is thus lifted completely beyond the limitations of a purely historical record and thereby given a cosmic significance. In this procedure we discern the intention of the authors to record supposed history metaphorically, thus constructing a vehicle for the revelation of ideas which completely transcend a narrative of events in time and place.

Although Jacob's attribution of various qualities to his sons is somewhat indirect in certain cases (see Gen. 49:3,4), the whole subject is nevertheless worthy of examination from this point of view. Deeply esoteric knowledge is revealed, such as the intimate relationships and correlations between archangelic regents of constellations and stars and their corresponding manifestations and expressions both here on this planet and within every human being. In this connection it is interesting to note that vast distances in space neither prevent nor reduce the functional interaction between the apparently far distant and remote on the one hand and the natural phenomena and inhabitants of this planet on the other.

Thus unity is presented as the underlying truth, while distance in space according to limited human perceptions is an illusion. In the eyes of humankind the cosmos consists of differing objects with varying degrees of materiality, while to Adept and archangel all are the products of one ever-active power throughout the field of divine manifestation. Although this field may be physically spatial, the energy itself is one and the same wherever expressed.

The Twelve Sons of Jacob
Personify Zodiacal Qualities

The various powers represented by the twelve signs of the zodiac and their planetary rulers and all the developed faculties and natural attributes of a high initiate are brought together under the direction of the will, to which they are utterly subservient. Thus the mystery teachings of the Chaldean, and sometimes the Egyptian sanctuaries concerning both the macrocosm and the microcosm are all revealed in these accounts of the Jewish patriarchs and of the founding of the Hebrew nation. The symbology employed is largely astrological. The attributions of the signs of the zodiac to the twelve sons of Jacob and tribes of Israel are as follows:

Jacob's Children and the Zodiac

Aquarius . . . . Reuben ("unstable as water").

Gemini . . . . Simeon and Levi (a strong fraternal association).

Leo . . . . Judah (the strong lion of his tribe, "a lion's whelp").

Pisces . . . . Zebulun (he "shall dwell at the haven of the sea").

Taurus . . . . Issachar ("a strong ass couching down," and therefore associated with stables, byres, etc.).

Virgo-Scorpio . . . Dan ("a serpent by the way, an adder in the path, that biteth the horse heels").

Capricorn . . . . Naphtali ("a hind let loose").

Cancer . . . . Benjamin (ravenous).

Libra . . . . Asher ("Out of Asher his bread shall be fat").

Sagittarius . . . . . . Joseph ("his bow abode in strength").

Aries . . . . Gad ("a troop shall overcome him; but he shall overcome at the last").

Virgo . . . . Dinah, the only daughter of Jacob.

The above correspondences are deduced from the words given by the dying Jacob to his sons and from his definitions of the future of each tribe of Israel (see Gen. 49:3–27).

Jacob Describes His Sons in Astrological Terms

Reuben, thou art my firstborn, my might, and the beginning of my
   strength, the excellency of dignity, and the excellency of power:
Unstable as water, thou shalt not excel; because thou wentest up to
   thy father's bed; then defiledst thou it: he went up to my couch.
   (Gen. 49:3-4)

These two verses which describe the character of Jacob's firstborn
son, Reuben, may well be regarded as mutually contradictory according to a literal reading alone. Evidently Reuben failed to live up to
the ideal in his father's mind as "my might, and the beginning of my
strength, the excellency of dignity, and the excellency of power."
Despite these great qualities, their expression through Reuben as he
grew up was greatly reduced, if not rendered impossible by the
characteristic of instability; for Reuben is described as being "unstable
as water." The zodiacal sign of Aquarius is indicated, however indirectly, and a correspondence with that sign applied to the eldest son.

Simeon and Levi are brethren; instruments of cruelty are in their
   habitations.
O my soul, come not thou into their secret; unto their assembly, mine
   honor, be not thou united: for in their anger they slew a man, and
   in their selfwill they digged down a wall.
Cursed be their anger, for it was fierce; and their wrath, for it was
   cruel: I will divide them in Jacob, and scatter them in Israel. *(Gen.
   49:5-7)*

The intimate association in their father's mind of Simeon and Levi
suggests a reference to the sign of Gemini, in which two aspects of
one power—generally called twins—are brought together, although
still manifesting diversity. The evolutionary procedure in nature, as
well as the task of the person with a geminian personality, is to elimi-
nate this tendency to divide because of opposite characteristics, and
to harmonize both motive and conduct from duality into unity. A person born under the sign of Gemini finds herself or himself capable
of a twofold self-expression. In the early phases of evolution these
can be antagonistic, as indicated by the characteristics of Simeon and
Levi, and so lead to difficulties until a harmonization has been
achieved. This is not an easy task, since the ideal on the one hand,
represented by one half or part of the geminian nature in people, and
the actual on the other hand may be at odds. The authors possibly

intended to draw attention to this antagonism and even hostility by describing the brothers as exhibiting anger and expressing it by murder.

> Judah, thou art he whom thy brethren shall praise: thy hand shall be in the neck of thine enemies; thy father's children shall bow down before thee.
> Judah is a lion's whelp; from the prey, my son, thou art gone up: he stooped down, he couched as a lion, and as an old lion; who shall rouse him up?
> The sceptre shall not depart from Judah, nor a lawgiver from between his feet, until Shiloh come; and unto him shall the gathering of the people be.
> Binding his foal unto the vine, and his ass's colt unto the choice vine; he washed his garments in wine, and his clothes in the blood of grapes:
> His eyes shall be red with wine, and his teeth white with milk. *(Gen. 49:8–12)*

The zodiacal attribution of the sign Leo to Judah is apparent, since the power of rulership and the office of kingship—both leonine—are appropriately described. If wine is taken as a symbol of wisdom distilled from knowledge (grapes), then evolutionary advancement and the later stages of the development of innate powers are being symbolically described. The intimate association of conduct and appearance with the vine, grapes and wine, even affecting the washing of Judah's clothes and the appearance of his eyes and teeth, may all be interpreted as indicating an attainment of such wisdom that the whole nature is "winelike," or expressive of wisdom in every undertaking.

> Zebulun shall dwell at the haven of the sea; and he shall be for an haven of ships; and his border shall be unto Sidon. *(Gen. 49:13)*

Dwelling beside the sea—the ancient port of Sidon—indicates that Zebulun must have been in intimate association with fishes. This may be read as a personification by Zebulun of the sign Pisces.

> Issachar is a strong ass couching down between two burdens:
> And he saw that rest was good, and the land that it was pleasant; and bowed his shoulder to bear, and become a servant unto tribute. *(Gen. 49:14–15)*

While procreative power is especially attributed to the bull—hence the sign Taurus—nevertheless the bull is a member of the genus *ox*, an animal widely used as a beast of burden in ancient times. Since asses, however, were also used this way, astrologers have presumably considered the association of these two families of beasts of burden to be so similar as to be interchangeable. In consequence Issachar, whom his father Jacob described as "a strong ass couching down between two burdens," has become associated with the ox, and so with the sign Taurus.

> Dan shall judge his people, as one of the tribes of Israel.
> Dan shall be serpent by the way, an adder in the path, that biteth the
>   horse heels, so that his rider shall fall backward.
> I have waited for thy salvation, O Lord. *(Gen. 49:16–18)*

The correspondence between the serpent and the scorpion gives rise to the possibility of the association of Dan with the sign Scorpio. The serpent, however, has been given at least two beneficent meanings in the language of symbols. One of these is comprehension, including wise judgment and spiritual intuitiveness—apt attributes of a lawgiver and judge. Thus it seems appropriate that Jacob should begin his description of Dan by referring to his future office of judge of the people of Israel.

A deeper and more esoteric interpretation is possible and even hinted at in the eighteenth verse where, in his father's mind, Dan is associated with salvation by the power of the Lord. A reference may here be discerned to the second meaning given to the symbol of the serpent, namely the divine, creative power present in the human body—the serpent fire or kundalini.

When this normally sleeping force is aroused into supernormal activity, the limitations of bodily encasement can be overridden and the person, thus freed, becomes aware of her or his own divine and eternal nature. In this aspect immortality, deathlessness, and assurance of the full expression of spiritual powers is reached.

> Gad, a troop shall overcome him: but he shall overcome at the last.
> Out of Asher his bread shall be fat, and he shall yield royal dainties.
>   *(Gen. 49:19–20)*

The zodiacal correspondence given by astrologers to Gad is the sign Aries, ruled by the planet Mars. In early phases of human evolution combativeness, whether personal or national, can lead to destruction. In the evolved person, however, it makes victory over the lower nature possible. Refinement then follows, producing the characteristics of gentleness and of readiness to direct arietic qualities and martial tendencies to an exploration of the previously unknown aspects of human nature, and to victory over all that would delay hastened progress towards this goal.

> Naphtali is a hind let loose: he giveth goodly words. *(Gen. 49:21)*

A correspondence with the goat family, and so with the zodiacal sign Capricorn, is probably indicated here.

> Joseph is a fruitful bough, even a fruitful bough by a well; whose branches run over the wall;
> The archers have sorely grieved him, and shot at him, and hated him:
> But his bow abode in strength, and the arms of his hands were made strong by the hands of the mighty God of Jacob; (from thence is the shepherd, the stone of Israel:)
> Even by the God of thy father, who shall help thee; and by the Almighty, who shall bless thee with blessings of heaven above, blessings of the deep that lieth under, blessings of the breasts, and womb:
> The blessings of thy father have prevailed above the blessings of my progenitors unto the utmost bound of the everlasting hills: they shall be on the head of Joseph, and on the crown of the head of him that was separate from his brethren. *(Gen. 49:22–26)*

References to archers, to Joseph's bow, and to archery in general would associate Joseph with the sign of Sagittarius. In view of his later contributions to the welfare of his family, the somewhat symbolical descriptions by Jacob of his son Joseph are quite apt from both the material and the spiritual points of view.

> Benjamin shall ravin as a wolf: in the morning he shall devour the prey, and at night he shall divide the spoil. *(Gen. 49:27)*

The description of Benjamin as a ravening wolf devouring its prey suggests both the sign Cancer and the parasitical disease of the same name. Although Jacob's daughter, Dinah, is not here mentioned, her maiden status may justify her choice by astrologers to represent the sign Virgo.

The Field of Machpelah

The closing verses of Chapter Forty-nine of Genesis, with their description of the death and burial of Abraham, Sarah and certain members of their family and culminating in the death of Jacob himself, can be interpreted as revealing some knowledge concerning the final stages of universal, racial and individual human evolution. The preceding descriptions of the characters of the sons of Jacob and of the corresponding tribes of Israel refer to phases of the gradual development and also to the eventual attainment of full expression of the twelve inherent or zodiacal powers locked up in the spiritual "seed" or human Monad. This dweller in the innermost of each human being who is evolving through the present period of manifestation (Manvantara) of our Solar System contains germinally within itself these twelve capacities. The words of Jacob to his sons in these closing verses may be read as veiled revelations of the ultimate stages of development to be reached by the end of the era, in its turn symbolized by Jacob's death and burial.

A hint of this achievement may possibly be found in verse thirty, where the name of the field in which the burial cave existed is given as "Mach-pelah." This word, especially in its first syllable, resembles a word uttered at low breath by certain officers during an important rite in freemasonry. If this interpretation is accurate, supported as it is by the inclusion of the word Machpelah in a description of the close of a tribal dispensation, then a reference may be discerned to procedures followed in the temples of the greater Mysteries of old, of which modern freemasonry is considered to be a representative.

The Path to Perfection

Esoteric philosophy includes the idea of the existence of a path of hastened progress, a way of self-quickening. By treading this path the goal of human evolution or twelvefold development is achieved ahead of the normal time—in advance of the rest of humanity. In this largely secret way of life, which includes victory over adverse attributes and the unfoldment of esoteric, theurgic and spiritual powers from within, a record of each phase of development is kept by an official in the hierarchy of the Adepts of this planet. The title of this Adept keeper of the records is Maha-Chohan, meaning "Great Lord" in Sanskrit.

The activities of the Great White Brotherhood are all directed towards the fulfillment of nature's grand design, and they are all entirely secret. These activities include the attainment of masterhood by those who pass through trials, tests and successive initiations leading to the final goal. References in the sacred language to such activities are, in consequence, heavily concealed behind a veil of allegory and symbol. As previously stated, this veil may be employed in these closing chapters of Genesis, most of the events described in them being without either historical or anthropological support. Even the existence of Jacob himself, his twelve sons and the tribes named after them is in doubt, as also are the events related about their journey to Egypt, their meeting with Joseph, and his beneficent treatment of them under agreement with the reigning Pharaoh.

Certain other words appearing in the closing verses of this chapter may be similarly regarded. Two of these are "cave" and "field" (v. 29). As already mentioned, the ceremonies of the greater Mysteries were always performed in complete secrecy, and in some cases in a crypt or other underground part of a temple. (Note that when partial descriptions are found in ancient literature—as of the Eleusinea, for example—they are always of the lesser Mysteries alone.) The word "cave" also suggests a deep recess, and is used allegorically to refer to the innermost depths of the human constitution where the Monad, or unit of pure Spirit-Essence, abides. The word "field" may in its turn refer to a universe or to a planet, and microcosmically to the Auric Envelope of the individual; for these three are the fields in which cosmic and human evolution take place, the Monad or divine seed having been planted there.

14

The Joseph Cycle

Genesis 50

Jacob passed from this realm, and Joseph wept bitterly. He issued orders for the ritual embalming of the body, which took forty days. And for seventy days all of Egypt mourned Jacob.

When the time of mourning was past, Joseph entreated Pharaoh that he might leave Egypt to bury his father in the land of Canaan. Pharaoh gave his blessing, and Joseph and his brothers and all of the household of Israel, along with the elders of the land of Egypt, journeyed to Canaan. At Atad, beyond the Jordan River, the traveling party paused in mourning for seven days. They then continued on to the field of Machpelah and buried Jacob there as he had commanded.

On Jacob's passing, Joseph's brothers feared that he would begin to treat them harshly because of the tribulation that they had caused him. They told Joseph that Jacob had ordered them to seek his forgiveness; they then fell down before him and offered themselves as his slaves. Joseph set their hearts at ease, telling him that their actions and his trials because of them had been used by God for the good of humankind.

Joseph lived to the age of one hundred and ten. Before he died he told his brothers that one day God would bring them out of Egypt and back to Canaan. He said, "God will visit you, and you shall carry my bones away from this place." Having said this, Joseph died.

Joseph Personifies the Initiate
Who Reaches Adeptship

The interpretation given of the narrative of the life of Jacob, particularly in the preceding chapter of this book, may also be applied to the account of the life of his son Joseph; for he, like his father, is united with his family and its descendants and with them journeys to the land of his birth where his father is to be buried.

Minor cycles overlap and the patriarch of one period of office generally participates in the closing years of office of his predecessor. After assuming leadership he continues the process of administration until he completes the cycle of his activities, and in his turn dies and is buried. A similar procedure is followed by hierophants in the lesser and the greater Mysteries.

The restatement of the enmity and perfidy of his brothers towards Joseph as described in this chapter of Genesis is noteworthy, particularly from the point of view of esoteric psychology. They are still afraid of him after Jacob's death, but he forgives them and cares compassionately for them and all their people. The numerous energies, qualities of character, motives and tendencies which the brothers personify, and which form part of the complexity of the nature of a human being, can indeed be the causes of war both between people and within each person. The very matter of the body, or rather the three *gunas* or attributes of that matter, can become unequally expressed, particularly during this present age when humanity is passing through highly individualistic phases of development. (The three gunas are *rajas*—activity, desire; *sattva*—harmony, rhythm; *tamas*—inertia, stagnation. They correspond to three aspects of the Trinity—Father, Son and Holy Spirit, or Brahma, Vishnu and Shiva respectively.) Indeed at this time strife is evident within each person—the true Armageddon, interior and mystical. When, however, the later phases of human evolution are entered upon, human nature becomes more harmonious and its diverse elements are increasingly under the control of the inner Self. In the language of symbols families are reunited, countries are subdued and harmony reigns, as was finally the case between Joseph and his brothers.

Adverse experiences of a single life, including especially those of childhood and adolescence, can establish areas of distress and disequilibrium in the human psyche. The tendency towards these disharmonies, and the karma of suffering from them, have both been brought over from a preceding life. Moreover, unless harmonized and healed some of them can be carried forward into succeeding incarnations. Before the higher initiations can be conferred, these warring and pain-producing factors must be reconciled. This is largely achieved by the reincarnating Ego which, Joseph-like, has become wise and powerful enough to bring about a restoration of health and interior harmony.

The very substance of which the mental, emotional, etheric and physical bodies are composed itself resists the spiritualizing and harmonizing process; for the elemental consciousness inhabiting that substance is traveling on the downward arc towards coarser emotional experiences and denser embodiment in physical matter [see Volume I, Part Three]. This involving consciousness of the matter of bodies is part of the subjective Devil or evil in humans, and is sometimes personified either by Satan or by the dark angels who are said to be at war with the angels of light. The human spiritual Self which inhabits these four bodies has, on the other hand, long ago embarked upon the path of return. Its objective is liberation from the imprisoning and coarsening influences of life in the physical and emotional bodies. An interior conflict is thus inevitable and continuous, and this is one possible microcosmic interpretation of Armageddon or Kurukshetra (the Hindu Armageddon described in the Mahabharata, the scene of the divine Discourses of the Bhagavad Gita).

Jacob and Joseph, as initiates approaching Adeptship or the completion of the human cycle, both achieved victory in this interior warfare, even though they suffered mystical wounds in the process [see the symbolic interpretation of mystical wounds, Volume I, page 20]. Their physical well-being and security, and the assembling of all the members of their families in the closing years of their lives, partly describe this psychospiritual attainment. The highest honors having been achieved, Joseph leaves his body at the age of one hundred and ten years and is, in his turn, buried with his forefathers.

The Jacob Cycle Closes

Joseph's grief at the death of his father, the embalming of the body, the request to Pharaoh for permission to take it to Canaan for burial and Pharaoh's consent (v. 1–6) can be interpreted as descriptions of the ends of cycles. Esoterically, these closures of cycles would include the following: the consummation of Manvantara leading to the onset of the night of Pralaya, whether of a Solar System as a whole (Maha-Pralaya) or of component Schemes, Chains, Rounds, Globes, Races and civilizations; the death and disappearance of the bodies of all organisms; the completion of a cycle of human existence; and the subsequent entry of the Monad into the superhuman kingdom of nature, which upon entering the perfected human Ego is conscious of oneness with its Source – a state of awareness symbolized by entry into the land of Canaan. The tears of Joseph shed upon his father's body not only tell of the grief of a bereaved son, but are also a possible reference to the "waters of space" into which, at their dissolution, all material objects disappear.

The laborious – but in actuality entirely unnecessary – plans for taking the body of Jacob all the way back to Canaan, and their fulfillment, also refer to a return of the essence and the substance of each completed cycle, of whatever dimensions, to the Source. This Source is precosmic Spirit-matter in a conjoined and relatively passive relationship.

As has been mentioned earlier, this change from activity to passivity, from form to formlessness, and from active life to peaceful rest is a fundamental, unchanging procedure of nature. It is one of the secret teachings of the ancient Mysteries, revealed directly to initiates by the use of metaphor and allegory to the outside world. Thus the death of a central figure refers to the end of a cycle, the choice of a specially chosen place for the tomb implies return to the Source, while the burial itself implies the resumption of that darkness which brooded over "the face of the deep" (Gen.1:2) in Pralaya, to be replaced by light when the new cycle dawns in Manvantara.

Doubtless the numbers of forty days for embalming and seventy days of mourning given in the third verse are also significant and can be allegorically and symbolically interpreted. The number seventy, reducible to seven, indicates the completion of a minor cycle, the end of an age.

The affirmation that on his journey to Canaan Joseph was accompanied by "all the servants of Pharaoh, the elders of his house, and all the elders of the land of Egypt" (v. 7) can hardly be taken literally. In consequence it must surely be regarded either as a great exaggeration to show the importance of Joseph's position in Egypt, or as an indication that in the cosmic sense the totality of objective, manifested existences is withdrawn into the quiescent state. The reference in the tenth verse to the crossing of the Jordan River may also be taken as descriptive of passage from one state of existence to a successor, the Jordan thus being employed as a geographical symbol for an episode or condition of fundamental change — in this case from activity to rest. The reference in verse thirteen to the field of Machpelah where both Abraham and his wife, Sarah, were buried, in addition to the meaning that was given in the last chapter, accentuates the idea that the close of every cycle (the death of Jacob) brings about a return to the identical condition into which the products of the earlier cycle had descended, namely passive, precosmic space.

The Joseph Cycle Opens

In the small compass of verses fourteen through twenty-one, where Joseph's brothers beg for his forgiveness and he promises to protect them, a new era begins. Since this era was new only for the brothers, and the personification of power (Joseph) remains the same, it may be assumed that only the closing subcycle of a major cycle is involved.

Of interest, more particularly in the human sense, is the account of the further reconciliation between Joseph and his brothers, their confession and request for pardon, and his complete and very generous forgiveness. Although related as applying to persons, the impersonal law of cause and effect is doubtless being revealed, together with the state of complete reharmonization achieved at the closing of the cyclic sequence of action and reaction. While this is of macrocosmic significance, the approach to Adeptship is also being referred to, since this state cannot be attained until every action has been followed by an appropriate reaction, every debt paid to both nature and humanity and a surplus acquired in favor of the participant. Then, and then only, can the human kingdom be transcended and the Monad continue its evolution as sage, rishi, Adept.

The superabundance of favor earned by many lives and many acts of selfless service to humanity (Joseph's beneficence) is a characteristic of the closing phases of evolution through the human kingdom and entry into a higher state. This is indicated by Joseph's ready forgiveness of the injury, even to the extent of the murder which his brothers had planned and attempted to carry out against him when he came into the field (Gen. 37:24). Not vengeance but pardon, not imprisonment or execution but forgiving love was shown by Joseph to his erring brothers. Similarly, Christ upon the cross prayed for those who crucified him, saying, "Father, forgive them; for they know not what they do" (Luke 23:34).

Joseph's Death and Burial

In the sacred language the death of a person, in the sense in which it is used in the book of Genesis, means both the death of an age and the end of the passage of the Monad through the human kingdom of nature. Thus in these concluding verses Joseph dies, is put in a coffin and is buried in the land of Egypt. Note that in the New Testament death may be regarded as a symbol for that condition of the mind in which it is totally unresponsive or dead to the influence of the spiritual Self. The active presence of the awakened Christ-nature, personified by Jesus, restores the dead person to life – to responsiveness to conscience and egoic inspiration. Thus Jesus raises from the dead the daughter of Jairus and Lazarus, the brother of Martha and Mary.

Although a limited number of cycles, their presiding Logoi, and the processes of involution, evolution and withdrawal into the Source are actually referred to in the Old Testament, nevertheless the wisdom revealed beneath the veil of allegory refers to all cycles, of whatever dimensions, that have ever existed and will ever exist. The underlying principles, laws and procedures are ever the same, and so will ever remain, and this is part of the greatness of the revelation deeply hidden beneath a supposed historical record of the history of the Hebrew nation which is found in Genesis, as also in the rest of the Pentateuch and in much of the Torah as a whole.

The seeker for wisdom must, however, be prepared to delve deeply, to discover and to interpret according to the classical keys the numberless treasures of spiritual and esoteric wisdom and law which lie beneath the surface of all allegorical writings, littered with distractions though that surface may appear to be.

*　　　*　　　*　　　*　　　*　　　*

So ends the great book of Genesis – a marvelous cup filled with the wine of the esoteric knowledge of the sanctuaries of ancient days. Temples of the Ageless Wisdom exist today, even if less easily discoverable, and in them are to be found the same teachings, laws, successions, initiations and radiations of the light of truth. World changes are not reflected in the Mysteries, which are repositories and conveyors of eternal and unchanging ideas. A sack of corn containing a silver cup awaits every Benjamin or child of Jacob who finds himself or herself called by a hierophant (Joseph) from the famine-stricken outer world, to the storehouse from which an elder (a Master) who has already completed initiation will, in prodigal abundance, supply a gift of the golden grain of eternal truth.

PART FOUR

Moses and the Exodus

15

The Burning Bush

Exodus 3

Moses was keeping the flock of his father-in-law, Jethro, a priest of Midian, near Mount Horeb. He led his flock into the desert and came to the mountain of God. There the angel of God appeared to him in a bush that burned but was not consumed, and Moses was amazed by this. As Moses approached the bush, God spoke to him and told him not to come any nearer and told him to take off his sandals because he stood on holy ground. God then told Moses that "I have seen the affliction of my people who are in Egypt . . . I know their sufferings" and that God had chosen Moses to lead the people to freedom in the land of Canaan.

Moses was startled by this revelation and told God that he wasn't worthy for such a task. God insisted that he not worry, saying, "I will be with thee." Moses still wasn't convinced and remarked that the people would ask the name of the God who sent him. "God said unto Moses I AM THAT I AM . . . Thus shalt thou say unto the children of Israel, I AM hath sent me unto you."

Moses was then instructed to gather the elders of the tribes of Israel together and tell them that the God of their fathers had appeared to him and that God would bring them out of Egypt into the land of Canaan—a land flowing with milk and honey. Moses was also instructed to tell Pharaoh that they had to travel three days into the wilderness to make a sacrifice, in order that they would have a reason for leaving Egypt. Because Pharaoh would not let them go unless compelled, God promised to smite Egypt so Pharaoh would obey. Because of God's influence, the Egyptians would look upon the Israelites with favor— each woman was thus to ask her Egyptian neighbors for jewelry of silver and gold and for clothing. The Israelites were to wear these out of Egypt in order to despoil the Egyptians.

The Symbology of the Mount

In the Bible Mount Horeb represents a geographical symbol for that elevation of consciousness which is the result of a fusion of the Atma (fire) with the Manas (water), the inmost Self with the higher Ego in its vesture of light, the vehicle of the higher Mind. As a result of this fusion, which is rarely attainable without esoteric assistance, buddhic consciousness is born, the unity of life is known and the faculty of direct intuitive perception is gained. Thereafter, the Monad-Ego acts increasingly as a unit. Life is viewed from that exalted level (on the Mount) and action is decided upon in the light of that view. After initiation in the greater Mysteries this exalted state is permanently attained. The inner Self, the imperishable Monad, can then commune with and direct the outer self, whom it reaches through the Ego in the higher Mind.

This is neither a sudden nor a temporary accomplishment. It gradually becomes a permanent state, being attained by virtue of evolutionary development and the esoteric assistance of a hierophant of the greater Mysteries. For those in whom the buddhic vehicle is not yet sufficiently operative, this high officiant is able to bridge the gulf between will and intellect, Atma and Manas. The hierophant brings the cosmic Atman (electrical, solar, fiery will-force) down through the Monad-Atman of the initiate, and causes it to penetrate into the vehicle of the higher Mind, where consciousness is focused at the time. This is the real "heavenly marriage" from which the Ego in the Causal Body receives that immaculate conception or spiritual fructification by which its innate and already partially awakened buddhic selfhood or Christ nature is developed or "born." This is the real Nativity, of which all nativities of saviors, heroines and heroes are allegories, and is their microcosmic significance.

The mountain, with its elevated peak and its stability and permanence also aptly symbolizes this fruition of many lives on Earth, ripened by the action of the cosmic Atman, which is to the seed-like powers inherent in the human Monad-Ego as the physical sun is to ripening fruit. In accordance with this method of allegorical revelation, the first verse of the third chapter of Exodus opens with a description of the condition of the immortal Ego (personified by Moses) after the first great initiation has occurred. He has become a shepherd of Souls and not of physical sheep, as is indicated by the statement that

the flock belongs to a priest and is therefore holy. He himself comes
through the desert, symbol of the preinitiate state, and leads his flock
from the desert (of spiritual aridity) towards the exalted state of consciousness which he has attained, as symbolized by "the mountain
of God, even to Horeb" (v. 1).

The Fire That Does Not Consume

> And the Angel of the Lord appeared unto him in a flame of fire out
> of the midst of a bush: and he looked, and, behold, the bush burned
> with fire, and the bush was not consumed. *(Ex. 3:2)*

The esoteric revelation is continued in verse two, in which Moses
sees the angel of God in the burning bush. In the microcosmic or
human interpretation, the angel seen in the high mountain symbolizes
the influence, the radiance and the directive power of the Monad to
which the initiate becomes susceptible or which, allegorically, he
"sees."

Though often destructive in the lower worlds—especially observable in the physical—fire is spiritually constructive. In essence, fire
is the conjoined will-thought of the Logos. When these two aspects—
will-power (fire) and intelligence (water)—of the human spiritual
nature are conjoined as a result of evolutionary attainment and the
assistance of a hierophant, the initiate becomes enfired. This will-
thought of the Logos, the cosmic Atma-Manas, is perceived, received
and employed by him or her. Egoically the initiate is enrobed in fire
and the aura is aflame. This spiritual essence of the creative element
does not consume, as does its dense counterpart or physical manifestation. At the physical level, matter in the present phase of its evolution is unable to respond to the high frequency of oscillation of the
element of fire. It therefore breaks up, or is consumed. At all levels
above that of the concrete mind this phenomenon does not occur. The
substance and the correlated forces of those planes of nature are not
disintegrated by the presence within them and the action upon them
of the spiritual essence or noumenon of the element of fire. This
phenomenon is symbolically revealed in an observation by Moses that
"the bush was not consumed."

The bush, like the tree, symbolizes both the coordinated activities
of generative life spread throughout the universe and the result of that
coordination. Macrocosmically, the tree of life is all nature viewed

as a manifestation of the one universal life-force, organic as well as inorganic, Source of the Spirit which vivifies every form of creation, contained as the vital "sap" in this tree. This life-force is not, however, a free energy loosely spread out as a general ensouling and vitalizing principle. On the contrary, though omnipresent it is contained within a vehicle, the general form of which may be thought of as resembling that of a tree or bush. The roots of this tree of life arise within, and draw sustenance from Absolute Being. The trunk or stem of the tree represents, and is formed by, the localization or focusing of the one eternal life within a cosmos. Currents of formative energy flow in accordance with the laws of polarity from the unpolarized state (the Absolute) into the polarized universe. The directive power is universal ideation or divine thought, which might be regarded as the bark and inner membranes of the symbolical tree. Branches, leaves and fruit represent the product of this polarization into root substance of the creative life-force.

If the eternal Source of all is regarded as the "above" and nature as the "below," then the tree of life grows downwards; the roots draw their sustenance from the spiritual heights and its fruit are formed of, and appear in, the material depths. However, as above and below are illusions, and only the one point or apex exists, this inversion is only applicable at the levels below the higher Mind. Actually, the eternal Source is within all nature. No movement in space, no change of location, not even any extension in dimension is involved in the productive process, the whole of which occurs at that point which is everywhere, with circumference nowhere. This, however, is inexplicable and inapprehensible to the formal mind, and the symbol of the tree was chosen to express the action of the Logos in drawing upon, polarizing and focusing into time-ruled manifestation the one eternal life-force. This spiritual truth is perceived by the initiate on or near the mount, and the meaning of the burning bush in the second verse is revealed by allegory and symbol.

> And Moses said, I will now turn aside, and see this great sight, why
> the bush is not burnt. *(Ex. 3:3)*

This verse draws attention to the microcosmic significance of the presence and activity of the life-force; for the whole universe is reproduced in the individual, and in humankind the processes of universal creation are repeated continuously. The humanity of a planet is the cosmos in miniature and each individual person—spiritual, intellectual, psychical and physical—is a duplication of a Solar System. Each person is to the human race as each Solar System is to the cosmos as a whole, namely both a component and a perfect reproduction on a small scale.

In the individual the creative point is the Monad, that center in the ocean of cosmic life at which the life-force is intensely concentrated and then directed into the universe, and on to the Planet which is the appointed field of evolution—there focused as a ray or thread. Thereafter, the potential powers concentrated in the divine, microcosmic point gradually awaken, and find expression through appropriate vehicles according to the laws of resonance. Subsequently, as a result of eons of evolutionary experience and development through the seven kingdoms of nature (three elemental kingdoms on the arc of forthgoing, the mineral kingdom as turning point, followed by the plant, the animal and the human kingdoms on the returning arc—C. Jinarajadasa, *First Principles of Theosophy*), these inherent powers of every Monad awaken to life and develop to full maturity in the perfected person.

The eighth kingdom, that of superhumanity, is then entered. The purely planetary limitations are outgrown. The forces of the Solar System find expression through the Adept, whose consciousness is in consequence expanded to include extraplanetary dimensions, levels and fields of awareness and supramental states of consciousness. This attainment, in its turn, leads to extrasolar extensions of awareness and universal states of consciousness, ultimately leading to the experience of full unity and self-identification with the cosmic whole.

The Illumination of Moses

This emergence, descent and ascent of the Monadic powers is made possible by the presence within the Monad of an infinite, intense potency, the creative life force, the source of the irresistible evolutionary impulse, the flame which is cosmic life. This fire of God is present and continually active in every person, and at initiation into the greater Mysteries the candidate achieves awareness of the fact. At Adeptship the candidate becomes a master of this divine energy. Such awareness is referred to as "seeing" in verse three, in which Moses (a personification of the initiate) is made to "turn aside"— from purely personal and physical considerations—"and see this great sight."

The human physical body is built upon the model of this fiery tree of life or burning bush. The spinal cord is its trunk. Its roots are at the spinal base, the sacrum, where in every vertebrate a reservoir of solar power is concentrated. The great "trunk" of the spinal cord along which the sublimated, creative impulse ascends, opens out within the cranium, and merges with the physical branch system—the cells, the nerves, the tissues, and the organs of the brain.

The fiery force rises beyond the physical head into the human superphysical worlds and bodies, reproducing the form of the tree of life in each of them. As evolution raises the level of awareness into supramental realms, these currents of force eventually flow up through the Buddhic and Atmic bodies into the Monad, which abides at a still higher level known as *Anupadaka*, "the Parentless." Thereafter, Monadic power and consciousness can be made manifest at any level from the Atma to the physical, the formative potency serving as the transmitting energy. Sacrum, spinal cord and brain in the physical body are then enfired. The electrical current plays on through psyche and mind, illuminating the Ego-personality, now conjoined. This state is symbolized in verse three by the burning bush. By this state of consciousness Moses liberated the Israelites (the Monad-Ego) from the bondage of Egypt (the lower personality). Thus illumined, he later led them through the desert (the despiritualized state) to the Promised Land, meaning supramental awareness and power.

> And when the Lord saw that he turned aside to see, God called unto him out of the midst of the bush, and said, Moses, Moses. And he said, Here am I. *(Ex. 3:4)*

Self-conscious spiritual illumination, instead of spontaneous and sporadic intuitive flashes, now becomes available to the enfired mind, symbolized by Moses. Symbolically, the Lord calls to Moses from out of the burning bush. Moses responds, answers to his true name, acknowledges the power and the command of the inmost Self (the Monad-Atma), the true God, the Deity which speaks from within the symbolical burning bush.

All calls and answers, sound and its echo, call and due response—accurate and true—from that of Adam (Gen. 3:9) down to the latest God-illumined person, mark the spiritualized state. Monad rules, Ego acknowledges and personalty ratifies. From highest to lowest, Spirit is in command of matter, universality is attained, separated personality is transcended. Joyful is that neophyte who, with Adam and Moses, answers the divine call with the words "Here am I," for thereafter the secret of magical power is known.

The Serpent Fire

And he said, Draw not nigh hither: put off thy shoes from off thy feet,
for the place whereon thou standest is holy ground. *(Ex. 3:5)*

In this famous verse precise instruction in the manner of advancing from outer darkness to inward light is conveyed. The words "Draw not nigh hither" warn against a premature, unprepared entry into the sanctuary of nature and of the human Soul. Grave dangers await the unwary Soul which, lacking the necessary knowledge and therefore the necessary reverence, dares to touch sacred things with hands which are still profane. The sanctuaries of the world were not devised and established out of secretiveness, but as safeguards; for the potency of the powers to which they give access is so great that misused, either witlessly or willfully, it can destroy bodily health and sanity of mind. Knowing this, the inspired authors provide all aspirants to spiritual light, and all would-be magicians with both guidance and warning in the quest of their goal.

The instruction to remove the shoes, while exoterically denoting reverence, actually refers to electrical laws of the esoteric cosmos. Full illumination demands bipolarized contact with the source of light. In humans that source is the solar, electrical, creative life-force stored in the center of the Earth, and sheathed in the human sacrum. These two reservoirs remain distinct and without interrelationship. When the way of light is to be entered upon, they must be brought within a common circuit. The soles of the feet, and especially the heels, act as anode and cathode, or positive and negative poles of that organic conductor which is the human body.

When, with ceremonial intent and under conditions established by a hierophant, the right and left foot are placed in contact with earth, a current of fohatic energy leaps from the fiery reservoir at its center. This enters the body via the feet and awakens into activity the previously sleeping fohatic fire at the base of the spine. The currents cross and wind around the spinal cord, the electric sap ascends the trunk of the microcosmic tree of life and the brain receives the charge, to become both enfired from below and illumined from above. This electric shock must be applied very gradually to every neophyte, and he or she must advance one foot at a time to the place of light, and in an ordered manner, according to unchanging rules. Eventually, with both feet bare and in utmost reverence with the fohatic energy at its maximum—in full self-consciousness—the neophyte reaches the light.

Moses received illumination in just this way. It also happens to every person in whom there awakens the desire to bring humanity to deliverance, and the determination to realize the power of a deliverer.

The Exodus—The Pilgrimage of the Human Monad

The historical basis for the story of the deliverance by Moses of the Israelites from the bondage of Egypt is not very strong. It is not supported by any historical records of other nations, whether of Egypt or adjacent countries. Such slight foundation as exists has been made use of by the group of Chaldean and Egyptian initiates among the Hebrew peoples. They saw the spiritual significance of the journey of the tribes into Egypt, their initial prosperity and later subjugation, followed by a revolt and departure. The journey of life through the limitations of matter, and the pilgrimage of the human Monad, were seen to be reflected and dramatically represented in such a story. Guided by their own initiatory experience and their knowledge of the sacred language and of the scriptures of other nations, they wove these wonderful allegories of the Pentateuch. In them the secrets of the Mysteries, the stages of the natural unfoldment of the human Soul and the spiritual quickening which was the effect of passage through the grades of the Mysteries are especially portrayed. Details of the various methods by which illumined states of consciousness are attained are given in these inspired writings.

This third chapter of Exodus, and particularly the verses which follow the ones already discussed, describe the measures by which the lofty vision and the awakened power of the inner Self force the outer self to succumb to its rule. The creative fire from the sun and the center of the Earth, up to now asleep in the human body, has become awakened. The three fires, which are one, have been dynamically interlinked. Currents of fiery electrical force now play through the human body as connecting link and conductor between Earth and sun. Outer self is then sensitized to inner God. The Monad-Ego assumes direction of physical development, thought and life, affirming and gradually manifesting complete dominance.

> Moreover he said, I am the God of thy father, the God of Abraham, the God of Isaac, and the God of Jacob. And Moses hid his face; for he was afraid to look upon God. *(Ex. 3:6)*

This sovereignty of the God within is described in verse six. The Supreme Deity of the Hebrews, the cosmic Logos and not the tribal God, is made to proclaim its existence and its rule to the Israelites through Moses, their chosen leader. Allegorically this affirmation portrays the attainment of increasing dominance of the outer by the inner Self, and the mind's recognition of and submission to this.

Note that God addresses Moses as an individual and names the three preceding patriarchs. Successive cycles of the manifestation of Spirit in matter in the cosmos are indicated. This allegory is concerned with the fourth and always the densest cycle, personified by Moses. In the human realm, the God of Abraham, of Isaac and of Jacob is the Monad which has passed through the preceding evolutionary phases, personified by those three patriarchs, and at last has brought the higher Self (Moses) and its personality (the Israelites) to the initiate (liberated) stage. The fact is allegorically portrayed that the turning point has been reached in humans, that matter is no longer to dominate Spirit, and that the Divine is to liberate the human. This is ultimately certain to occur, for the cosmic and the microcosmic are inseparable. The little manifests the great, and the great is expressed with gradually increasing fullness in the little.

The glory of the vision by which the initiated person is illumined is so great that at first it is unendurable. The intensity of awareness, the vividness of the higher consciousness, the rapid frequency of oscillations are at first so far above the normal as to be beyond human power to bear. The initial experience dazzles both intellect and mental eye, so intensely that they must be turned away from the awe-full presence upon which they have gazed. Symbolically, "Moses hid his face; for he was afraid to look upon God."

> And the Lord said, I have surely seen the affliction of my people which are in Egypt, and have heard their cry by reason of their taskmasters; for I know their sorrows; *(Ex. 3:7)*

These verses of Exodus describe the experiences of the yogi in the higher states of yoga (the system by which realization of the divine in the human and in the universe are perceived as one). Each is a well-known state in that great science of the Soul so wonderfully expounded in the systems of Indian philosophy and esoteric training. Indeed, the word "yoga" might well be given as the key to the whole life of Moses from birth to death; for his every recorded action and experience allegorically portrays the progress of the successful yogi. The esoteric training of members of all nations, given and received in their Mystery Schools, is in basically the practice of the science of Raja yoga (the system of developing spiritual and esoteric powers and union with one's higher Self—see OG). Knowledge of that science provides one of the keys to the interpretation of scriptural allegories, and especially the application of these to the microcosm (of the human realm) after one has become a candidate for initiation and later an initiate of the greater Mysteries.

Verse seven, in which God tells Moses that he has seen the trials of the Israelites at the hand of the Egyptians, indicates the stage in the progress of the initiate to Adeptship—and foretells the approach to it—at which karma is to be balanced, debts are paid and the Soul finally is weighed, tested, and delivered from debt and the dominion of death. Symbolically, God knows the sorrows of humanity and decides to end them. Actually the Monad determines swiftly to pay all just debts and be free.

The Promised Land

> And I am come down to deliver them out of the hand of the Egyptians, and to bring them up out of that land unto a good land and a large, unto a land flowing with milk and honey; unto the place of the Canaanite, and the Hittites, and the Amorites, and the Perizzites, and the Hivites, and the Jebusites. *(Ex. 3:8)*

The descent of the living, fiery will-force as illuminant and source of power from the Monad (the Lord), through the higher Self (Moses) into the higher Self in the personality (the Israelites in Egypt) is one of the results of the initiatory process. In consequence, the person becomes wise, pure and strong to resist worldly temptations and sensual cravings. In due course self-deliverance from bondage occurs, and the initiate enters and establishes herself or himself in a field of awareness where these desires have no power.

In verse eight, God promises to deliver the Israelites out of their bondage in Egypt, into "a land flowing with milk and honey." In general, the Promised Land is a symbol of the condition of consciousness of the higher Self, which is interiorly and bountifully supplied from an infinite Source with all its life needs. In the present case this condition consists in particular of awareness in the vehicle and world of universal life called the buddhic plane (the fourth of the seven planes of the Solar System counting from below, that of the unalloyed, indwelling, universal life and Soul; consciousness at that level includes a state of inexpressible sweetness, happiness and serenity—"Buddhi is bliss"). The buddhic vehicle (of the Christ-nature), itself the container and deliverer of pure spirit, or Atma to the Ego and personality, is well described as a land flowing with milk and honey, or rich in both essential nutriment and pleasurable sweetness. Consciousness at that level to which the initiate is raised abides in a state of infinite abundance, in which the thought of lack cannot arise. It is a state of unalloyed happiness which no shadow of pain can ever dim. Established there, the evolving Ego is in the presence of the eternal and infinite source of life and in a condition of balanced harmony, the result of which is pure bliss. To this land, or actually to this state, the Ego and personality of the initiated person—symbolized by Moses and his people delivered from Egypt—are elevated by the sacrament of initiation in the greater Mysteries. The whole nature becomes infused with the light, life and joy characteristic of that region of awareness. The reference in verse eight to the six tribes indicates this fact, for they are said to abide there and the Israelites are promised habitation with them. Thus the sevenfold person, each part represented by a named nation, is brought to the purported Promised Land, which is the initiate state or salvation, liberation, Nirvana.

This is the promise and the possibility when the degree has actually been conferred. Thereafter, the newly initiated must bring the lower vehicles to subservience, culminating in the full response of the lower self to the rule of the higher Self. This subjugation is not achieved without great difficulty, and in its human and initiatory implications the account continues allegorically to describe those difficulties and the ways to overcome them. They are symbolized in the narrative by dissension among the Israelites themselves and the resistance of Pharaoh to their departure.

God Beholds the Oppression of the Israelites

Frequently throughout the Scriptures the truth is enunciated that from human suffering the will to self-liberation is aroused. From the point of view of the author, pain plays a significant, if not an essential, part in the liberation of the human Soul from the bondage of desire, the limitations of physical existence and the mortality inseparable from it. In this case it is the oppression of the Israelites by the Egyptians which causes them to cry unto the Lord for deliverance. The sheer pressure of untoward circumstances brings them to that state of consciousness at which the relative desirability of the purely material and the spiritual ways of life are truly evaluated.

The virtue of discrimination is born of suffering. It is pain, limitation and loss which literally drive people to forsake the world and the ways of life where these are experienced, and to seek those realms where they are unknown. In verse eight, therefore, God affirms that the cry of the Israelites has been heard and their oppression observed. A gradual psychological transformation from acquiescence in bondage to determination to win freedom is described here by means of symbol and allegory.

> Come now therefore and I will send thee unto Pharaoh, that thou mayest bring forth my people the children of Israel out of Egypt. *(Ex. 3:10)*

The solution of the problem of suffering and the way of liberation from it are indicated in this verse. The higher Self (Moses) must put forth its power upon the mental, emotional and physical bodies (Pharaoh and the Egyptians), for only in this way – Ego-inspired and Ego-empowered – can transmutation occur and liberation be achieved. The Monadic impulse, symbolized in Exodus by the Lord, empowers the initiated Ego (Moses) and directs it to achieve the deliverance of the Ego in its personality (the Israelites in Egypt) from the bondage of matter and the sense of separateness (Pharaoh and the Egyptians).

Moses Feels Unworthy for the Task Ahead

Without the interior impulse, and thus bereft of divine power and insight, even the human immortal Ego shrinks from the task of bringing the human personality out of the relative chaos of purely animal existence into the sublime order of a spiritualized mode of life – the true Exodus. Indeed, for many incarnations, despite the steadily increasing influence of the Manas (mind), the higher Self is impotent to elevate its lower nature, or that manifestation of itself which during incarnation becomes imprisoned and distorted in a physical body. However, when the fiery power of the awakened Monad flashes down into the inner individuality — or, symbolically, the Lord speaks to Moses — then the higher Self, spiritually empowered, knows that it can dominate the lower and proceeds to do so.

Immediately following the reception of that initiation in which the inherent Monadic power is enhanced and directed into the Ego-personality, the task of forcing the physical person to ratify the egoic decision is difficult to fulfill. However, once the Monad is awakened, it will brook no denial and little delay. An imperative command, as well as an assurance of full support reaches the mind-brain of the spiritually awakened person.

This is the secret of all great reformers, deliverers and geniuses of the power of service to their fellow humans. Their inmost Selves, their Monads, have come into direct relationship with their conscious self through the channel of the higher individuality, and particularly its mental aspect and attributes. According to the type of human temperament (see Hodson, *The Seven Human Temperaments*), either wisdom-love provides the driving power and direction or intellectual illumination and mental resolve lead to embarkation upon a career through which the Monadic impulse can be expressed. A third path is that of the spiritual leader who as ruler, lawmaker and magician leads his or her people — that section of the human race which is responsive to this person — towards a higher state of existence. This, for the most part, is the path described in the story of Moses. In verse eleven, where Moses tells God that he is unqualified for the task of freeing the Israelites, it is shown that even the greatest of world leaders experience a sense of disability before undertaking such a mighty task.

> And he said, Certainly I will be with thee; and this shall be a token unto thee, that I have sent thee: when thou hast brought forth the people out of Egypt, ye shall serve God upon this mountain. (*Ex. 3:12*)

Here, in symbol, the true test and assurance of verity of spiritual experience is given. That test consists of the continued persistence of the inward driving power and of the ruling idea, and of entry into an exalted state of consciousness. The mountain is the symbol of God-consciousness, a region of awareness which is above the Earth even though compounded of earthly substance. The embodied Ego is lifted above its earthly limitations onto the spiritual heights and there fulfills the spiritual command or, symbolically, serves God upon the mount.

"*I Am That I Am*"

In this phrase in verse fourteen is defined and described the supreme revelation. The inmost human Self is brought to a realization of the ever-enduring spiritual principle of which it is a part. The phrase "I Am That I Am" indicates self-existent Being, and therefore describes the one eternal, conscious, creative life, the essence of all essences of Being, the One Alone, the Tetragrammaton, and its Source implicit within itself and in its divine name.

This revelation is final. This self-manifestation of the Supreme Deity in and through a fragment of itself decides for all time the issue between human Spirit and matter to an illumined human mind. Material proclivities, while they may still make their presence known, no longer have power to hold and grip in a worldly mode of life the now illumined inner Self.

Verse fourteen contains the magical affirmation which every Adept eventually makes in full consciousness, and which aspirants to Adeptship are taught in Mystery Schools to utter. The ineffable name is an instrument of magic. Knowledge of its syllables and the manner in which they should be uttered bestows theurgic power. The thaumaturgy which follows this revelation of the ineffable name is only possible as a result of the deliverance of that name to Moses, who personifies the initiate.

The whispered words of power and of esoteric ceremony, the secret signs and words split up into their letters and their syllables, all have reference to the ultimate secret, the "lost word," which every candidate for Adeptship is seeking. Moses sought, and in verse fourteen finds, the ultimate hidden name. Thereafter, hesitation vanishes, action is performed and success achieved. Symbolically, by means of theurgic powers based upon a knowledge of the name and the nature of God, the Israelites are delivered from enslavement by Pharaoh. By God is meant the divine in humanity and the divine in nature. When the former is discovered by an individual, the latter is self-revealed. Thereafter the individualized Deity, which is a human, knows that the two are one and wields the power of both.

And God said moreover unto Moses, Thus shalt thou say unto the children of Israel, The Lord God of your fathers, the God of Abraham, the God of Isaac, and the God of Jacob, hath sent me unto you: this is my name for ever, and this is my memorial unto all generations. *(Ex. 3:15)*

The deliverance by the Deity of its name, and the insistence upon the fact that by this name both the allegiance of the people and their escape from bondage would be achieved, refer to a mighty truth; for the name is but the expression of creative, energizing and redeeming power in terms of thought-imbued sound. Spiritually, the name is the announcement and the definition of that power. Knowledge of the divine name, and its subsequent utterance, release that power. Its discovery, therefore, places in the hand of the finder unlimited power when the name is that of the Deity itself—hence the necessity for the veil of allegory and symbol.

In the case of humans as represented by Moses, the name of the Deity is simply the definition and description of Monadic attributes and powers. When once a person has realized this—her or his own "lost word"—their entire existence is changed. From this time forward, "they are what they are," namely an immortal God. Moses, the initiate, had intuited this truth. By its means victory would be gained, even against so mighty an opposition and so greatly superior a power as that of the Egyptian nation.

A message is thus delivered to every aspirant to Moses-ship, meaning every Soul that would win freedom from the bondage of sense and self (Egypt) and enter into that realm of pure bliss, unfading and unalloyed, which all of humankind is seeking (the Promised Land). Knowledge of the existence of that realm is preserved as the holiest secret hidden within the "cave" (1 Kings 19:9,13) of the heart. The physical heart is not implied here, but rather the heart or center of human existence where the indwelling Deity abides. "Find your own name, utter it, and so win freedom from bondage and enter into bliss"—this is the message of the authors of these passages, illumined and empowered by knowledge of their own name as each one was, and as every comparable initiate before and after them has been and ever will be.

The sovereign secret is the spiritual name, meaning the interior, spiritual nature and power of the human God-aspect. As the Deity is the self-existent One, so the God in each person is his or her own self-existent divinity. The divine name, therefore, is: "I AM THAT I AM." Here the Pentateuch reveals its direct descent from the far more ancient Indian mystery tradition in which the summit of attainment by the yogi is self-discovery, which implies and includes discovery of that Self of the universe with which the individual is forever at one. The victorious aspirant chants *"Soham,"* meaning "I am THAT, THAT am I," uttering in Sanskrit her or his divine name, or affirming Self-existence.

In Egypt, too, the name was the most divine part of a person, its discovery and utterance the highest human achievement. Down through the ages the search for and rediscovery of the hidden name, the lost or secret word, has been the golden thread running through symbolic ceremonials and many mystic rites—particularly those of freemasonry.

The emphasis placed by the Deity, when addressing Moses, upon both God's divine name and worship by the three preceding patriarchs is of both historical and mystical significance. The elevation of the concept of the Godhead to a level far beyond that of a tribal deity of one particular generation was doubtless necessary to a people living under foreign domination in a foreign land. As already explained, the fourth phase in any cycle of involution and evolution is always the deepest and the darkest. The bondage in Egypt represents that densest phase. While each of the three preceding eras had its own subcycles of emergence, descent to the deepest level and ascent or return, none of the three brought the Children of Israel (unfolding life) to such depth of darkness as did the oppression by Pharaoh.

Moreover, after this fourth and darkest phase the upturn begins. The day of deliverance from a fourth into a fifth cycle is at hand, which will symbolically bring about the reestablishment of the Hebrews in their national home. Mystically interpreted, the new, fifth era under Moses will be marked by the entry of consciousness and life into a higher level of awareness.

Verse sixteen, in which God tells Moses to gather together the elders of Israel, illustrates the psychological necessity for the gathering together of all the forces of human nature into a unity, and the direction of these forces towards the end in view. The initiate, as also all truly converted people, is compelled to integrate ("gather together") and elevate the whole nature to the new level of consciousness. For this purpose all the various attributes, superior and inferior, must be unified and brought to collaboration with the will and aspiration of the illumined higher Self, typified by Moses. The power of the Monad is the means by which the exaltation is attained ("the Lord God"), which at last finds means of penetrating via the Ego (Moses) to the personality (the Israelites), and liberating it from its purely human and material limitations (bondage in Egypt). Symbolically, through their leader, to the end of their deliverance, the Lord God "visits" the oppressed Hebrews.

God Promises to Liberate the Israelites

There is a phase in human evolution in which despair and hopelessness are the predominant state of mind. The path leads through a darkness unillumined by light or any possibility of light anywhere along the road. The tasks of life are so heavy, make such demands upon mental and physical strength, that the Soul can be temporarily bereft of hope. For long ages nations may endure this phase, as they pass through fourth cycles or subcycles in their evolution, and must meet and pay off their karmic debts. Individuals may feel during certain years of their lives that they are shut in by an oppressive darkness and burdened by inescapable responsibilities. Necessities of life must be obtained, and the conditions of labor make such excessive demands upon their strength that despair and hopelessness descend upon them. Actually, however, such situations, whether national or individual, are neither hopeless nor unending. Eventually the lords of karma lighten the load, and deliverance is brought about. The dark, imprisoning phase of the cycle draws to an end and freedom is attained. The inner Self then has power to elevate, inspire and infuse with happiness the previously imprisoned consciousness of the lower self, and elevation of Spirit and expansion of consciousness are experienced.

This psychological phase of darkness and subsequent transition to light is traversed both in the natural course of evolution and also prematurely—and in an intensified form—when initiation into the greater Mysteries is conferred, as was the case with Moses; for all initiates pass quickly through normal human experiences in highly concentrated form. Their sufferings are intense and the strain to which they are submitted is almost overwhelming, but the heights of exultation to which they are later elevated are very great indeed.

These three psychological experiences and necessities of evolutionary progress—national, individual and initiatory—are all described in the story of the Children of Israel, and especially in the book of Exodus. God's promise to liberate the Israelites in the seventeenth verse indicates the descent of redeeming Monadic power (the voice and message of God) into the responsive higher Self (Moses), to pass eventually to that fragment of the higher Self (the Israelites) which is incarnated in the mental vehicles (Egypt and the Egyptians).

> And they shall hearken to thy voice: and thou shalt come, thou and the elders of Israel, unto the king of Egypt, and ye shall say unto him, The Lord God of the Hebrews hath met with us: and now let us go, we beseech thee, three days' journey into the wilderness, that we may sacrifice to the Lord our God. *(Ex. 3:18)*

From this verse onwards the method of self-elevation and self-liberation begins to be described by means of allegory and symbol. With deep discernment the author indicates the true means of redemption, and there uses the unvarying symbol. This consists of the creative, and therefore recreative, power of the Monad. Its symbol is the voice, its outpoured energy and life is the word.

In the fourth Gospel, John, in conformity with the unvarying rule, bestows upon the redeemer the title of Logos (the Greek translation of "the Word"), the doctrine of which is applied here both to primordial creation and to that recreation and transformation by which spiritual redemption is attained. Symbolically Moses (the higher Self) is informed by the Lord God (the Monad) that the all-sufficient Monadic will and life are now available for the attainment of salvation.

This power must then be effectively applied to the personality, and particularly to the physical human, symbolized by the King of Egypt. The plea of a desire to "sacrifice to the Lord our God" indicates the spiritual motive for the whole endeavor. The distance of three days journey into the wilderness may be interpreted as the passage of purely physical consciousness from that level through emotion and mind (arid, without spiritual sustenance) into the region of the higher Self, which is beyond and above them.

God Will Smite Egypt

The inertia of the physical substance of which the physical body is built, and the habits of self-centered thinking, self-indulgence and self-will, inevitably render difficult the liberation of the Soul. Therefore Moses is warned that the King of Egypt will not let his people go (v. 19), and that there will be severe resistance.

Success is, however, utterly sure, because the power of the awakened Monad is practically infinite, while that of the habit-ruled physical human is finite. Resistance is not overcome without a struggle (v. 20). The body must be subjected to austerities, to a spiritual rule and discipline which will at first appear harsh and cause inevitable suffering.

Eventually the power and pressure of the highest in humanity overcomes the resistance of the lowest. The passions are subdued, the physical nature is first humanized and then spiritualized, until at last personality and higher Self are combined in pursuit of the ideal. Symbolically Egypt collaborates with Israel in the attainment of liberation (v. 21 – "And I will give this people favour in the sight of the Egyptians," referring to the gifts of jewelry), and the faculties and powers of the lower self are transmuted and received as riches by the higher. The evolutionary fruits of the dark cycles are very great indeed, at least equal to, and sometimes greater than, the fruits of the cycles of light. The very stubbornness of matter-blinded humanity evokes an added measure of willpower and an added intensity of effort in its application, which together produce greatly enhanced faculty and effectiveness.

These evolutionary fruits are all described in verse twenty-two as jewels of silver and gold and as clothing. Silver symbolizes the Atmic will. Jewelry made of this refers to the successful and rhythmic expression of that will at the physical level. Gold typifies abundance of the life-force, of spiritual percepti᾿n and of intuition. Gold jewelry represents their manifestation in ᷉᷉d through the lower self. Fine clothing indicates the glowing a᷉᷉ᵕ iridescent vesture of light, the microcosmic *Shekinah* (Heb. for the "visible glory of Yahweh"), with which the Soul is enrobed when deliverance has been won. All these riches of the Soul are attained through incarnation in the flesh. They are the fruits and results of bodily life, bodily resistance, bodily effort, from which the experience and the ultimate transmutation of the Soul grows in spiritual stature, in richness, in beauty and in light.

Thus the book of Exodus, with its system of symbology, is of universal significance. It describes the laws of liberation which cosmic Solar Systems, Races, individuals and initiates must and do obey. The nature of the esoteric forces and the decrees of the esoteric laws – those secrets of the sanctuaries by which individual heroines and heroes are enabled to emancipate themselves from the bondage of matter and desire—are also revealed. Therefore, the revelation is couched in mysterious terms. The symbolic language is used to conceal the secret knowledge and power from the profane. However, truth and its consort, wisdom, shine brightly through the somewhat transparent veil.

16

Instructions from God

Exodus 4

Moses told God that the Israelites wouldn't believe that God had sent him to liberate them from Egypt. So Moses was given three miraculous signs to illustrate God's power. For the first, Moses was to cast his staff upon the ground. When he did so it became a serpent. When Moses grasped it by the tail it became a staff again. For the second sign Moses was told to put his hand on his chest beneath his cloak. When he took it out it was full of leprosy, but when he put it under the cloak and drew it out again the hand was healed. For the third sign, Moses was to take water from the river and pour it upon the dry ground, where it would turn to blood.

However, Moses was still troubled because he felt he wasn't an eloquent speaker. God grew angry at Moses' reluctance and appointed Aaron as Moses' spokesperson.

Having sought the permission of his father-in-law, Jethro, Moses took his wife and sons, put them upon an ass, and returned to Egypt with "the rod of God in his hand." However, God then told Moses that when he went to Egypt to liberate the Israelites, God would harden Pharaoh's heart against this.

On the journey to Egypt, when Moses was at an inn, God met him and sought to kill him. Moses' wife Zipporah then circumcised her son, and told Moses that "a bloody husband thou art." As they traveled on, Aaron met them near the mountain of God, and Moses told him all that had happened.

In Egypt, Moses and Aaron met with the elders of Israel, and Aaron told them all that God had said to Moses. When Moses showed the people the signs, the people believed and they bowed down in worship.

The Staff and the Serpent

In this chapter the symbol of the serpent is once more introduced into the narrative, in which it is made to play an entirely supernatural part. God makes the staff of Moses turn into a serpent, and then back again into a staff. A most deeply esoteric revelation, which in those days was completely confined to the sanctuaries, is made in this and later chapters; for the actual means is revealed by which the Soul or noumenon of both universe and humanity is extricated from entrapment in matter.

The symbol of the serpent can be interpreted in many ways — both exoteric and esoteric. In general, it is the symbol both of wisdom and of the wise, who in the sacred language are frequently referred to as serpents. The *nagas* (serpents) of Hindu literature are none other than the ancient rishis, liberated yogis, Adepts. The serpent is chosen as the symbol of wisdom for various reasons. It glides secretly and for the most part unseen on the surface of the globe, just as wisdom — whether revealed from God or inborn — is a concealed power potent to either illumine, if rightly employed, or destroy if misused. The smooth sinuosity of the snake and of its movements aptly portrays the harmonious and rhythmic self-expression of wisdom in both the universe and the human in whom it is awake and moving. This person is enlightened from within, or secretly.

The serpent regularly sloughs its skin. Despite this seasonal change the reptile itself is unchanged, but appears in a new and glistening covering. So wisdom, while remaining ever the same in essence, is self-manifest in ever new forms, none being able to hold it permanently. The serpent's tongue is forked or bipolar. So also is wisdom, being capable of degradation into low cunning employed for meanest motives, or of elevation into lofty intuition according to unselfish ideals. Snake venom can destroy or heal according to its use and dosage; wisdom, when degraded, poisons the Soul, but when rightly used it is an antidote for many ills.

The eyes of the serpent are compelling, even hypnotic. Wisdom, once awake in an individual, brooks no resistance, breaks all bonds and ultimately rules with impelling power. The wise, also, are irresistible in their might, even though appearing to be lowly and making no claim to high regard. Nevertheless they live near to the source of life, just as the serpent lives near to the roots and seeds of living things.

When the serpent's tail is in its mouth an endless circle is made, implying the eternity of wisdom, and even eternity itself. Esoterically, however, processes of cosmogenesis are indicated by the union of a symbolized positive and negative, or the entry of the tail into the mouth. All generative processes are, indeed, indicated in that form, which leads to the deeply esoteric significance of the serpent—namely as a symbol of the universal, divine, creative, ever-active life-force. This is Fohat in its dual polarity, sometimes symbolized not as one serpent with tail in mouth, but as two mutually intertwined. Here are indicated the laws of electricity, under which all formative processes occur.

The driving force from within which leads to inceptive activity in organic forms, and to chemical affinity in inorganic ones, is indeed bipolar. The aptness of the choice of the serpent as a symbol for this power would seem to be supported by the fact that its tongue is forked. A reference is thus made to the positive and negative currents of the great breath, continually breathed forth as Fohat into and through every atom of every world, to become omnipresent and perpetually active throughout the whole universe. This fact was both concealed and revealed in ancient allegories, in which Jupiter and other male creative deities changed themselves into snakes for the purpose of seducing goddesses. Their progeny were the demigods, many of whom later attained full deification.

A serpent with tail in mouth, two serpents intertwined, or one encircling a rod, staff or pillar all symbolize the electric energy of Fohat in action in the material universe and therefore in humanity, the microcosmic temple of the universe.

In humans the rod or staff refers both to the spinal cord and to a canal or etheric and superphysical channel in its center, passing from the root of the cord in the sacrum along its whole length and into the medulla oblongata and brain. This canal is the vehicle for the primordial life-force, a measure of which plays down from above in the generative act. The current is unipolar, or even of neutral polarity, since it plays upon and produces its effects in both the male and the female organism. The historic esoteric name for this canal is *Sushumna,* but generally that name is only used when by esoteric means the same neutral force is made to play not downwards, but upwards along the spinal cord. Before such reversal of the flow of originative energy can be achieved, the positive and negative currents must be aroused and must themselves, like twin serpents, flow upwards, intertwining as they flow to induce an ascent of the accompanying neutral energy.

Entering the brain, this triple power so illumines the human mind of that he or she becomes as a god (possessed of theurgic powers). As discussed earlier in this volume, this fact is revealed in Chapters Two and Three of Genesis, where a man and a woman, Adam and Eve, represent the oppositely polarized currents; the tree of knowledge of good and evil (especially the trunk) corresponds to the staff, and the tempting serpent to Sushumna. Thus Adam and Eve are forbidden to eat of the fruit of this tree, since by so doing they would become as gods. The intensely heightened vibrations of the brain, the glands, the cells and the substance in the ventricles cause the brain and cranium to be responsive to egoic and Monadic life and consciousness. Spirit then predominates in the individual; matter loses its power. Symbolically, through the agency of an interchangeable serpent and staff, the Israelites are freed from bondage in Egypt.

In verse three of this chapter of Exodus the order was given to cast the staff upon the ground, after which it became a serpent. The shaft of Atmic fire which forms the core of the force which plays along the Sushumna is brought down to the densest physical level, or symbolically is cast upon the ground. When that occurs the relatively dormant, positive-negative life-force resident in the sacrum is awakened into activity. Each polarity then pursues a mutually intertwining, serpentine path around the Sushumna canal. Symbolically stated, the staff or rod becomes the serpent.

Again as previously discussed, this process may produce a certain shock and some pain. The initiate momentarily shrinks from it, but still persists. Moses is therefore made to flee before the serpent. When, however, he unites his own will with that of the hierophant and sublimates the creative force, compelling it to flow upwards from the pelvis, it becomes in his hand the magician's wand of power. Symbolically, as in verse four, Moses takes the serpent by the tail and it becomes a staff again in his hand.

As portrayed in Egyptian art in which serpents are intertwined around rods or pillars, the tail is at the foot of the pillar, meaning in the sacrum. The head of the serpent is at the upper end, where frequently a lotus flower is blooming. This, too, is a universally used symbol. The opening of the force-centers in the superphysical bodies, consequent upon the arousing and the upward flow of the serpent power, is depicted by such emblems. The historic esoteric names for the positive and negative currents are *pingala* and *ida,* and the triple upward flow is most perfectly revealed by the Greek symbol of the caduceus.

The Greek god Hermes is the Moses of the Greeks, in that he is both messenger from God to humanity by virtue of holding in his hand the caduceus—just as Moses held in his hand the rod—and deliverer of Persephone from Hades, just as Moses delivered Israel from bondage in Egypt. The holding of the caduceus (or staff or serpent) in the hand is itself a symbol implying mastery of a power, and the possession of knowledge and skill in its employment.

Note that the transmutation of staff into serpent could only occur at the command of the Deity and by his or her magical power. Actually, the descent of the Monadic Atma through all the vehicles and down the spinal cord into the sacrum is essential to the premature full awakening of the triple creative fire, and its successful sublimation and use as a magical tool. To bring this power of Atma down is one part of the office of the hierophant of the greater Mysteries. Since after this transformation a new life is begun, the act has always been correctly termed initiation. The initiate is one in whom has been aroused the power to liberate herself or himself from the limitation of matter, desire, and self-separateness into the freedom of universal consciousness, life and power. This is part of the inner meaning of the strange story of the magical power by which Moses overcame the resistance of Pharaoh to the departure of the Israelites.

In the first three-and a half phases of all cycles this power drives life and consciousness downward into matter, into generation, and in organic life to generative activity. It is therefore presented as evil, or contrary to the highest good. Temporarily this is true, since pure Spirit, unsullied life and innocent consciousness become stained and aware of passion as a result of the serpent-inspired descent. Ultimately, however, the self-same force liberates Spirit, life and consciousness, individualized as humans, from the grip and stain of material life and physical generative processes.

In the Garden of Eden, representing the period of the downward arc, the serpent is the devil and his temptations lead to the generative act, and to loss of innocence and banishment from Eden. In the initiate and the Adept (typified by Moses and Christ) the serpent force, transmuted and spiritually employed, becomes the redeeming power. This, in part, is the revelation of the serpent symbol in the book of Exodus. It represents both the creative and the redeeming agencies (the dark and the light serpents of the caduceus) in nature and in humanity.

An incursion into esoteric physiology is necessary for an exposition of this subject, as symbolized by the mutually interchangeable serpent and staff; for the staff has its own specific meaning in the sacred language. In the universe it is the fohatic pillar or current of formative power by which the universe is created and sustained. It is a pillar less in its shape than in its supporting function of a rod or staff breaking into leaf or flower, as portrayed on the tarot cards and in the allegory of Tannhauser. When this process has been fully accomplished, the lower nature is subject to the higher; the vehicles of consciousness acknowledge the rule of the higher Self. This is stated symbolically in verse five, where it is promised that the Israelites will recognize that Moses is divinely inspired. ("That they may believe that the Lord God of their fathers, the God of Abraham, the God of Isaac, and the God of Jacob, hath appeared unto thee.")

The Leprous Hand

The hand inside of Moses' cloak turning leprous (v. 6) portrays the dual process of complete self-purification in the lower nature, and particularly as regards motives for actions, and also the withdrawal from the physical self of the power to act in self-will against the dictates of the inner Self.

The outer self is not, however, deprived of the power of effective action; for at will the hand becomes whole (v. 7) and therefore available for purified, selfless action once more. The hand as a component symbol in the sacred language has deep significance. It is itself a synthesis of sevenfold humankind, consisting as it does of skeletal palm and back, four fingers and a thumb. Each of these several parts has its correspondence with vehicles and planes of consciousness. The skeleton represents the Atmic core of the human, while the Ego directing the function of the hand represents the Monad. The body of the hand—the enclosing muscular mass of the skeleton with its arteries, veins and lymphatic vessels—corresponds to Buddhi, the life-supplying and conveying principle and vehicle of Atma, without which it is inchoate and universal. Atma, in its turn, is actionless without its buddhic vehicle and Buddhi-vitalized lower principles.

Bone tissue is the hardest, densest constituent of the body. Such hardness corresponds to the immense driving force behind the emitted Atmic power by which atoms are formed. In terms of energy this potency is to all substance what the skeleton is to the supporting frame. Atmic shafts are to nature, or the evolving universe, what the skeleton is to the forms of all vertebrates and the shell is to crustaceans.

The palm, the back of the hand and the muscular tissue connecting them, which together form the main body of the hand, serve both as container of the skeleton and conveyor of life impulses to the fingers and thumb. This tissue corresponds to the life principle or Buddhi, which serves as vehicle for the Atma. Fingers and thumb, in their turn, are the organs of ultimate action and so together represent the body. The blood and the neurotransmitters correspond to the astral and the etheric bodies respectively. The five digits each have their significance and their function as conveyors of energy. The thumb corresponds to the will-force and the bone which is covered by Buddhi (the enclosing muscular mass), to the flesh. The first and second fingers are in resonance with the higher Mind and the lower mind respectively, and the third and fourth with the astral and etheric bodies, their forces and their functions.

Thus the thumb is physically the instrument of power, and through its extremity the will-force of the Monad most directly flows. This explains its choice as the digit for anointing and other ceremonial acts; for the thumb, being itself a vehicle for pure Spirit and attuned in terms of resonance to the Atmic principle and plane, of all parts of the hand most readily accepts or receives, and conveys additional power invoked and employed in magical rites.

Having three joints, each of the four digits corresponds symbolically to the three higher principles—will, wisdom and intelligence—and also to their reflections as the three lower—concrete mind, emotion and physical body—with the hand itself as synthesis. The nails are provisions of nature for certain life needs and purposes. Being denser than muscles, they have a similar significance to skeleton and thumb. The whole hand itself is the instrument of self-expression in action for both the inner Self and the outer self, just as the sevenfold human being similarly serves the Monad.

At initiation and after the sublimation of the creative force, the whole human being begins to be subservient to the Monad. Either it can be temporarily paralyzed to set the Monad free, or it can be used as an active agent. This is implied symbolically by God causing Moses to place his hand onto his chest—that is, near to the heart—where it turned dead white as if leprous, though it was easily able to be restored to the normal color of good health. The act of placing the hand near the heart also symbolizes the bringing of the outer instrument of action, the personality, close to and as a result responsive to the inmost Self—the real heart of the total human being.

Hand over heart signifies voluntary surrender of the outer to the inner Self in terms of both consciousness and action; for the heart also represents the inner Self in its intellectual principle, the Ego in the Causal Body, through which direction is given in the personal life and from which the causes of action arise—hence the name Causal Body.

The whiteness of Moses' hand symbolizes both the utmost purity of the whole person, and particularly the lower self, and its complete irradiation by Atma, the symbolic and the actual color of which is white. Thus the incident recorded in this chapter of Exodus is of deep significance, being both descriptive and instructional concerning progress through the grades of the greater Mysteries.

The hand raised in blessing and the hand clasped in greeting constitute significant gestures. Both may convey decidedly beneficent influences. Neither action, in consequence, should be performed perfunctorily but always with due intent. The handshake is an especially intimate form of communion and greeting. Rightly understood and performed, it brings about an interchange of forces embodied in all the seven principles of human beings.

As an agency for exorcism and for healing, the hand is unique among all the parts of the body, again because of the fact that in its construction and correspondences it represents the total human being—body, Soul and Spirit. Its choice as a means for the conveyance both of forces for these several purposes and of secret signs is therefore easily understandable. Even the knuckles of the fingers themselves are of the same significance as the fingers, while the wrist represents the connecting current of power between the Monad and the sevenfold human. Only the Adept can contact this current. Only such a one, therefore, can truly redeem or raise fallen humanity.

Turning Water into Blood

The third wonder which was given to Moses to perform, the third sign which God gave to Moses to convince the Israelites that indeed he was the one chosen and accepted by God, was the turning of water into blood (v. 9). Three types of magic were to be performed, three degrees of power to be received and demonstrated. The first concerned the serpent fire, its awakening and its use to enfire the spinal cord, or to change the "staff" into a serpent. The second describes the purification of the lower self, symbolized by the hand and its intimate communion with and subjection to the inner Self, represented by the heart within the breast.

The third sign symbolically depicts the final and full transmutation of earthly desire, typified by water, into universal love born of experience of the nature of the all-pervading, all-sustaining lifeforce—here indicated by the use of the word "blood." This is the crowning act of self-illumination and self-redemption. Substance, per se, is also represented by water, and the life-currents by which forms are vitalized are depicted by blood. The attainment of the power to construct forms, and temporarily to vitalize them, is included in this third degree of exaltation.

Blood is intimately associated with the heart, invariably the emblem for the higher Self in its vehicle of intellect and light. Spiritual lifecurrents, which are received by and rhythmically transmitted to the lower self by the Ego, are also symbolized by blood. The transference of the center of consciousness from the outer self to the inner Self is a power designated by this allegory, which therefore implies a cessation of reliance upon temporal, worldly supply and a turning to the eternal, spiritual and infinite Source.

Blood itself is a complete entity, its various components being in correspondence with the seven vehicles of humans. Arteries and veins represent those of form, while the pulsing fluid indicates the vehicles of life. The heart is the intermediate and linking principle which bestows the individual pulse-rate or beat upon the life-giving fluid; it therefore corresponds to the Ego. To turn water into blood at will is to demonstrate the fact that the psychological and intellectual conditions have become established by which the individual thereafter lives in and as the inner ruler immortal, and no longer as unillumined and purely worldly human.

Three degrees in the ancient Mysteries are depicted in allegory and symbol in this most revealing chapter of Exodus. Thaumaturgic powers are attained by those who pass through these degrees of training and initiation in the greater Mysteries. Chemical, or rather alchemical changes are implied in the alteration in the color and condition of the hand, as also in the turning of water to blood. The oxygen which, with two parts of hydrogen, is a constituent of water is introduced into other chemical combinations to produce blood. Moses was, in fact, an esotericist, as his several magical acts demonstrate. He is a personification of a fully initiated person endowed with and capable of employing initiate powers. His hesitation to fulfill the commands of God, each of which drew forth and placed at his disposal greater powers, is not dissimilar to that of the disciple Thomas, who insisted upon visual and tangible proof that the risen Jesus really was his Galilean Master (John 20:24–29).

While in the magical acts the Atmic will, the serpent fire and the life-currents are all involved and manipulated, in the hesitation and questioning the intellectual principle is depicted. It is essential that the mind of the initiate and would-be magician be fully informed and have mastered the forces, principles and laws by which, at the physical level, esoteric phenomena are to be produced.

"I am Not Eloquent"

In verse ten, where Moses tells God that he isn't eloquent enough to convince the Israelites, a revelation is made under a veil of unusual self-doubt of the real power by which the thaumaturgist performs feats. The creative power of sound is employed, whether audibly as vibrations of the air or inaudibly as vibrations of mind-stuff, impinging upon and molding into desired shapes first the *akasa* [the subtle, supersensuous, spiritual essence which pervades all space – TG], second the etheric and third the physical substance in which the phenomena are performed.

Although spoken to by the Lord – meaning inspired, directed and molded by the inmost Self – the initiate in his or her mind, and later in the body, must be empowered before physical results can be achieved. Symbolically, until then the initiate is "not eloquent" or is "slow of tongue." Eventually, as in the Egyptian Mysteries, the initiate becomes "Maa-kheru" or true of voice. The tongue, larynx, pharynx, trachea, vocal cords and breath are the physical organs of speech, aided by teeth and lips in the formulation of consonants and words. Esoterically employed, these organs are also the vehicles of esoterically uttered sounds by which sets of vibrations are initiated in the akasa and then expressed in the ether – its densest counterpart or manifestation – and ultimately at the solid physical level. Moses personifies a thaumaturgist in the course of his training, and for those who can perceive them many secrets of the sanctuaries are contained in these chapters.

> And the Lord said unto him, who hath made man's mouth? or who maketh the dumb, or deaf, or the seeing, or the blind? have not I the Lord?
> Now therefore go, and I will be with thy mouth, and teach thee what thou shalt say. *(Ex. 4:11–12)*

Initiate powers do not pertain to the mortal human. They are manifestations of the divinity within, by which alone the power to create phenomenally may be exercised. The Lord in these verses symbolizes the inmost Self. The Lord's power, expressed as speech to Moses, represents that measure of Atmic will by which the thaumaturgist must be both inspired and empowered. The human capacity for inspiration is affirmed here. The inmost Self bestows at the appropriate time both power and knowledge upon the aspirant to God-like faculties.

Aaron as the Voice of Moses

At this point in the narrative a second character is introduced. Aaron, the Levite (or priest), is about to become the partner and voice of Moses (v. 13–14). This collaboration denotes an intimate blending of and close cooperation between the mind and body (Aaron) and the inner Self (Moses). These two aspects of human nature become conjoined in the higher grades of the Mysteries, both of them being empowered by and acting as agents of the Monad for the ultimate deliverance and perfecting of the inner Self and of the outer self in the mortal vehicles, represented by the Israelites as a whole.

Aaron, in another sense, is the person who in the course of evolution has sought out the inner Self and become self-dedicated to the spiritual life. Therefore he is a Levite or priest. He is to become the voice of Moses to Israel and to Egypt: meaning that the powers of the inner Self must be made manifest through the outer and that the vocal organs are mentally and physically employed, both phenomenally and to recreate the whole inner and outer being.

The Anger of the Lord

In verse fourteen, God expresses anger at Moses because he is trying to escape his destiny and responsibility—God then appoints

Aaron as Moses' spokesperson. The attribution to God of a capacity for anger is one of the many errors which occurs in the scriptures. The creator of the universe and of this Earth, the Supreme Deity, is an incarnation of immutable, impersonal Law. The attribution of human error and weakness to so mighty a Being is a misinterpretation of the text.

No such error could have been made by the original initiate authors, men of the spiritual stature of Enoch, Melchizedek and Moses. Unless the anger of the Lord has a symbolical significance, such as his allowance of blood sacrifices and the destruction of neighboring tribes, such a god is but a tribal deity.

That tribes of those days displayed bloodthirsty characteristics is undeniable, as also is the fact that they attributed their gratification of blood-lust to the fulfillment of the commands of their deity. Therefore in its literal meaning, the use of the phrase "the anger of the Lord" (v. 14) and the attribution to the deity of bloodthirstiness by the authors of Exodus may be better understood. Even when mystically interpreted, the Lord as the human Monad directing the higher Self, both in its human pilgrimage and through the grades of the Mysteries, would be incapable of any human feeling whatsoever. The human Monad may be justly regarded as an intensely brilliant center for the radiation of spiritual light, a fiery spark in the creative flame endowed with divine intelligence, the whole being manifest at the level of pure spiritual essence—the Soul of things. Neither discordant nor disunited concepts can ever arise in the consciousness of any Being at that lofty level.

In one way only may the attribution of anger to God possibly be regarded as meaningful. The operation of the law of cause and effect brings suffering to those who fall into error. Discordant, separative, pain-producing and self-debasing acts provoke the operation of that law. The karmic reactions inevitably take the form of restriction, disease, pain. All of these effects endure as experiences in consciousness until effect has matched, and therefore balanced, cause. Then the discordance is cancelled out and attunement or equilibrium is re-established. The restoration of equilibrium is the fundamental function and ceaselessly applied influence of the spiritual principles of harmony, which is at the heart of all creation.

Since the human afflictions resulting from discordant actions, meaning those which disturb the equipoise of nature, so often appear to come from invisible sources, they have been erroneously attributed to the anger and the action of an imagined, personal deity. This could only be even approximately correct if by deity was implied immutable Law.

Expressed in terms of esoteric philosophy, the verses under consideration describe the thrust of Spirit operating upon physical matter and the forms that are produced from this action. This is for the result of evolutionary progress and the production of vehicles of consciousness of ever-growing beauty, sensitiveness to Spirit, and perfection. Microcosmically, the verses describe the insistent pressure of the Monad upon the higher Self in the direction of self-illumination, self-spiritualization, and the redemption of the outer, personal self from the bondage of matter, desire and separativeness.

This action of the Ego is portrayed by Aaron, who personifies the evolutionary stage at which brain, mind and life have begun to be illumined by the light of spiritual truth and directed from within. Symbolically, Aaron is to become the spokesman and mouthpiece of both Moses and God. He is also to display those esoteric and magical powers to which Moses has attained.

Moses-Aaron represents the Ego-personality ("brothers"–Ex. 4:14) of initiates passing through the grades of the Mysteries. The story of the relationship and activities of the principal characters is a mystery drama of great beauty and significance, a veritable revelation of the esoteric wisdom taught in the Mystery Schools of Egypt and Chaldea. The statement made by God that Aaron "cometh forth to meet thee: and when he seeth thee, he will be glad in the heart" (v. 14) indicates that the outer self had turned its attention towards the inner, had forsaken the ways of the world and the flesh, and was treading the way of the Spirit. The vital moment of the union of heart, mind and will, of the interblending of the outer and the inner Self, is about to arrive. Spiritual ecstasy is, indeed, the result of that blending. Initiation produces gladness of heart.

> And thou shalt speak unto him, and put words in his mouth: and I will be with thy mouth, and with his mouth, and will teach you what ye shall do.
> And he shall be thy spokesman unto the people: and he shall be, even he shall be to thee instead of a mouth, and thou shalt be to him instead of God. *(Ex. 4:15–16)*

Again the formative action of the Monadic will, now dominant in the personality of the initiate, is indicated. The voice of God is the ruling power forevermore. Symbolically God (the Monad), through the mediation of Moses (the Ego), puts the words (Atmic power) into the mouth of the outer self (Aaron).

The rhythmic and repetitive language of verse sixteen almost suggests that it is taken directly from a Mystery ritual. The meaning has already been indicated. The Monad-Ego shall rule the personality. The outer self shall recognize the rule as if it were divine, as indeed it is.

Instruction in the Mysteries

And thou shalt take this rod in thine hand, wherewith thou shalt do
   signs. *(Ex. 4:17)*

Again, this verse indicates the means of expression of Monadic rule and egoic inspiration as well as of physical exaltation and magical power. They are the controlled current of the serpentine, creative life force awakened and directed upwards in and along the spinal cord, frequently indicated by a rod held in the hand. Holding the rod in the hand signifies both mastery of and power to employ at will those esoteric forces for which it, the spine, is a vehicle.

The rod or wand of the magician is also a physical instrument of magic. It is made of either metal-alloy, ivory, ebonite, transparent amber, or certain carefully selected woods. Its preparation is a science and, having been correctly made according to precise directions as to length, diameter and shape, it is highly magnetized with energy from the human aura. It is then consecrated according to certain rites, as a result of which operation a spiritual principle is added to the auric energy and the physical substance, giving to the rod a triple nature. Thus made into the semblance of a living thing, the rod readily becomes a vehicle for superphysical forces directed into and through it for the purpose of producing esoteric phenomena. Certain of these forces active in and around the spinal cord are directed by the will down the arm, through the hand and into the wand, which thus becomes a potent esoteric instrument—a rod of power indeed.

The four elementals of earth, water, air and fire become obedient to the will of the holder of such a rod. The phenomena produced by Moses, whether purely hypnotic or actual, were partly the result of the exercise of this dominion. He was especially successful with the elementals of water, as the narrative states (v. 9), while the plagues of locusts and flies (Ex. 8, 10) were brought about through the agency of the elementals of the air.

This intrusion of all kinds of supernatural events, including the voice of the Supreme Deity, into this historical narrative indicates that the Pentateuch is as much a revelation of esoteric and philosophic wisdom as a history of Israel. The origin of the documents — namely the sanctuaries of Chaldea, Assyria and Egypt — is clearly indicated by the precise, if allegorical, revelation of esoteric science. Chapter Four of Exodus is a treatise on the serpent fire and the instruments of magic — spiritual, psychological, corporeal and external. The revelation is only verbal, and is therefore incomplete. Furthermore, it is couched in the form of allegory. The real revelation is made by means of demonstration by the teacher and of experiment by the student, the two being face to face. No amount of perusal of books on esotericism and magic, however direct the language, will by itself bestow esoteric power. Although useful as a basis and in saving the teacher's time, it must nevertheless be supplemented by illustration, demonstration, and the awakening in the student of the necessary powers of vision, evocation and directive will. These are only obtainable either within the sanctuary or from those that have already received the knowledge and the instruction to convey it to a chosen recipient.

The darker arts, the debasement of knowledge and power, may be learned from certain apostates who have betrayed the sanctuaries and their wisdom. Every student is seriously warned about these practitioners of the dark arts. Their true nature may always be discerned, since sooner or later they display the selfish — and sometimes sensual — grossly material motives by which they are moved. The absence of the slightest desire for personal gain is the hallmark of an esotericist of the White Order, just as its presence unmistakably indicates a practitioner of the Dark Order. The student must ever be on guard. Even as Moses' hand was turned as white as snow, so must the will, mind and action of the would-be white magician be self-purified from without and within. The initiate who thus has placed a hand on the heart and made it all-white may find in the Bible all that is needed of external verbal instruction in the mysteries of the hidden powers of nature and of humanity.

The scriptures constitute a manual of esotericism, and that is their true value to humanity. The whole Bible is alive with spiritual and esoteric wisdom and knowledge. It is therefore also a vehicle for spiritual and esoteric power. The person that has eyes to see as she or he reads—let that person see. Having read and seen, let the seeker, with the goal of effective service to humankind, aspire to the wisdom of the sanctuary. Then a representative from the Holy of Holies, one of the world's initiates, will reach out and draw the student towards the portals of a temple of the ancient Mysteries.

The Bible is not a single, isolated piece of literature. It has neither beginning nor end. It is as a chapter of the world scriptures, begun long before the first chapter of Genesis was written and was still in the process of construction and continuation after the writing of the book of Revelation. The Bible is as a jewel, an opal of many flashing hues set beside innumerable other jewels, each a divine revelation to a people and an age. Only at the end of the world period, the close of the seventh cycle of the Seventh Race, will the Earth's inspired writings be complete. Even then these writings will be only one unit for the fourth of the seven epochs of planetary activity. By the seventh epoch, however, that which is now an undercurrent will have become the main stream of revelation. Deeper layers will by that time form the esoteric wisdom of the highly illumined Seventh Race.

Copies of every world scripture that has ever been written, from the remotest times when the first Adept teachers began to instruct primitive humanity, are preserved within the libraries of the guardians of the esoteric knowledge of this planet. No single book worthy of preservation, whether for its intrinsic merit or for its historical place in the stream of divine inspiration given to humankind, has been allowed entirely to disappear. It is for the humanity of a future age that the Adepts, the true keepers of the sacred light, have thus preserved and will continue to preserve the spiritual wisdom revealed to and discovered by later generations.

In verse eighteen, Moses asks permission of his father-in-law, Jethro, to go to Egypt. This reveals that law of the sanctuary under which no initiate may leave the sacred precincts without the permission of the hierophant, here personified by Jethro, the priest of Midian. Moses, in this context, represents those messengers who are sent out from time to time from the still-living and still-operative sanctuaries of the world. Like them he is to go forth, illumined by both the light of his own Monad-Ego and the wisdom of the ancient Mysteries, to teach and redeem humankind. Success depends upon the power of the sanctuary of which the initiate is a member. Jethro thus says to Moses, "Go in peace."

> And the Lord said unto Moses in Midian, Go, return into Egypt: for all the men are dead which sought thy life. *(Ex. 4:19)*

Here the inner compulsion matches the command of the community and its head. Doubly empowered and doubly inspired, the initiate — when the time is ripe — goes forth to liberate the human spiritual Selves (represented by the Israelites) from their submergence in, and domination by, their lower selves and the material world (as represented by Pharaoh and Egypt respectively).

Moses Begins God's Assignment

In verse twenty is repeated an age-old glyph constantly appearing in the Bible — namely that of the head of a family with his wife and their offspring journeying upon an ass. As previously interpreted, the higher Self, inspired by the Monad-Atma (God's voice), is represented by Moses. The higher Mind within its vehicle — the Causal Body — is typified by Moses' wife Zipporah, and the product of their union (the sons) is spiritual wisdom. The ass upon which they ride has previously been stubborn, but is now tamed and docile, and it represents the four-fold lower self. This is a quaternary consisting — in one classification — of the formal mind, the emotions, the vital force in its etheric vehicle, and the physical body. Thus the sevenfold human, unified and harmonized in purpose and mutual relationships as a result of evolutionary attainment and the influence of the sanctuary, continues her or his development and fulfills her or his mission in the world.

In this case the authors are careful to indicate both the esoteric awakening, status and power and the means by which the mission of liberation is fulfilled, namely "the rod of God in his hand." Thus in verse twenty there is depicted a Jewish Hermes — Tehuti — God-inspired, God-empowered, serving as divine messenger, shepherd, teacher and deliverer of humanity; for one as this is the true initiate of all ages and all times.

God Hardens Pharaoh's Heart

Again, as so often elsewhere in the Bible, the spiritual law is enunciated allegorically by the strange apparent inconsistency of the action of God. The law is that Spirit must descend into and arise from and above matter, that life must first submit to the imprisonment of form and ultimately mold form into perfect responsiveness and beauty, that consciousness must achieve self-consciousness through insistent effort to overcome the resistance of the vehicles in which it is forced to incarnate.

The universe, viewed from without, appears to be submitted to the action of two opposing powers, each apparently fulfilling an opposite purpose. Spirit is imbued with the inherent characteristic of expansion, and matter with that of contraction when once it has been impregnated by Spirit. Thus the inception of the process of the creation and evolution to perfection of a universe constitutes also the commencement of a kind of cosmic warfare between these two seemingly hostile agencies. The opposition is, however, only apparent; for when the universe is viewed from within—that is, from the point of view of Spirit—rather than from without and the point of view of matter, then the very conflict is seen to be the sole means by which an orderly and predesigned expansion, through forms of ever-growing beauty and sensitivity, can be achieved.

The spiritual consciousness behind all creation, the one Universal Mind, is therefore not actually guilty of setting up conditions within the fields of manifestation—namely the conflict between Spirit and matter—by which its own designs are rendered extremely and unnecessarily difficult to fulfill. Viewed from without, life may appear senseless and chaotic. Viewed from within, a law of existence is seen to be at work. This is allegorically revealed in verse twenty-one, where God promises to harden the heart of Pharaoh against letting the Israelites leave with Moses. With a strategy that is strange and incongruous, as so often, being employed as a clue—God announces the intention of deliberately preventing, at least for a time, the fulfillment of the command which God had given to Moses. Apparent inconsistency is one of the recognized veils by which in the sacred language profound truths are concealed, even while by the very nature of the veil attention is drawn to them.

> And thou shalt say unto Pharaoh, Thus saith the Lord, Israel is my son, even my firstborn:
> And I say unto thee, Let my son go, that he may serve me: and if thou refuse to let him go, behold, serve me: and if thou refuse to let him go, behold, I will slay thy son, even thy firstborn. *(Ex. 4:22–23)*

These two verses reveal the fundamental macrocosmic and microcosmic truth that the divine triplicity (the Lord, the Mother and the

Son—Osiris, Isis and Horus worshipped at Thilae, and Amar, Mut and Khonsu at Thiles), symbolized by an upward-pointing triangle, is reproduced in the material cosmos and in humans. This reflection (the Egyptian Father, Mother and Son) is, in its turn, symbolized by a downward-pointing triangle of exactly the same shape and size.

The geometrical laws known to be manifest in the triangle, the numerical principles and facts which it displays, have their cosmic significance when applied to the creative, evolutionary and transforming processes. These laws, principles and facts also pertain to the reflected divine triplicity, which is represented in symbol by the downward-pointing triangle. Nature is the faithful mirror of cosmic truths. As the reproduction in a mirror is illusory, though real and exact in appearance, so in philosophy the material worlds are regarded as an illusion in their relation to the ultimate reality. The original and the reflection, the reality and the unreality, form the subject of the revelation in these two verses. In the first the divine triad is described. The Lord is the Father or first aspect, the apex of the upward-pointing triangle. The Mother is nature herself, and particularly precosmic substance, represented by an angle at the base of the triangle. The Son is the product of their union, namely the universe itself with its indwelling life, symbolized by the other angle of the triangle.

In terms of human consciousness the Father is the human creative will, the Mother is the creative intelligence or higher Mind, and the Son is creative wisdom, referred to as Israel, and like the universe, emerging only at a certain phase in the process of emanation and evolution. It is this "Son" which is all-important, and therefore must be saved.

The downward-pointing triangle represents the three lowest material planes, with the physical as apex and the emotional and mental as angles at the base. Egypt is made to represent this reflected triad, whether as material nature in her threefold aspect or as the latter of the bodies of the mortal personality—physical, emotional and mental. The purification of the lower, that the higher may be emancipated from its limitations while manifested in it, is portrayed in the rest of the allegory.

The plagues which beset Egypt (Ex. 7–11) simply refer to the tribulations through which nature in the cosmos, and the lower human self must pass in the refining and self-liberating processes. The lower self, represented by Egypt, naturally resists. Thus, despite the tribulations Pharaoh is repeatedly made to harden his heart. Although the whole is made to appear as the result of action and intervention by God, actually purely natural processes are described. For the guidance of initiates, however, the laws of self-liberation are also revealed in the allegory.

The son referred to in verse twenty-two, and personified by Israel, is the illumined spiritual Self which must, and inevitably will, become free. The second son of verse twenty-three, personified by Egypt, is the temporary, evanescent and illusory sense of selfhood of the outer person, and this sense must be destroyed in the process of redemption. Thus, at the beginning of the conflict which is about to occur the basic principles are enunciated in these two verses. All that follows is but their outworking and their application to the purpose in view, namely the perfecting and completion of an evolutionary phase or dispensation, and the attainment of Adeptship by humanity.

"The Lord Met Him and Sought to Kill Him"

The sequence of the narrative does appear to be interrupted in verse twenty-four. The Lord, who has up to this point been the ally and adviser of Moses, now seeks to kill him in an inn. If this break in the motif is merely literary and the consequence of a multiplicity of authorship, then it may be dismissed. If, however, its inclusion has a purpose, as is not uncommon in the Pentateuch, then instruction may be gained by a consideration of the history of a minor event in the life of Moses.

Israel, the son who must be preserved, and Egypt, the son who must be destroyed, are shown as aspects of one and the same individual, whether the evolving universe or illumined person in his or her inner and outer individualities. In such a case the inn symbolizes the Ring-pass-not of a universe, or one of its components which has reached the phase of the withdrawal of Spirit-Life from matter-form. In humans the inn symbolizes the Auric Envelope, or enclosing sphere marked by the extreme range of auric emanation, within which individual integrity is preserved and the process occurs of the ensouling of substance and form by spiritual life and other sources of supply. The Lord is pure Spirit, Moses is its material manifestation, and the age-old conflict between the two, which reaches its height at the phase being described, is depicted in this verse. Microcosmically, all action in allegorical narratives occurs within the human Soul. All is a subjective experience. It may well have been the intention of the authors to allegorically state this fact at the beginning of the description of the great conflict between Moses and Pharaoh.

"A Bloody Husband Thou Art"

In verses twenty-five and twenty-six, where Zipporah circumcises her son, the arrangement of the symbolism is somewhat confusingly changed. Moses becomes the Monad-Atma, the spiritual will, Zipporah becomes the spiritual Soul, the immortal Self in its vesture of light, while the son is the lower personality, the outer self. In its spiritual meaning circumcision symbolizes the cutting off of physical sexuality, and the transmutation of the creative energy and capacity so that it may be exercised in sublimated form as creative genius. It also represents the power by which objective results may be thaumaturgically produced. This transmutation is achieved only with strenuous endeavor and the severest of self-control. The complaint of Zipporah ("a bloody husband thou art") represents the cry evoked from the Soul when the turning point in its existence is reached, one of the marks of which is deliberate renunciation of the gratification of desire, especially sexual—the conscious sublimation of the sex drive.

These verses are thus in harmonious relationship with those descriptive of the transformation of a staff into a serpent (v. 3), or the awakening and directing of the serpent fire along the spinal cord. Circumcision in its symbolic meaning is utterly essential to that process, because awakening of the serpent fire, if done prematurely, can awaken completely uncontrolled sexuality. This would produce deep degradation of the Soul. It is almost impossible to redeem the Soul if this occurs, for after the death of the body in which esoterically stimulated sexual excesses occur, the inner Self experiences a loss, a veritable rending away of a part of its own being and life. It is this danger which, in part, necessitates the careful selection of candidates for initiation and the receipt of esoteric power and knowledge, and also the secrecy with which the sacred rites are always surrounded for the protection of such candidates.

Put simply, these verses of the fourth chapter of Exodus reveal the conditions essential to success in thaumaturgy. In its inner significance, this implies complete self-mastery and the capacity for that true magic by which all that is unrefined in a human being and in humanity is, by a supreme effort of will, transmuted into the fine gold of a purely spiritual and illumined individuality. This is the objective of the various grades in the greater Mysteries, this is the goal before every initiate.

In its microcosmic interpretation the story of Moses, like that of all the great legendary heroes and heroines of antiquity, describes the passage of the inner Self through those evolutionary stages in which a person is transformed from a matter-blinded, desire-ruled, normal human being into a self-redeemed Adept. The power of achievement is that of the innermost spiritual Self, the Monad. The transforming agency is the transmuted, creative, serpentine force, which is an absolute necessity in the conquering of sexual desire and the sublimation of this force. Then, and then alone, is the God inside of a person able to act outwardly and to perform upon this person and upon surrounding nature those seeming miracles, that true magic, accounts of which read so strangely in the descriptive allegories which emanate from the world's esoteric sanctuaries.

17

The Passover

```
┌─────────────────────────────────────────────────────┐
```

Exodus 11

God told Moses that there was one more plague (the tenth) to bring upon Pharaoh and Egypt. When this actually occurred, Pharaoh would not only let Moses' people go, he would throw Moses and the Israelites out of the land.

Moses went to Pharaoh. He told him that God had instructed him that at midnight death would pass through the land of Egypt and strike down all of the firstborn in the land—from Pharaoh's own eldest child, and even to the firstborn of "the maidservant that is behind the mill and all the firstborn of beasts." He also told him that as a result there would be a great cry of mourning throughout the land. But the children of Israel would be untouched. Having said this, Moses left the presence of Pharaoh in great anger. True to what God had said, even hearing of this plague, Pharaoh remained stubborn and would not let the children of Israel go.

In the sacred language the final and highest sacrifice is implied by the loss of the firstborn, the dearest amongst all offspring. Even as jewels and precious metals are symbols of the highest products of inorganic nature, so the firstborn of animals and humans represent the highest products of organic kingdoms. At the close of Manvantara, described in allegory by the tenth plague of death of the firstborn, nature's fruits in all her kingdoms must be transferred from form to the life of a manifested universe. As form they are lost. As life they are saved. The loss is depicted as an unreturned borrowing

235

and as a death. The gain is described as favor to the Israelites, who throughout the allegory stand for life and consciousness, as the Egyptians stand for form and vehicle. Night for matter is day for Spirit. To consciousness limited to form, loss of form is as darkness. Therefore at the hour of deepest darkness (midnight) God will and does smite the Egyptians, depriving them of their firstborn.

Three instances are described, namely those of Pharaoh, of maidservants, and of beasts. These may be regarded respectively as the abstraction of life from the worlds of thought, emotion and physical substance at the approaching close of the epoch. This withdrawal in fact is not a punishment, nor is it achieved with pain, except perhaps by the initiate for whom it forcibly foreshadows, far in advance of the natural time, the normal ascent of consciousness from matter and form into Spirit and Life.

In nature the process is unhurried, normal and not associated with either loss or death, extending as it does over millions of solar years. In the initiate, passing consciously from the human to the superhuman kingdom and onwards, there must be intense effort, sacrifice and strain. The surrender in Gethsemane (Matt. 26:39) and the passion of the crucified Savior (Matt. 24:46) describe that sacrifice in another allegorical form—particularly of the renouncement of the self-centeredness and separateness for the selflessness and realization of unity of the Adept. This is the true "firstborn," which later is slain. It is the dearest human possession and the hardest to give up, having necessarily been attained and sustained throughout the purely human phase of evolution. The reversal of this motive for living is acute. The instinctual reason and basis for the thoughts and actions of a normal person must be relinquished and replaced by those diametrically opposed to them. This enforced reversal is achieved with the same anguish that a parent endures at the death of a firstborn. It must be thorough, complete beyond the possibility of falling back, and so must be established throughout the lower mind (Pharaoh on his throne), the emotions (the maidservant behind the mill), and the physical consciousness in the brain (the beasts in the field).

"A Great Cry throughout All the Land of Egypt"

The great cry of mourning throughout the land (v. 6) is of deep and twofold significance. In nature it is as an announcement of the close of a creative epoch. In the initiate it is the cry expressive of the anguish of the Soul as it is forced by the unyielding Monadic will from I-ness to I-less-ness.

Nature herself is creative sound made manifest. Her every form is the product of thought-charged sound. She is the Logos made flesh, or incarnate in physical vehicles which are imbued with but one instinctual purpose—to resist disintegration, to survive as forms. When these perish the life-force fears extinction, is anguished at death. Symbolically, a great protest arises throughout all the land of Egypt—the universe of formulated substance. This occurs normally at the close of Manvantara when all forms perish and return to cosmic dust. The totality of instinctual resistance and the fear of annihilation may well be portrayed as a previously unheard "cry."

As Christ upon the cross is said to have called aloud *"Eloi, Eloi, lama sabachthani,"* which translated is "My God, my God, why hast thou forsaken me?" (Mark 15:34), so every initiate at the corresponding stage and grade in the greater Mysteries utters the cry of the Soul when it perceives itself forsaken by form, and has not yet seen itself as pure life.

The intervening period, brief though it is, is one of intolerable anguish, of an aloneness in the cosmos, which is beyond description and which at the time seems to be irremediable and without possible end. As the Soul passes through this phase, consciousness is finally withdrawn from Self and circumference, and is established in the One Self and at the center of cosmic awareness. Once achieved, whether by nature at the close of the age or by a person at the close of life in the human kingdom, the attainment is final. Therefore there shall be no cry "like it any more" (v. 6).

In these significant verses God as Law is about to make a clear distinction between the opponents by injuring the one and preserving the other. The life of the Logos is about to be withdrawn from its material encasement. To that life the process brings freedom; to the forms it means death and disintegration. The authors have previously allegorically described the effect of the decree upon forms. Concerning life itself, however, resurrection, ascension and liberation—in their mystical significance as states of consciousness—are natural results of evolutionary progress.

> And all these thy servants shall come down unto me, and bow down themselves unto me, saying, Get thee out and all the people that

> follow thee: and after that I will go out. And he went out from
> Pharaoh in a great anger. *(Ex. 11:8)*

The complete submission of matter and of its inherent consciousness, characteristic of the final phase of objective manifestation, is again described by Moses' utterance in this verse. It is stated to be imminent despite the apparent resistance that will be met with at first. Events move on irresistibly, and eventually all will be fulfilled. The "great anger" expresses not bad temper, but the fiery intensity of the will to ascend and attain the freedom characteristic of the penultimate state of evolution. In the initiate on the threshold of Adeptship this is a passion and a thirst. By sheer force of will the last barriers and limitations are overcome. Matter is forcefully subdued, its inherent attributes brought to subservience, ahamkara is finally renounced and its power broken. The subsequent disaster to the Egyptians in the Red Sea is an allegory of the disintegration of forms (the army and its equipment) and the return of their substance to the free, precosmic condition – the Red Sea.

> And the Lord said unto Moses, Pharaoh shall not hearken unto you;
> that my wonders shall be multiplied in the land of Egypt.
> And Moses and Aaron did all these wonders before Pharaoh: and the
> Lord hardened Pharaoh's heart, so that he would not let the children
> of Israel go out of his land. *(Ex. 11:9–10)*

These "wonders" are not achieved without resistance and great effort. Indeed, the last act of the great epic is the most dramatic of all. Whether microcosmically at the death of any sentient form, or macrocosmically at the close of an evolutionary epoch and at the final initiation, resistance to disintegration, annihilation and the end of I-ness is passionate. To the *Arhat* (the initiate of the fourth degree who has entered the highest path and is thus emancipated from both self-separateness and enforced rebirth) on the Cross it seems that matter summons all its powers, and nature all her allurements, to resist and prevent that final renunciation and self-emancipation which necessarily precede the attainment of Adeptship.

The last struggle, which sometimes immediately precedes the death of a human or an animal body, is an example of the tremendous effort of form to prevent disintegration. The birth of every new form involves the loss of an old one. Attainment of a new and higher level of consciousness demands a renunciation and the disintegration of the predecessor. In the universal sense this is true of both forthgoing and return. The immersion of life in forms and the descent of consciousness into vehicles are accompanied by an inevitable, if temporary, loss of the preceding states of freedom and of peace. The human Ego suffers severe privation on being born into a physical body as a baby. According to an esoteric tradition (see SD, Vol. 3), one-third of the Monads to whom the Earth was appointed as an evolutionary field refused to descend into human bodies and, in consequence, were incarnated by force.

The "war in heaven" (Rev. 12:7) refers in part to this refusal, and the true "angels that sinned" (2 Pet. 2:4 and Jude 6) are not celestial inhabitants in disgrace, but rather human Spirits which have descended into matter. This aspect of involution and its effect upon consciousness are allegorically described in the tribulations of the Israelites as they groaned in bondage to the Egyptians. On the downward arc it is matter and form, represented by the Egyptians, which gain; and it is life and consciousness, represented by the Israelites, which suffer loss.

On the upward arc the situation is reversed. The Egyptians suffer from the plagues and the Hebrews do not. This is a very correct portrayal of the opposite effects of the two phases of manifestation. On the downward arc, life and consciousness are limited. On the upward arc, matter and forms are destroyed. The fable of the Phoenix illustrates this truth, which is also made manifest at every birth and death. Whether of larva from egg and winged insect from chrysalis, or of consciousness in mammalian forms, this is the law of life.

Throughout this long narrative of the ten plagues, as elsewhere in the Old Testament, the God of Israel is sometimes portrayed as a peculiarly cruel, bloodthirsty and vengeful deity. The Passover, with its blood rite and the murder by spiritual means of all the firstborn of the Egyptians and of their beasts, may seem repellant to some truly devout minds.

How, then, is this to be explained? Some have said that this can be explained by the worship of tribal deities. If so, how is it that such an ignorant people were able to produce authors capable of the noble language and the lofty idealism of other parts of the Old Testament? A second explanation is that the whole story is an allegory. Interpreted allegorically the Bible, despite its limitations, presents an exposition of the doctrines known and taught in the ancient Mystery

Schools. The Bible constitutes a coordinate revelation of theosophical wisdom. It should be read as allegory particularly by those who demand consistent, rather than contradictory, accounts of the nature and activity of the Supreme Deity and of the involution and evolution, under its direction, of the universe and its component parts.

Nowhere in the Bible is this revelation of truth by allegory more wonderfully achieved than in the narrative of the ten plagues. That such a combination of catastrophes, magically caused and magically removed, should have passed unrecorded by so record-minded a people as the Egyptians is difficult to believe. Yet, save in certain carvings, there is no reference by Egyptian historians to either the arrival and long bondage of a foreign race which became half a million strong or the ten terrible plagues by which the Egyptian people became veritably an accursed nation.

Exodus 12

God spoke to Moses and Aaron and told them that this month was to be the first month of the year to them. God also told them to give the following instructions to the people of Israel: On the tenth day of the month each household was to choose a male lamb without blemish, and on the fourteenth day of the month, in the evening, the lamb was to be slaughtered. After having sprinkled the door posts and lintel of their houses with its blood, the people were to roast and eat the lamb, together with unleavened bread and bitter herbs. They were to eat this meal quickly and dress for traveling.

God told Moses and Aaron to tell the people that "I will pass through Egypt this night smiting the first born in the land, both man and beast . . . but when I see the blood I will pass over you."

At midnight, true to God's word, the Destroyer moved among the dwellings of Egypt, and the firstborn in each household in Egypt died, along with the firstborn of all the cattle. And a great cry of mourning went up through all the land, for there was not one household untouched by the hand of death, save for the Israelites. Pharaoh immediately sent for Moses, ordering that both he and his people must leave Egypt immediately, including their flocks. He also asked Moses to bless him before he left.

And so it was that the Israelites finally departed from Egypt, after dwelling there for four hundred and thirty years.

The tenth plague of the death of the firstborn and the events by which it was said to be followed may be interpreted as descriptive of the final phases of a cycle of manifestation, whether major or minor. The numerical references indicate completion and consummation. The symbols of the slaughtered lamb and kid, the blood-sprinkled lintel and doorposts, the unleavened bread, the death of the firstborn of one nation and the preservation of another living as near neighbors — all these alone, interpreted according to the classical and universal method, point to an esoteric revelation by means of the allegorical language of the ancient priesthood of the sanctuaries.

Chapter Twelve opens with the purported instruction to Aaron and Moses by the Supreme Deity to institute a blood sacrifice and feast, which were to be observed by the Hebrews throughout succeeding ages. This first observance was to be followed by an action so morally questionable as to cause one to wonder just what kind of deity had performed them. Whatever the sins of the Egyptians they had not deserved this national catastrophe, coming as it did upon nine others of great severity. If, however, it can be shown that a fable is being related for purposes of esoteric revelation, then the otherwise unacceptable narrative — involving the Deity in passions and brutality usually characteristic of humankind — becomes worthy of closer attention. Thus interpreted the verses are descriptive of both universe and humanity, and therefore of every other order of created beings.

> And the Lord spake unto Moses and Aaron in the land of Egypt, saying, This month shall be unto you the beginning of months: it shall be the first month of the year to you. *(Ex. 12:1-2)*

Philosophically interpreted, God is Law. Mystically God is the Monad, the innermost Self — whether of cosmos, angel or human. In humans, Moses is the Monad expressed as an individuality at the level of the higher intellect, or the Monad-Ego. Aaron, his brother, represents the executive mind, which by virtue of initiation is fully responsive to and directed by the Ego (Moses). Macrocosmically, the land of Egypt is the physical universe — nature with its ensouling principles. Microcosmically, Egypt is the physical nature of humanity. The first verse thus describes the Monad-Ego of a highly developed person while in physical incarnation.

A certain degree of unfoldment is indicated by the statement that God spoke to Moses and Aaron, and also by their later obedience. Applied to humanity, this ability of the Monad to address and obtain complete cooperation from the Ego during physical incarnation implies that the very last stage of human development has been reached, since a final subphase is indicated by the events which follow (See figure, p. 148).

The second verse indicates that passage from one evolutionary phase into its successor is about to occur; for the number ten (the last plague) represents culmination and synthesis, and number one the opening of a new creative cycle. For humanity these two evolutionary phases are the completion and fulfillment of purely human existence, and entry upon the superhuman stage of development. For Race, Planet, Round, Chain, Scheme and Solar System, the completion of a major cycle of manifestation and preparation for transference or "passover" into its successor are allegorically described. In the sacred language months represent minor cycles and years major cycles of manifestation; for the real Passover includes exodus from Egypt and, by divine intervention, successful passage across the Red Sea.

"They Shall Take to Them Every Man a Lamb"

Speak ye unto all the congregation of Israel, saying, In the tenth day
of this month, they shall take to them every man a lamb, according
to the house of their fathers, a lamb for an house. (*Ex. 12:3*)

In this revealing verse many symbols are used. Speech itself represents the creative and directive power of the Monad, whether of human or of universe. Spiritually formative and ordered activity is therefore implied by the first word of the verse. The congregation of Israel represents the powers of the Monad-Ego, now coordinated, unified and susceptible to divine guidance and employment. The word "congregation" is aptly chosen by the translators, who themselves were frequently in receipt of Adept inspiration. An ecclesiastical term is thus used for the combined families which made up the Hebrew nation then resident in Egypt. The powers and faculties of the higher Self are to be employed for Monadic purposes. The tenth day indicates the culminating subphase of the cycle.

The sacrificial lamb or kid is ever the symbol of the Logos in its aspect of preserver, while its blood represents the one life in its vitalizing, sustaining activity. This life is the foundation of the universe. It is the electrical and vital potency of the Logos, which is the active basis of all atomic substance.

The command that each "man" shall take a lamb "according to the house of their fathers, a lamb for an house," implies the attainment of fully conscious realization of the divine presence within, the very inmost human nature. A high state of yoga is described here, one in which the individual is self-identified with both the universal life and its divine Source. A condition of awareness is being described rather than active obedience to a command. The Arhat in its final phase of Arhatship is about to become an Adept, and the required level of consciousness—that of full illumination—is symbolically portrayed.

The term "house of their fathers" is a symbol for the Causal Body, which has been the vehicle of the Monad-Ego throughout the long series of physical lives. Each mental personality is, in fact, a father to its successor, since from its achievements and by its actions the future is formed (karma). In this sense only are the iniquities of the parents visited upon the children (Num. 14:18). The spiritual house —home, source and container of powers—is, in fact, the human Causal Body or the Augoeides (self-shining divine fragment).

In this human principle the divine presence, meaning the power, life and consciousness of the Monad, is manifest. Throughout long ages that presence is inactive, germinal, asleep, as at the beginning of the voyage during which the tempest was stilled by Christ (Mark 4:38–39). As the initiate stage is approached, the presence becomes active from within the individual, and is recognized or felt by the outer personality. At initiation the two are conjoined, and in consequence the Logos of the Soul assumes increased control of and manifestation in the physical self. At Arhatship divisions disappear, and Monad-Ego as personality becomes one being. Each of these three, with its awakened powers, has become part of the "congregation" or a component of the single being—which is the audience—both hearing and obeying the divine voice. This is the evolutionary phase now being described. The phrase "take . . . a lamb for an house" means that each illumined individuality becomes completely aware of, and fully responsive to, the presence and creative action of its Logos ("the Lamb of God"–John 1:29) as the spiritual creator and sustainer active from within the Causal Body.

Human beings are at differing stages of unfoldment when the time arrives for the dissolution of a universe or component part. Some have become spiritually individualized; for the process of individualization is repeated at the Atmic level where the Monad itself is discovered, and at the same time unity with and within the Logos or "lamb" is recognized. Others are not so fully developed. They shall not be neglected but, by a process of sharing, be drawn upwards into the Source and receive that Source into themselves.

The blemish that the lamb shouldn't have (v. 4) in this case would be a still-remaining trace of I-am-ness. This must be eliminated and outgrown. Remember that every being, person and thing mentioned in a truly inspired allegory represents a human component—a principle or a power, a state of consciousness, a virtue or a vice. The "lamb" within humankind may be regarded as the product of the ram—itself a symbol of the positive potency in nature and in humans—but gentle and childlike.

In humans the lamb represents the conjoined Atma-Buddhi, the cosmic will (Atma), focused in a single individual, and embodied in and conveyed into the higher Mind by the vehicle of intuitive wisdom (Buddhi). The ram, on the other hand, represents the same cosmic will expressed by reflection, and reversed in the outer self as procreative passion manifesting in and through the physical body. When active, the creative power renders the person intensely individualistic. When spiritually expressed, however, individuality is reduced to a minimum. Before maximum attainment becomes possible, that still remaining trace of separateness must be eliminated. Symbolically, the lamb to be slain "shall be without blemish."

Remote though these distinctions may appear to the purely human mind pursuing purely human interests, for the aspirant to Adeptship they are of supreme importance. The transmutation of the creative faculty from all desire for physical procreation into selfless participation in the divine emanative activity (creation) is an absolute essential. It comes about quite naturally in consequence of normal evolutionary progression. In the individual who has outstripped evolution and seeks to attain to early Adeptship, such transmutation is achieved only by a supreme effort sustained without yielding for many years and even for many lives.

The Mystery Schools, being nurseries for the guidance of future Christ-like humans and superhumans, receive and assist all such embryonic Adepts. There the experience of predecessors, knowledge of the laws ruling self-enforced attainment, and personal guidance and support are given to all candidates. This information is also made available to every human being, but through the vehicle of the sacred language it is safeguarded from misuse and premature application for unworthy motives. It is the heart of Sophia. It is Isis in her highest aspect. It is divine wisdom – Theosophia.

The true mythology of all nations, meaning those inspired legends which emanated from the ancient Mysteries, the scriptures of the world, and the religious sacraments in their pure form are all revelations of the secret wisdom. To the unprepared there exists only exoteric literature and exoteric religion. For the disciple there is revealed face to face "the [esoteric] mysteries of the kingdom of heaven" (Matt. 13:11), and the means by which that kingdom may be realized. Symbolically described, the method is "to sacrifice a lamb without blemish" and to do with its parts as is similarly described in the following verses.

> And ye shall keep it up until the fourteenth day of the same month: and the whole assembly of the congregation of Israel shall kill it in the evening. *(Ex. 12:6)*

"The whole assembly" of the Hebrews represents the totality of the spiritual, intuitional and intellectual human nature, whether as individual or as a collective. When the state of Arhatship has been attained, however, the Arhat must have become ahamkara-less throughout the whole inner being, must have eliminated even the faintest trace of a tendency to act self-willfully or for personal benefit. The possibility of such action rests upon the presence within the consciousness of the delusion of separateness or I-am-ness. When that delusion has been outgrown or forcibly set aside ("killed"), the danger of the exercise of the spiritual, creative will for personal purposes disappears. This high attainment, utterly essential to passage from the human to the superhuman kingdom of nature, is described in symbol by the injunction contained in this sixth verse, thus removing the brutality inherent in its literal reading.

In terms of the principles or bodies of humans, the ram is used in the sacred language to represent the highest – the creative, spiritual will resident in and active through the physical body as procreative power. That power is threefold in its polarities, namely positive, negative, and neutral or balanced, this triplicity being symbolized in the ram by the brain within the skull and a horn on either side.

When descending from the Source, whether in humans or in nature, this triple energy follows a winding path, the positive and negative currents intertwining round the neutral polarity, which serves as stabilizer and director of the power. In the Grecian Mysteries and elsewhere this was symbolized by the caduceus, the rod of Hermes, or by the ram's head with its curved horns. The ram-headed creative gods of Egypt were symbols of this actively applied threefold, creative power.

The lamb is without horns and is newborn. It therefore aptly represents the creative power in its highest spiritual state, or newly emanated and at no great distance from the mother source. Thus the lamb is an appropriate earthly symbol of a spiritual power in its purest form.

The term "Logos" is used in the Logos Doctrine in reference to the same power; "the Lamb slain from the foundation of the World" (Rev. 13:8) is none other than the Logos of a Solar System who, as an emanation from the spiritual Source or cosmic Logos, voluntarily sacrifices itself when actively engaged in the process of the emanation of a Solar System. When uttered, the creative Word (John 1:1) causes matter to assume preconceived forms. When outpoured, the divine life sustains those forms. The Word is the lamb and the life is the blood. When the Word is uttered, the lamb "dies" to self-sufficient, full consciousness as a purely spiritual Being, and the outpoured life is symbolized by the blood of the lamb. That which the Logos does voluntarily throughout Manvantara the initiate must also do—namely surrender individuality for universality. Symbolically the lamb must be slain and the blood creatively employed, as the narrative later makes clear.

The fourteenth day of the month may be interpreted as a reference to the final phase of Manvantara, when the seven cycles of the process of forthgoing and the seven of return have been completed. The double seven represents a completed dual process. In humans, the fifth initiation is indicated by the addition of the two digits—one and four. Thus the attainment of the state of the *Asekha* Adept is being described in this most remarkable twelfth chapter. Evening, in this verse, may be read as referring to the close of a creative period or "day."

The Feast of the Lamb

And they shall take of the blood, and strike it on the two side posts
   and on the upper door post of the houses, wherein they shall eat
   it. *(Ex. 12:7)*

Exoterically these actions have the double purpose of providing both a sign by which God may be guided and flesh food for a feast. It is, however, contradictory to assert that the Deity who created heaven and Earth and performed the marvels related in the Bible could not tell the difference between an Israelite and an Egyptian, as is indicated by the text. Creative deities do not require physical signs to guide them throughout universes of their own creations. An esoteric interpretation is clearly intended.

The key is provided by the method and form of sprinkling the blood of the lamb, three times – on two uprights and a crosspiece. This represents the symbol of the threefold creative life-force by which all things were made (John 1:3). Two pillars and a conjoining crosspiece are used to symbolize that triple life-force, as are the caduceus, the pillars at the entrance to King Solomon's Temple (1 Kings 7:21), and all other similar arrangements of symbolic forms. The sign by which the homes of Israelite families were to be distinguished from those of the Egyptians was that of the presence or absence of the symbol of the outpoured, active, creative life-force – namely blood.

In the cosmos the two apparent opponents are Spirit and matter, life and form, consciousness and vehicle. In humans they are the Monad-Ego and the mortal personality respectively. At the time period being described, the firstborn of an Egyptian family was to be slain and that of a Hebrew family to be preserved. The firstborn of the Egyptians is a symbol of the first product of formative activity, namely the archetypal universe or divine idea. The firstborn of the formal orders of creation is that same archetype projected into matter. When the process of return approaches its close, as in the period represented by the tenth plague, the projected mold is withdrawn from, or dies to the worlds of form. This, however, does not occur at the levels of life at which the pattern still exists. Only at the very last moment of Manvantara, when the whole universe finally falls back into absolute existence, does the firstborn, the prototype, cease to exist, being reabsorbed into that absolute from which it emanated or was born. The firstborn of the Egyptians, therefore, are slain (v. 29) and the firstborn of the Israelites are preserved (v. 27).

In the case of humans becoming superhuman or thereafter ascending the scale of superhumanity, the firstborn is the archetypal human, the Adam-Kadmon or Monad. On entry into Nirvana the Monadic presence is withdrawn from or dies to the vehicles in which individuality was inherent. These are symbolized by the Egyptians. The Monad does not really vanish, however. It is preserved, but is manifest only as pure Spirit. This procedure is due to no individual action of a personal God, but to immutable and impersonal Law. The transcendental truth is, however, veiled and yet revealed in an allegory of divine intervention written in the sacred language, and couched in terms appropriate to the outlook of a wandering tribe.

In humans, the presence of Monadic power and life within the vehicles in which individuality is inherent produces the sense of separated self-existence or ahamkara. To purely human consciousness this is the firstborn in two senses. First, it is the earliest experience of the newly formed, individualized being; and second, it is the promise and power of self-preservation.

This Monadic presence and its effects in and upon the mortal personality must be renounced by, or die in and to, the human being who is self-conscious in mind, emotion, vitality and flesh. The illusion of separated selfhood, of I-am-ness, must be outgrown and renounced before I-am-all-ness can be known. Yet I-ness is not absolutely lost. Paradoxically, in the nirvanic state it remains even while absorbed in the I-am-ness of the universe. Symbolically, the firstborn of the Egyptians are slain and those of the Israelites are preserved.

To eat the flesh of the lamb (v. 8) is to absorb the creative, cosmic principle, the Logos of the universe, into one's highest spiritual Selfhood. This is, in fact, the experience of the one who has attained Nirvana, who receives the One Self of all into her or his own highest Self. This does not violate a Euclidean principle that the lesser cannot contain the greater. At all levels of consciousness below that of the abstract intelligence, this principle does hold true. At all levels above, it does not. Inexplicable though the paradox is to the formal mind, it is not so to awareness in the subtler vehicles. In denser substances form limits and largely rules perception which, while manifestating there, must obey the laws of matter. On higher planes intellect rules and transcends those limitations of form that are appropriate to the lower realms. To the consciousness thus elevated, as a result either of normal evolutionary progress or of enforced development and expansion on the path, the experience of entry into Nirvana—as previously stated—is less that of being absorbed into than of absorbing the nameless cosmic principle and power. The lamb is one of the symbols chosen to represent That, Paramatma when in creative activity. When a human being is made to consume the flesh of the lamb, entry into Nirvana is being described by means of allegory and symbol.

To the spiritual beings who are the components of Races, Rounds, Chains and Schemes, the culmination of an epoch at the close of Manvantara brings the threefold experience of withdrawal from material encasements, of absorption in a spiritual sea of infinite life and power, and of receiving that sea into themselves.

To eat the flesh of the lamb is also symbolically descriptive of a certain mystical experience entered into by every high initiate. This occurs not only at lofty spiritual levels and in the nirvanic or Atmic body, but also to initiate consciousness in the form worlds. The three separate constituents in the average person – mental, emotional and physical – are fused into one being in the initiate. At Adeptship that single unit of consciousness and action completes a process which began as an instinct during the preinitiate stage, and became self-conscious at the first great initiation.

This process consists of the gradual realization of the intimate relationship of the essential human life principle with that in all nature; for the same life principle exists in every form, every individual and every kingdom. The love of nature, the response to its beauty and its order, the realization of dawning sentience in the plant and of intelligence in the animal all arise from recognized kinship with it. The flashing, many-colored opal, the flower, shrub and tree, the lamb or other playful young, the full-grown products of each kingdom, the mountains, the varieties of trees and birds and beasts – all these delight because humans see in them something that is part of themselves, a life that is akin to their own.

The mystical experiences and expansions of consciousness which occur in the higher vehicles deepen the sense of unity with life instinctively felt in the lower vehicles, and especially in the physical body. This growing knowledge is one of the marks of evolutionary progress. It culminates in the Adept as full and continuous realization of the unity of the life in every living being in every kingdom of nature, and at every level of consciousness.

Such a concept is no longer theoretical, nor is it founded alone upon an intellectual recognition of a fact in nature. It is a living and intense vital experience. The pulse of the one life throughout all creation is felt within and known by the fully illumined superhuman.

Nature is as a unit to the Adept, and that in part is the secret of her or his power. All that appears phenomenally as outside of the Adept is known in its noumenon as part of the Adept and the Adept as a part of it. The life in the superhuman is not her or his life. It flows through such a being in its course as it flows through all beings and things, vivifying all just as it vivifies the Adept.

Although the one life is so intimately a part of all living things, it is nevertheless aloof, impersonal, free. It is the omnipresent One Alone. None can possess, retain or hoard it. It flows on its own courses, on its own mission, doing its own work. It links all, yet binds none and by none can be bound. Eternally free, the one life submits itself to the seeming limitation of temporary restriction as the life principle of myriads of forms, none of which can exist or subsist without it. It is the substance of the universe.

At Adeptship, that realization of the unity which gave to the purely human being joy in nature becomes conscious knowledge of identity with the ocean of the one life and with its Source, which is absolute life or life transcendent. At first initiation the initiate has become absorbed in the limitless ocean. It is then that the real truth begins to dawn upon her or him. That strange truth is only fully realized at Adeptship when, paradoxically to purely human consciousness, that boundless sea is absorbed. The Adept is expanded to include the whole, even though its limits are unknowable.

In the supra-Euclidean, formless worlds, consciousness, freed from limitation or having become Adept, knows by experience that the seemingly lesser can contain the seemingly greater, that the apparent part can absorb the apparent whole. Indeed lesser and greater, part and whole, lose their significance as terms of reference at these levels of consciousness to which the liberated Adept ascends. The ideas of center, circumference and intervening area have lost their usual meaning. All is center and center is all. The liberated individuality is the center, therefore the all. This is salvation, Nirvana, moksha (the release—Dhyan Chohan), and is implied in the mystical process of eating the flesh of the lamb (Rev. 5:13, 12:11, 22:1), or absorbing the one creative life-force, power or Word (John 1:1). It is a mystery which only full experience can resolve.

This attainment is couched in the terms of the sacred language because consciousness of unity with the one life bestows power upon those by whom it is attained. From within themselves forms and beings in all the sub-Adept kingdoms may be greatly influenced or even controlled. Minerals, plants, animals, humans, elemental beings and fairies can be brought under the dominion of the will of him or her who can even temporarily know and affirm unity with their inner essence. Such power is, however, capable of grave misuse, to the serious detriment of both victim and misuser. This is black magic, and so knowledge — which is power — must ever be veiled, as also must be the directions which place knowledge and power in the hands of humans. This necessity is the very reason for the invention and use of the sacred language of symbols.

The ten plagues as narrated in the first twelve chapters of Exodus are allegories descriptive of stages of development of human awareness, knowledge and power, and of experience appropriate to each stage. The tenth plague describes culmination at the end of an epoch, and brings that particular revelation to a close. Thereafter, as before, other aspects of truth are revealed in the Mosaic literature. Many books are missing and whole passages have been excised; others have become confused in the course of transmission down the centuries, but enough remains to shed a great light upon the mystery of life for those that have eyes to see.

> Eat not of it raw, nor sodden at all with water, but roast with fire; his head with his legs, and with the purtenance there of. *(Ex. 12:9)*

Interpreted symbolically, these injunctions indicate that the manifest Logos or "lamb" is self-expressed only at the highest levels, as represented by the primordial element of fire. At that level alone, therefore, may that One Alone be perceived and absorbed. Even a remaining tinge of the attributes and limitations of the levels below would violate the experience. It is therefore ordered that no water must be used. Furthermore, at the primordial level to which evolution has at this stage brought the divine pilgrim — which is life itself in its wholeness — homogeneity or uniformity is resumed.

Similarly, in the consciousness of the initiate seer no taint of impurity must remain; otherwise the splendid vision will be denied. Once these conditions are met, the one life as totality, as indivisible unity, is perceived, known and blended with the human individualized current of itself. The sacrificial lamb must therefore be cooked and eaten whole.

The lamb is to be killed in the evening (v. 6), eaten during the night, and its remains destroyed by burning in the morning (v. 10). In this procedure resides a key to the time period under consideration, namely the end of an epoch. Evening signifies the approach of night or Pralaya, and therefore the final phase of any cycle.

The narrative is still describing prophetically the conditions and actions which mark the close of the last cycle, as symbolized by the ninth plague. The feast is to occur in the night, meaning that all the fruits of the cycle, having been sublimated to the highest states or "fired," are absorbed into the divine consciousness, which has now been withdrawn to that level. The lamb is a symbol of the creative principle of cosmos, or the Supreme Deity. Its flesh represents substance when imbued with creative life, thus becoming the matter of the universe. Enfired or "roasted," that flesh represents the Divine at the highest level of manifestation as creative fire—the universe of form purged of all impurities—in fact sublimated.

The Divine may only be known and the phenomenon of its absorption into the individual (or feasting) may only be experienced in such a condition and at such a level; for the symbols apply equally to the condition of both substance and consciousness. For the Adept, therefore, the Feast of the Passover (the roasted flesh of the lamb), begun in the evening, refers to the state of consciousness attained as the result of a certain initiation and in preparation for its successor, symbolized by the tenth plague. That state of consciousness, normal for a Race at the end of the penultimate creative cycle and attained far in advance by the Adept, is one of complete self-purification—particularly from I-ness—though also from the taint of material tendencies, notably those of overactivity and inertia. Only then may the nirvanic state be entered and the Adept not only be reabsorbed in full consciousness into the One Alone but also be able to experience absorption of that One Alone into herself or himself (John 6:54–57).

Night then falls upon cosmos (universe) and microcosmos (humans) so far as the relevant phase is concerned. The dawning of the following day symbolically heralds the opening of a new cycle. Nothing remains of the evolutionary residues of the preceding epoch, the instructions concerning such residue being that "that which remaineth of it until the morning ye shall burn with fire" (v. 10).

> And thus shall ye eat it; with your loins girded, your shoes on your feet, and your staff in your hand; and ye shall eat it in haste: it is the Lord's passover. *(Ex. 12:11)*

"Loins girded" symbolizes readiness for a new evolutionary journey, or entry into a succeeding epoch of creative activity. "Shoes on your feet" means readiness to traverse the new round of the tenfold spiral, step by step. A "staff in your hand," together with shod feet, completes the creative triad. To eat in haste refers to the increased speed of the evolutionary process at the end of cycles, and especially to the enforced self-quickening to which the Adept has submitted. In this condition both creative life and the highly evolved person are properly prepared to "pass over" to a new and higher cycle.

The Firstborn of Egypt Are Slain

During the minor Pralaya following a minor Manvantara the creative and evolutionary processes do not cease. The fruits are harvested, winnowed, and stored or established within both the divine and the human consciousness. The action of smiting the firstborn of the Egyptians and of their cattle (v. 12) has been partly interpreted. The firstborn are the eldest of the progeny and symbolically represent the most highly evolved. To smite them is to transfer them from form to life, from matter to Spirit; to withdraw them from material encasement and transfer them to the freed, spiritual state.

The apparently murderous action of God is an allegorical description of a natural process, which occurs in the cosmos and the Race at the close of an epoch under law, or at the direction of God. The Egyptians represent the matter side of cosmos and the Israelites the side of Spirit. The most highly evolved (eldest) spiritual Souls that are still embodied in matter are, at the command of God, freed from that encasement.

The firstborn also represent the full fruits of the evolutionary cycle, namely all those spiritual Souls who have completed the pilgrimage. These, at its end, are freed or liberated. The firstborn of the Israelites, in their turn, represent the fruition of earlier cycles who have already become coworkers with law. They are the Cosmocratores, the Sephiroth or creative Intelligences who, as the first fruits of preceding Manvantaras, minister as directors of the evolutionary processes throughout all cosmoi. They have already been "slain" in the symbolical sense. Therefore God is made to pass them over (v. 13), the sign of their stature and office being two vertical posts and a conjoining horizontal one marked with the blood of a lamb (v. 7).

The Gods of Egypt are the nether powers, the opposing influences, the now highly developed attributes, forces and Intelligences appropriate to nature in her maternal aspect. They have served a useful purpose, but now are needed no more. The dissolution of cosmos will bring their existence to an end (see Hodson, *The Kingdom of the Gods*, Part. 3). In another sense the Gods of Egypt are those human beings who, by virtue of esoteric knowledge and will, have become highly developed in evil practices. However, the end of the major cycle brings judgment upon them. The vehicles of consciousness in which they have maintained a semi-independent existence as rebels against the law now disintegrate. The Monadic essence (the spark and its rays) is transferred from the closing cycle to its successor, and must therefore begin the evolutionary pilgrimage from a very early phase. In this sense judgment is executed upon them.

In verse thirteen, God promises to pass over the houses marked with the blood of the lamb. In the macrocosm this simply implies that at the end of Manvantara forms disintegrate, matter returns to a semiquiescent state, while the incarnate life, consciousness and beings still persist. They are liberated by the dissolution of the universe, continue in the inner worlds during the subsequent Pralaya, and resume active manifestation at the dawn of the new epoch. This is a fundamental process occurring universally, as throughout the seasons in the plant kingdom and during the individual life cycles of every animal organism. In humans death corresponds to the tenth plague, during which the substances of the vehicles return to their several sources and the higher human principles are withdrawn from the deceased body into a spiritual state, to reemerge at the opening of the new cycle.

In the embryonic Adept the purely human attributes, ahamkara and all the taints of matter—particularly passion and inertia—are extirpated and disappear or die, destroyed by the Monad-Ego made perfect, or "the Lord." The Adept passes from the human to the superhuman kingdom of nature, to begin and follow the next round of the ascending spiral of evolutionary progress. There greater attainments await the evolving being in an infinitely ascending series, each of which closes with the disintegration of limiting forms, evolution beyond existing states, and the passing over of consciousness to greater freedom and power and to a larger universalization.

Each major cycle is composed of ten subcycles, and at the completion of each the hold of matter (the Egyptians) is loosened and the power of Spirit (the Israelites) is increased and made more fully manifest. This is the key to the ten plagues in terms of individual evolution.

When God tells the Israelites that they are to keep the passover "throughout your generations," the quasi-eternal nature of the law of cycles is enunciated. Inevitably and unchangingly this law rules all life processes. It is personified by Tehuti or Thoth in the Egyptian Mysteries, and by Chronos in the Greek. It is the basis of time, whether abstract or concrete. The appearance, movements and dissolution of bodies, Races, continents, Planets, Solar Systems and cosmoi are with uttermost exactitude governed by the ticking of the cosmic chronometer, which is the law of cycles and periodicity. This, to consciousness within these forms, is as the period of solar night and day, the everlasting rhythmic ebb and flow of the tides of creative life. Therefore to evolving Monads it is as "a memorial" for ever (v. 14).

Leavened and Unleavened Bread

Seven days shall ye eat unleavened bread; even the first day ye shall put away leaven out of your houses: for whosoever eateth leavened bread from the first day until the seventh day, that soul shall be cut off from Israel. *(Ex. 12:15)*

This verse may be taken as a prophetic description of the coming Pralaya. Leavened bread is a symbol of life-filled, atomized, basic protoplasm. Unleavened bread is that protoplasm unvivified by the presence of the life-force, the leavening agency. Bread is thus used because it is made from grain, and grain grows out of the earth or "Mother." Mother-substance is primordial space out of which the "daughter" substances are formed, in their turn to give birth to universes when vivified by "Father"-life.

Grain symbolizes matter that is the product of the action of the formative Father-Mother, and gestates within and is born from the womb of the latter. Creative power under Law uses this grain or direct product of the universal matrix to form Systems, Suns and Planets, and these are represented as the loaves of bread. Before such utilization can occur, the secondary substance must become charged with electric energy, or be leavened. In terms of matter, leavened bread is a symbol of productively active material which during Manvantara nourishes universes and their component bodies. In terms of consciousness, grain is the symbol of will-mind, the germ represents the will itself, the protoplasm the mind, and the enclosing membrane the ahamkaric sense or individualizing, enclosing, separating agent. The husk is the formal human mind throughout each life cycle. Leavened bread is a symbol of the will-charged mind by which the individual Ego is fed, inspired, mentally nourished.

The vehicle for will is the second principle, the conveying spiritual life or Christos within. In consequence, Jesus the Christ feeds the multitudes (of existent beings) with a few loaves (Matt 14:17–21) – the ever-continuing miracle "by which all things live, move and have their being." In the miracle the addition of fish to the bread points to the necessity for the presence of the individualized life principle, of which the fish is a symbol. In terms of human consciousness there must be wisdom before intellect can be fully illumined or nourished.

Unleavened bread is a symbol of will-thought universalized, or without the individualizing action of the creative life. Those who partake of unleavened bread during Manvantara have achieved the generalization of consciousness and are fed from the universal Mother Source. This is the state of the Adept, and of every member of the human race at the close of an evolutionary cycle.

A kernel of grain is also a symbol of the human Ego, the immortal, evolving human principle. The germ is the Monad-Atma, the chemical constituents are the inherent qualities and powers, and the epidermis is the Auric Envelope, particularly of the Augoeides. The husk symbolizes the mental attribute of accentuated and apparently self-sustaining egohood, or egoism.

To multiply itself the Ego must be incarnated in mortal bodies, even as the grain must be planted if it is to bear fruit. The husk must have been removed and the enclosing skin must decay before the fertilized seed can produce the shoot and stem upon which a whole ear of grain can grow, and the one bring forth much fruit. (This would seem to be allegorically affirmed by Christ – see John 12:24.) In order to become fruitful by the production of germinated, developed and multiplied egoic powers, humans must use or "plant" those powers in the material worlds. They must further permit the husk and skin to lose the ability to limit the inner development. Symbolically, the husk must be removed and the epidermis must decay, meaning that dependence upon the separative, self-enclosing illusion of I-ness must cease. Then alone can fruitfulness in the evolutionary sense be achieved and full nutriment of the lower self by the higher Self be brought about. Again, as in the miracle of the loaves and fishes, it is the intuition with its universalizing action and revelation of unity which makes this process possible.

All inspired allegories are dramatizations of fundamental law, ever active during creative periods. By such dramas the rules of life are revealed to those who at first could not perceive them in any other way. These allegories of the nations are narratives descriptive of the order of things, knowledge of which is delivered by the Adept teachers to every Race and subrace at a certain stage in its development. This knowledge is imparted in obedience to that law of laws under which only what is given forth can live, and that which is retained inevitably dies. That principle is enunciated in the famous words of Christ: "Except a corn of wheat falleth into the ground and die, it abideth alone: but if it die, it bringeth forth much fruit" (John 12:24). The dying of the grain is that self-same death of the Christ upon the Cross (Matt 27:50–56), and of the Logos of a universe or "the Lamb slain from the foundation of the world" (Rev. 13:8).

Consciousness itself is subject to evolution and to expansion of range. From becoming capable of awareness throughout the whole physical body it is extended successfully throughout the superphysical bodies, from the lowest up to the highest. These are seven in number, and the attainment of awareness in each of them occupies an evolutionary period or day. The realization of the universality of divine consciousness and life in the seven vehicles is accompanied by its increase in range throughout the plane of each vehicle. This implies an actual widening of the sense of self-ness in all other forms of life in an ever-expanding measure, and at the close of the seventh day culminates in technical omnipresence over the whole field of evolution.

The Adept forcibly achieves this development far in advance of the rest of humanity. Instead of the normal, relatively slow process through Round, Chain and Scheme, Adeptship is attained by conscious effort, which is at least dual. On the one hand Adepts force themselves to progressively surrender the sense of I-ness, to deny to themselves every sensation of individual identity, which includes the relinquishment not only of personal possessions, but even of awareness of their own existence as a separate being. This is the "death" enacted in all initiatory rites. On the other hand, by prolonged contemplation they extend the experience of harmonious attainment in consciousness with the life of other beings around them until self-identification with them is achieved, and by practice this becomes normal. As this is successively attained in vehicle after vehicle, they become at one with worlds positioned at increasing distances from themselves. This culminates in at-one-ment with the totality of the appointed field of evolution. In a solar Logos this consists of oneness or omnipresence throughout the whole Solar System, attained at the close of the seventh day (Maha-Manvantara) of its cosmic manifestation.

To this process of extension of self-identity with other selves there is no finality. Manifested cosmoi are innumerable, since all are themselves evolving through the continuous process of emergence from the Absolute and eventual withdrawal into it. The Absolute may therefore be defined—in a literal sense only—in terms of consciousness as unlimited cognition in space and time, both potentially in Pralaya and actually in Manvantara, without cessation and without end.

Yet awareness in itself is, in fact, a denial of Absoluteness. Only the unmanifested can be totally beyond the limits of either space or time, for it includes every possible phase, from transcendence in Pralaya to immanence in Manvantara, and therefore is inconceivable, except in theory, to a mind in manifestation. Apperception in the highest Being reaches to the very threshold of this state, this being the evolutionary summit.

To eat unleavened bread is to transcend individuality or to participate in and live in and by the one life in its eternal self-existence in homogeneity. Freedom of creative action at what is miscalled a distance (miscalled because consciousness of localized space at that level is inconceivable) is one of the powers gained by the attainment of omnipresence. To use an analogy from physiology, to the totality of the blood content of the body, distance is without significance, for it is omnipresent. To blood flowing through a particular area, or endowed with self-consciousness, an illusory sense of distance and separation from the blood flowing through other areas might conceivably exist. Such illusion would correspond to the sense of I-ness in people. That temporarily localized portion of the total bloodstream flows on without pause to another continuous area of the body, and could conceivably fall under the same illusion there, and so on throughout the whole circulatory system. In the same sense this applies to the Ego-ness of the human life principle as a person passes from one incarnation to its successor, and becomes subject to an illusory sense of selfhood in each. Actually the human Ego is part of an ever-flowing totality of manifested life, within which no separated individualities can possibly exist.

As at the completion of each circulatory circuit the blood returns to the place where it emerged, namely the heart, so at the close of each Manvantara all life returns to that unnameable agent from which its impulse to rhythmic circulation is derived. When at the outermost capillary limits, blood is flowing through its greatest number of separate vessels. When in the heart, however, it gathers into its greatest volume. In like manner consciousness reaches its extreme of multiplicity and individuality of self-manifestation at the lowest level of density of the substance and forms in which it is expressed. Thereafter, it withdraws in a succession of Manvantaras — or pulsations of life — to its Source, where there is unity.

In terms of human evolution, those phases in which ahamkara reaches its heights correspond to the capillary phase in the circulation of blood, and to periods of deepest density in the evolution of universes and their components. Similarly, those phases in which ahamkara is reduced to a minimum correspond to the period at which blood is withdrawn to the heart and universes to their very highest condition. Initiates and Adepts force themselves to transcend the illusion of localization and to live in the state of consciousness which exists at the center or heart of life.

The whole of this procedure is allegorically implied and described in the narrative of the ten plagues. The preliminaries to the tenth plague refer to the approach to the final evolutionary stage — whether reached naturally or by enforced evolution — at which all returns to the center and source not of life itself, which is sourceless, but of the impulse to rhythmic circulation. To that starting point the spiritually awakened deliberately force their way. Within it the Adept, by the exercise of the will, maintains her or his position, this being the meaning of Adeptship attained during pre-Adept evolutionary periods.

Adepts are of at least two orders, the Nirvanis and those who renounce Nirvana in order to assist in the swifter attainment of Adeptship by all below that state. The former sink into a relatively pulseless existence. Beyond time, space and the illusion of personal identity, they are "out of circulation" so far as all worlds below those at the nirvanic level are concerned, though doubtless active on higher planes. Those who renounce the state of identification with pure cosmic being forcibly maintain a measure of sublimated individuality, even as during their ascent they forcibly break the power over themselves of the illusion of self-ness. On the threshold of absorption into supreme self-less-ness, and therefore of supreme rest in everlasting serenity, they sacrificially refrain from entering it before the close of the Man-vantara during which they attained Adeptship. At its close they, too, will return to the heart of all life, and there remain throughout Pralaya. Both full Nirvanis and Adepts who have renounced Nirvana for the present period have reached the condition allegorically described in the tenth plague. Their progress to that state is described symboli-cally by the number ten, as also is the progress of life as a whole and of all its temporarily individualized manifestations.

Days of Holy Convocation

In verses sixteen through twenty, God sets down some of the parameters of Mosaic law. For example: "in the first day there shall be an holy convocation, and in the seventh day there shall be an holy convocation to you" (v. 16). The first and the last "days" or phases of any sevenfold cycle of involution and evolution—or "week"—are days of holy convocation, because in them the evolving entity is at the nearest position to the point of departure on the journey of forth-going, or is in the most highly spiritual state. On the first day this state still inheres, and at the last day the despiritualizing influences of the material mind-phases have been overcome. The evolving life and consciousness have reached the highest degree of spirituality at-tainable in the particular sevenfold cycle or week. Furthermore, the manipulation of matter, or "work," is less in those phases than in the other five. [This procedure is fully described in Volume I, Part Three.]

"Cut Off from the Congregation of Israel"

> Seven days shall there be no leaven found in your houses: for whosoever eateth that which is leavened, even that soul shall be cut off from the congregation of Israel, whether he be a stranger, or born in the land. *(Ex. 12:19)*

The dire punishment awaiting those who eat leavened bread dur-ing the preliminary phases of the tenth plague, namely that of being "cut off from Israel," is deeply significant. The only lost souls in a universe are those whose mental and astral vehicles have become severed from the two highest principles—the spiritual Self which is the source of will (Atma), and its vehicle which is the source of wisdom and intuition (Buddhi). For those who "eat leavened bread during a period set aside for the partaking of unleavened bread only," the severance of the mortal soul from its spiritual Self can occur.

In such a case the personality, ensouled only by a measure of the intellectual principle (Manas), eventually sinks into oblivion – which is the opposite pole of existence to that of the supreme spiritual awareness of Nirvana – or is "lost." The two highest principles, which are everlasting and indestructible, having become separated from the manasic vehicle, must later resume the cyclic pilgrimage and again reach Egohood. At the appointed time, in order to become Nirvanis – a much later development – they must successfully lay aside the limitations of egoistic mentality.

To be cut off from Israel is to be severed from one's highest Self – the greatest of all catastrophes. That the mere eating of leavened bread, even in violation of divine ordinance, should be punished by exile for life is surely too harsh a judgment. If taken literally as a statute in Mosaic law, then such judgment is indeed severe. If regarded as an allegory and rightly interpreted, however, the ordinance is a statement of inviolable, natural law.

To recklessly turn back during the later stages of the pilgrimage to perfection is to return to the restrictions of earlier stages and to undo the achievements of the cycles, thus becoming the victim of an outgrown past. In terms of human consciousness, unleavened bread signifies the primordial, nonindividualized state. To partake of it at the close of a cycle is to enter into realization of unity, to outgrow the limitations of individuality, and to forswear the heresy of separateness. The primordial state is reentered in full awareness and is known not as a restraint due to helplessness, but as a condition consciously attained and just as consciously established and maintained. Deliberately – and in no other way can the highly evolved fall so low – to return to diversity after unity has been reached is to surrender the fruits of the eonic pilgrimage. When this turning back as an individual to a past out of which the Race has evolved occurs, then the soul is cut off from that Race and can no more progress with it to final liberation.

The Actions of Moses as Profound Allegory

In the words of Moses Maimonedes (a Jewish theologian, 1135–1205 A.D.): "Every time that you find in our books a tale the reality of which seems impossible, a story which is repugnant to both reason and common sense, then be sure that the tale contains a profound allegory veiling a deeply mysterious truth; and the greater the absurdity of the letter, the deeper the wisdom of the spirit."

If this view is accepted and applied to the interpretation of the Pentateuch, it is discovered that in the Bible the laws upon which the creation and evolution of a universe are founded are sometimes enunciated in terms of divine actions and divine commands. The abstract is made concrete, the unmoving is dramatized, and the ever active is indicated by means of actions in time. Regarded in this way Moses represents the principle of vehicleship which, in operation during Manvantara, makes actions at the lowest levels by the highest powers both possible and comprehensible. Moses, as the spokesman of God, is the state of consciousness and matter by virtue of which creative will is enabled to produce, ensoul and transmute the planes and worlds of dense substances. This interlinking principle is described and shown in action by means of the allegories of communion between God and God-illumined people. Moses receives the divine commands and conveys them to the Israelites, by whom they are obeyed. In consequence, the preordained results are produced upon the Egyptians.

The doctrine of *Avatara* (the incarnation of a deity), or of Self-manifestation by a highly advanced Being or Power in and through a prepared and dedicated person still living in the world in order to reach the masses of humanity, is revealed throughout the Bible by means of the deliverance of verbal instructions by God to a chosen recipient—in the present case, Moses. This representative in turn conveys the orders and celestial influences to the inhabitants of the mundane world. Throughout the Old Testament spiritual overshadowing alone is described. In the New Testament a full Avatara is implied in those passages in which Jesus identifies himself with the Logos and is portrayed as a veritable presence of God on Earth (John 10:30—"I and my Father are one").

The emanation, involution and evolution of cosmoi and their components may be regarded and described in terms of more complete manifestations of the Divine. At each stage the Logos becomes Self-manifest in and through the products of that stage. The full presence, if not the full manifestation, marks the completion of a phase, particularly on the downward arc. On the upward arc Self-manifestation by Deity is progressively achieved, and at the close of Manvantara the universe itself is a total Avatara of the Logos. All this is implied and described in the first five verses of the first chapter of the Gospel of St. John, which might be called the Gospel of the Avatara.

The appearance of the still wounded body of the Christ to the disciples in a room with closed doors (John 20:24–27) may, in addition to its exoteric meaning, be interpreted as an allegory of Self-revelation by God of the universe during the phase on the journey of return at which the imprint of matter on Spirit is still observable. The power of Spirit over matter is not yet complete, ultimate fulfillment of the cyclic pilgrimage being symbolized by the later ascension of the perfected body, robed in light, to the highest spiritual state — "the right hand of God" (Mark 16:19).

Moses receives and conveys the divine commands, and so portrays partial Avatarship or overshadowing. Jesus portrays full Self-manifestation of Deity, and so is a perfect Avatar on those occasions when he is identified with "God the Father" — whether by himself or by the Evangelists.

18

The Red Sea

Exodus 14

God commanded Moses to encamp the Israelites between Migdol and the Red Sea. Moses was then told that Pharaoh and all his armies would finally give honor to God.

By this time Pharaoh had changed his mind about letting the Israelites leave, and he pursued them with an army of six hundred men and chariots. On seeing the approaching army, the Israelites panicked and cried out against Moses, blaming him for their predicament. But Moses told them not to be afraid, because God would do the fighting that day.

The angel of God, in the form of a great pillar of cloud, stood behind the Israelites and shielded them from the sight of the Egyptians. Moses was commanded by God to stretch out his staff to the sea. When he did, it caused an easterly wind to blow all night, and the waters of the sea divided and stood like walls to the right and left. This allowed the Israelites to cross the sea on dry land. When in the morning the Egyptian army pursued them, the wheels of their chariots came off on the floor of the sea. The Egyptians panicked, for they saw in this the hand of God.

With the Israelites safely on the other side, God commanded Moses to once again raise his staff over the sea. The walls of the sea caved in on the Egyptian army and destroyed them. When the Israelites saw this, they believed the word of God, and of Moses.

At the close of Manvantara, the period being described in these verses, the manifested returns to the unmanifested state. Spirit, life, consciousness return from where they came, into a state of pure (un-modified) spiritual essence. In that state all is lifeless from the point of view of objective, creative activity, productivity and evolutionary movement. This condition is symbolized by the wilderness on the other side of the Red Sea. The Israelites, therefore, move into the wilderness after they have crossed the Red Sea on dry land, Moses having parted the waters with his rod.

The two walls of water, one on either hand, held back by the up-raised rod of Moses, represent the positive and the negative qualities of matter, while the empty space between signifies that neutral third which comes into existence when the oppositely polarized energies have been perfectly controlled. The attributes of activity and inertia have, at the close of Manvantara, been totally mastered and made subordinate to that of rhythm.

In the physically living Adept the two vital forces of ida and pingala have been perfectly controlled. The spinal cord itself, the true rod of the magician, has become vivified by the third fiery power of creation—kundalini shakti—to liberate consciousness from vehicle and enable the illumined Adept to pass to realms beyond human ability to perceive. These realms or states of being are symbolized by the wilderness. Actually, however, they lead to the summit of the highest attainable level of awareness, portrayed by Mount Sinai, and thence to the Promised Land, which is *Para-Nirvana.*

As throughout the Pentateuch, the command of God to a patriarch or leader and the results of obedience to this command are actually descriptive of natural procedures associated with the emanation and withdrawal of universes, and of evolutionary attainments by advanced Beings according to the law of forthgoing and return.

> And behold, I will harden the hearts of the Egyptians, and they shall follow them: and I will get me honour upon Pharaoh, and upon his host, upon his chariots, and upon his horsemen.
> And the Egyptians shall know that I am the Lord, when I have gotten me honour upon Pharaoh, upon his chariots, and upon his horsemen.
> *(Ex. 14:17–18)*

The "honour" of the Lord granted to Pharaoh and his hosts implies the complete domination, first, of matter in the universe by Spirit and, second, of the vehicles of the Adept by consciousness. The armed cohorts of Pharaoh, the chariots and the horsemen all symbolize the basic substance of a universe with its inherent material tendencies in opposition to the rule of Spirit and consciousness.

Level by level, from lowest physical matter to the most highly refined yet still material state, epoch by epoch and eon by eon, Spirit overcomes resistance or symbolically gets "honour" upon matter, represented by Pharaoh and his hosts. Throughout the total period of manifestation the conflict is long, the battle arduous. The inherent consciousness in protoplasm is itself divine and eternal. It can never be destroyed. It must be refined, directed and subordinated to cosmic will and cosmic law.

The Angel of God

Eventually pure Spirit, stainless and unalloyed, is withdrawn into its Source and pure matter. It is sheer substance undifferentiated and unillumined by consciousness, and therefore without design once more becomes the cosmic sea of space (see Gen. 1:2 – "And the earth was without form, and void . . ."). The law under which this occurs is personified as an angel (v. 19). The pillar of cloud which had guided the Israelites by day now stands behind them. Since at this stage consciousness is self-guided, self-illumined, it no longer needs external guidance. It has once more become the effulgence of which it is a manifestation. Hence the cloud is said to be light and to give light to the Hebrews, and yet to cause darkness for the Egyptians (v. 20). The radiance of Spirit is always as darkness to those who are unable to perceive it.

The shaping of the cloud into a pillar again indicates the deeply esoteric nature of the narrative. The oppositely polarized vital forces that ascend within the human body along the spinal cord, from sacrum to brain, call forth the intermediately polarized third current. By the aid of this aroused threefold energy (kundalini) full illumination, full liberation from the body, and ascension to the highest states of consciousness are made possible.

The unillumined (Egyptians) and illumined (Israelites), of whatever degree or at whatever stage of development, are always separated by a dark gulf (v. 20). In such circumstances, for the unillumined it is as night and for the illumined it is as day. The separation is inevitable, natural, a fact which becomes strikingly evident at the close of Manvantaras, major and minor. All that is highest withdraws itself from all that is lowest, and the two part forevermore.

In the mortal bodies of the Adept this self-same process must consciously be carried out if a physical personality is to be retained.

Longevity—attainable by every Adept—demands that all the coarser substances, conditions and attributes of the vehicles of mind, emotion, vitality and flesh must be completely eliminated. As they are expelled, finer matter replaces them; this means new vehicles of carefully selected substances are built into the mold of the old ones. The appearance of the Adept is basically unchanged, except for the spiritual light which irradiates from within and the utterly ennobled and spiritualized condition which is apparent in every phase of the personality. In allegorical language, the Adept has separated the Egyptians (coarser substances) from the Israelites (finer matter) by means of the instruments of the magician. These are the three electrical, fiery currents of creative energy fully aroused, interrelated, controlled and drawn up from sacrum to crown to constitute the rod of power. This is the column of strength, of establishment and of stability, three in one, by which the fully illumined "temple" (the mortal, personal vehicles) is supported and sustained. It is the pillar referred to in the New Testament in the statement: "Him that overcometh will I make a pillar in the temple of my God, and he shall go no more out. . . ." (Rev. 3:12). This symbolical pillar both conjoins and keeps apart the states of light and darkness in the universe and of spirituality and spiritual blindness in humans.

"The Waters Were Divided"

The underlying theme of the life lived, the teaching given and the effort made in the sanctuaries of the mysteries is this very process of attaining self-illumination, brought about by the ascent of the divided, yet intertwined, triple creative fire or vital forces (kundalini). By applying this interpretation the constantly veiled references by the authors of the Pentateuch to these forces can be more readily understood, for such authors were either candidates for initiation or initiates themselves, writing allegorically under the direction of hierophants. These first five books of the Bible may even be regarded as a thesis, by virtue of which proficiency is demonstrated. Since realized immortality was the prize for which they labored, these initiates may be said to have been "writing for their lives." A gift—one of epochal significance and value—must be given to the world if karmic merit is to be attained and proficiency demonstrated. The Christ taught: "Give not that which is holy unto the dogs, neither cast ye your pearls before swine, lest they trample them under their feet, and turn again and rend you" (Matt. 7:6). Indeed, the secret wisdom must ever be available to the seeker, yet concealed from the unenlightened; for the word "swine," when used in the allegorical language, is a symbol for those who are as yet at the stage of evolution at which primitiveness blinds them to spirituality. There is neither condemnation nor abuse in the term; it is merely descriptive of people at a certain evolutionary stage. Esoteric knowledge must simply be withheld from them. Nevertheless it must ever be offered to the illumined who are able to make of it a veritable elixir of life.

> And Moses stretched out his hand over the sea; and the Lord caused the sea to go back by a strong east wind all that night, and made the sea dry land, and the waters were divided. *(Ex. 14:21)*

The outstretched hand of Moses typifies the fulfillment of the function of those officials in the government of Solar Systems, planetary groupings, Planets and Races known as the Manus. At the close of every epoch in the lives of the portion of cosmos in their charge, these Beings gather together the fruits of the age that are the seeds from which in future aeons successive universes and their harvests will be reborn. These are coordinated under their direction, conserved through the intermediate Pralayas, and led through the waters of interspace to the opening phases of the next stage in their unfoldment. This is the cosmic significance of the complete story of Exodus; for it allegorically reveals the alternating periods of emanation and withdrawal of cosmoi, universes, Solar Systems, Planets and all that exists and evolves in these systems.

In his patriarchal as well as his magical offices, Moses is a type of all Manus, as were his predecessors. In these capacities he wields all the powers, faculties and attributes of both the Spirit and the matter of the evolutionary spark under his direction, and is able to lead the human Monads to a like attainment. For him space (the Red Sea) is an obedient servant and substance (the Egyptians) is his slave. The east wind by which the waters are driven back is a symbol of power from God, the divine breath directed by one who is both an aspect and an agent of creative will and law. The land may represent the vast aura of the Manu within which the spiritual Souls move in security from one eon to its successor. All happens in the darkness of night, which is a symbol of the interval between two creative days.

In human individuals the self-same process is enacted within the Causal Body, which is the personal "Ark" or dry land. In the human as microcosm, the Monad-Ego is personified by Moses. At death the conscious, creative ray of the egoic Self which had entered the physical world in the body of a child is withdrawn. With the fruits of life's experiences carefully preserved, this ray cleaves the interspace to return to its Source (see Hodson, *The Miracle of Birth*). The substance of the various vehicles of consciousness in which the projected ray had been clothed is thereafter dispersed and returns to its appropriate sphere—that ocean of substance from which it had been drawn, as symbolized by the Red Sea.

In every individual a "Moses" watches over this process. An appropriate Intelligence, one of the Dhyan Chohans, under karmic law guides the returning ray (the Israelites) and sees that utter justice is done, and that all the powers and faculties developed in the life which has closed are preserved as the inalienable attributes of the God-Self within. Throughout the great narrative the Egyptians are made to represent life-imbued and creatively responsive matter or substance, and the Israelites the conscious, creative rays. The two great antagonists, Moses and Pharaoh, in this sense represent respectively creative will-thought and the differentiated substance upon which it operates. These are, in fact, the eternal enemies—light and darkness, God and Devil—while the evolutionary field, whether macrocosmic or microcosmic, is their battlefield.

All that is done by a superior Being for members of the subhuman and human kingdoms of nature, the Adept performs for herself or himself. The Adept is a master builder who, having completed the construction and the establishment, without and within, of the temple of her or his own Being, now proceeds to the construction of temples of steadily increasing dimensions in the larger cosmos in which she or he serves. The Adept is the highest product of the age and time. The seniors in the sanctuaries have been to the Adept as a Moses, have guided and directed the Adept through all the dangers and ordeals inseparable from the fulfillment of the determination to quickly reach the spiritual heights by a self-enforced process of quickening.

Moses is thus the hierophant of the mysteries and his rod the thyrsus. The Red Sea, displaying the quality of obedience (driven back on either hand by the upraised rod), symbolizes the threefold fiery current of creative powers in nature (kundalini) and in the candidate for Adeptship. The east wind is the hierophantic power, the solar Atma, by which every hierophant fulfills the duties of office. The dry land is both "the way of holiness" (Is. 35:8) itself and the sushumna or central etheric canal within the spinal cord and brain, with its two intertwining, ascending currents of positive and negative, rhythmically flowing, creative power. The two great walls of water, reared up and held on either hand by the rod of the magician, represent these positive and negative forces under perfect control. Thus, in the terms of the sacred language of the Mysteries, Moses leads the Israelites out of the land of Egypt and through the parted waters of the Red Sea towards Sinai and Canaan.

The Mysteries themselves are similarly preserved from age to age, and conveyed from one epoch and one individual to their successors. In this sense the Israelites as a whole represent the Mysteries, Moses personifies the hierophant, and the national talismans and other contents of a sacred ark symbolize the hidden wisdom, the unchanging, eternal truths which it has been the function of the Mysteries to preserve and deliver to succeeding generations.

The Israelites Enter the Red Sea

Mastery of the forces of nature, whether external or interior to a person in the physical body, depends upon the ability to control, to separate, and thereafter to manipulate the positive, negative and neutral currents of the electrical energy of which nature consists. The Adept is taught the secret of this power in the Mysteries, and by training and practice acquires the necessary capacity for its control. The human will, when spiritualized and united irrevocably with the cosmic will, is relatively omnipotent in its action upon the forces and Intelligences of nature (Devas). The fully trained initiate can so direct the currents of cosmic energy that the appearance, position and condition of existing natural objects can be changed. Others can be made to appear seemingly out of nowhere, though actually made from the materials in the inexhaustible storehouse of substance which is the akasa. In this process, control of the three currents of the creative energy is essential. From within, the Adept similarly brings under the direction of the will the same three electrical currents. Thus charged, the whole body becomes as an electrical system, a series of circuits, with spinal cord and brain as main conductor and cable.

Psychologically, a corresponding process must have been brought about in the superphysical bodies and the levels of consciousness for which they are an expression. These, too, are arranged in pairs with a neutral third, which is the Ego itself. The chief duality is the inner Self and its vehicles, with the interlinked higher and lower Manas as third. Three other pairs consist of the vehicles of the inner will (positive) and of the etheric and physical bodies treated as a unit (negative), the vehicles of intuition (positive) and emotion (negative), and the vehicles of the abstract (positive) and the formal (negative) minds. The components of these three dyads must be so controlled that they can be readily separated the one from the other, the positive from the negative—the Ego standing between. This achieved, all the powers of the spiritual Soul of the initiate can shine out and act with full potency through either polarity between the two, or through both of them. The division of the couplets following their full mastery is therefore the key to all magical operations, whether external or interior, and whether physical, psychical or spiritual. Throughout the scriptures of the world this psychospiritual fact is displayed in allegories, in which pairs of the same order are made to appear one on either hand of the hero or heroine. Examples are: Samson, who met his death by destroying the pillars of a house (Judges 16: 29–30); Hiram of Tyre, who set up two pillars in the porch of the temple of King Solomon (1 Kings, 7:21); and Hercules, who, on his way to perform his tenth labor, set up two pillars—now known as Gibraltar and Ceuta.

In the verses of Exodus now being considered, the waters of the Red Sea are divided by Moses and made to stand as walls, one on either hand of the path of dry land upon which the Israelites passed to the further shore (v. 22). All triplicities in the sacred language in their thaumaturgical meaning refer to this attainment. It is for this reason that Christ is made to be crucified between two thieves. The central figure, the Lord Christ, is the spiritually and intuitionally illumined inner Self of the initiate, and the two thieves represent the concrete and the abstract minds. This is made clear by their differing remarks to the crucified Lord—mockery by one and a request by the other to be remembered by the Lord when he came into his kingdom (Luke 23:39–43). The whole manifestation of initiate power occurs in the spinal cord and the brain, or upon Golgotha—"The place of a skull" (Mark 15:22).

In Greek mythology, the infant Hercules is attacked by two serpents. He seizes them, one in either hand, and strangles them. In the myths of nations the meaning of the winged sandals and helmet of Perseus, as of all other divine aerial navigators, has the same significance. Similarly the bow, string and arrow of Eros, and of all other divine archers, also have the same interpretation, for these myths constitute the real "treasures in heaven" (Matt. 6:20) of all peoples.

The two thieves, one on either side of the crucified Christ, are also represented by the two organs—the pituitary and pineal glands—which in their normal condition permit the exercise of concrete mental powers, but at the same time make the manifestation of abstract intelligence difficult. They are therefore called thieves, for under normal circumstances they "rob" the lower self of the influence, vision and power of the higher Self. These two organs, as stated above, are the pituitary gland, which is the vehicle of the emotions, and the pineal gland, in and through which the purely mental activities find expression. The very fact that they permit awareness of emotional and mental states within the brain—valuable from the purely physical point of view—causes them normally to be unresponsive to, and therefore actually to shut out, the more delicate perceptions possible to higher mental and intuitional states. In this sense, therefore, they are thieves.

Evolutionary progression produces changes both in the superphysical bodies and powers of humans and in their corresponding physical organs of manifestation. In the case of the two glands, the range of responsiveness increases to bestow upon the brain within the skull more delicate perceptions. They then come to be used increasingly by the Ego to permit the expression in the brain of the powers of the abstract mind and the faculty of intuition. In the sacred language this process of the extension into spiritual realms of consciousness (abstract thought and intuition) of capacities that previously have been limited to relatively lower manifestations and propensities is referred to as a "death." Sometimes this progress is described as a beheading of the central character, and sometimes as a crucifixion. No death occurs in reality, but only an extension into higher regions of consciousness, abiding in which the individual is less responsive to—or is "dead" to—the lower levels of awareness, namely the acutely self-centered, prideful, concrete mind.

The walls of water held back, one on either side of the dry bed of the Red Sea over which the Israelites passed allegorically represent these physiological, intellectual and spiritual changes and attainments. Once completed, the Ego is free of the body, out of which it passes at will—the true exodus. Symbolically the Israelites, led by

Moses under the direction of God, escaped from the bondage of Egypt by means of a phenomenal division of the waters of the Red Sea into two walls, one on either side of dry land.

The initiates and Adepts of the sanctuaries of the greater Mysteries by such means as these reveal their knowledge to the world in obedience to the law that all who have sought and successfully found must share with all humankind. The verbal interpretation of the allegories and their component symbols does not itself constitute the true revelation. Beyond the intellectual perception of natural laws and of their application to the development of powers remain the practices by which the laws may be applied, and also the attainment in full awareness of the powers which result. The real secret does not consist of words and sentences, but rather of experience in consciousness and the practical wielding of esoteric power. No purely verbal instruction can provide this experience, although it can lead to that intellectual perception which is a necessary precursor to individual discovery.

The Pursuit by the Egyptians

Elevation of consciousness cannot be achieved without a corresponding heightening of the frequency of oscillation, and an increased responsiveness by the material vehicles and their specific organs. Body, bodily magnetism, vitality, emotions and formal mind—the mortal personality as a whole and its essential parts—must be purified, refined, spiritualized. In accordance with the allegorical method of writing, the Egyptians, attracted by a desire to share in their treasures and profit by their labors, must pursue the departing Israelites.

The polarization of the two opponents is itself a reflection and physical expression of a similar process occurring in the higher vehicles and states of consciousness. Therefore, the Egyptians must be made to pursue the Israelites into the Red Sea, using the self-same path of dry land ("the way of holiness") with its walls of water piled up one on either hand (the controlled and directed thoughts and emotions). If full success is to be attained in raising one's center of awareness, then the whole nature of the lower self must thus pursue or follow the higher, and so the statement is correctly made that "all Pharaoh's horses, his chariots, and his horsemen" enter the Red Sea (v. 23).

The correspondences are peculiarly exact, for Pharaoh himself— as the Monarch—represents egoic consciousness limited to and conditioned by the physical body in the waking state. The horses of Pharaoh represent that life-force which is the driving power behind and within the activities of mind, emotion, vitality and body. The chariot is the whole personality within the enclosing superphysical aura, the skin of the physical body being represented by the sides and floor of the chariot. The wheels represent mobility, the capacity to respond in relatively free motion to the impulses of the life-force. The pole of the chariot by which the horses are harnessed, and along which their strength is conveyed to the vehicle might be regarded as the Etheric Double, the storehouse and conveyor of vital energy.

The horsemen of Pharaoh's army, like the knights on the chess board, represent the mental body, thought-power and thought-produced forms. Armed with the spear or sword of will, these horsemen can either destroy as warriors or protect as knights. The two squares straight and one square oblique which constitute the knight's move in chess—again not unconnected with the Mysteries—correctly represent the physical body, the astral body and the concrete mind through which thought-power finds expression, or "moves." Thus the whole of the lower self (the life-force, the directing Intelligence and their vehicles) "pursues" the higher in its escape from the bondage of purely material existence and the limitations of ahamkara.

> And it came to pass, that in the morning watch the Lord looked unto the host of the Egyptians through the pillar of fire and of the cloud, and troubled the host of the Egyptians. *(Ex. 14:24)*

The Monad (the Lord) assumes increasing mastery over the physical self (the Egyptians). Now linked to the body by the ascended triple serpent fire—symbolized by the upheld rod of Moses and the two walls of the waters of the Red Sea, representing the positive and the negative currents of kundalini—the innermost Self sees the mortal personality through a pillar of fire and a cloud. In the sacred language, to be seen by God means to come under the observation and direction of the all-seeing eye, the witness, the Monad, ever united with the One Self of All. To this the human race will eventually come; to this the Adept has already achieved.

The Egyptians Flee from the Israelites

The Monadic "gaze" (as in Luke 22:61—"And the Lord turned, and looked upon Peter . . .")—directed current of spiritualizing power and influence — inevitably troubles all in the outermost self which is not yet totally redeemed from ahamkara, excessive activity, inertia, the stain of matter and the illusion of maya. Even to the very end of human evolution, both in the Race and in the candidate for Adept-ship, these despiritualizing influences remain, however greatly diminished may be their power over consciousness. They are repre-sented by the Egyptians, their armies, their chariots and their horsemen (v. 25). All must be destroyed (drowned) and their remains returned to the ocean of the substance of the universe (the Red Sea). At the close of Manvantara, this comes about by the natural processes of evolution of humanity. The Racial Monad has freed itself from these limitations of matter and maya. The four lower principles have lost their power to bind.

In the Adept the innermost Self, consciously at one with the Logos — symbolized by God — has "gazed" upon all that remained of the erstwhile human being. In the personality — troubled, deprived of the capacity for self-initiated motion, forced to follow in uttermost sub-servience the ascending consciousness — all power to bind is finally destroyed and Adeptship is attained.

The removal of the chariot wheels of the Egyptians (v. 25) sym-bolizes the denial by the Monad of the power of the substance of any vehicle for self-initiated action or motion; for the Monad rules with an intensity of will which is irresistible. As described in this verse, all efforts to resist, evade or escape the Monadic gaze and frustrate the Monadic will are lost at this stage to the outer self.

The Sea Engulfs the Egyptians

The "sea" engulfs the lower self and all of its attributes, in the sense that consciousness has become universalized. This affects every thought, emotion, impulse and instinct, all of which now bear the im-press of generality. Ahamkara is indeed left behind on the western shores of the Red Sea (the geographical location of Egypt), and all separative tendencies in any vehicle, including the physical, totally disappear. In terms of consciousness this is the meaning of the over-whelming of the Egyptians in the midst of the Red Sea.

The totality of the lower nature, everything in the erstwhile human individual, must become subject to this process of complete self-purification and self-universalization. Not one vestige of the lower self in the series of physical incarnations must remain unillumined, unempowered and not freed from the ahamkaric bond. Thus the whole company of the Egyptians who followed the Israelites is absorbed into the Red Sea (v. 28).

Nature achieves this completeness at every level throughout all her kingdoms by means of reiteration, constant stress—often up to the breaking point but never beyond it—and continual retesting of achieved results under differing circumstances. This is the reason and necessity for the continual recurrence of similar experiences throughout the hundreds of human lives by means of which the Monad-Ego attains perfection. Nature, however, does not waste time, does not unnecessarily prolong the periods of rehearsal and repetition. As soon as the desired attainment is reached and fully established in all the vehicles of consciousness, as well as in consciousness itself—the Egyptians and the Israelites respectively—the inherent evolutionary impulse moves the unfolding life and the conscious life-centers (human and subhuman) into another and higher class in the great school of life.

The candidate for Adeptship who seeks to advance ahead of the rest of fellow humans must voluntarily submit himself or herself to the inevitable strain, tension and attention essential to the swifter progress that is desired. No gaps may be left. The minutia of experience and its fruits must all be included in that concentrated form of living which is known as the path; for only so may totality of advancement be achieved. This especially applies to the twin barriers to progress on "the way of holiness," namely the impurity or stain of matter and the sense of separated selfhood. So difficult to eradicate is the stain, and so deep-rooted in both vehicles and consciousness is the sense of I-am-ness, that constant and concentrated watchfulness and self-discipline alone can ensure the desired result.

When treading the path, humans become a willing collaborator with nature. All of her laws must therefore be obeyed, her design followed in detail, and so produce her products in all their beauty unmarred by evidences of carelessness or haste. Thus in verse twenty-eight it is said of the hosts of Pharaoh that "there remained not so much as one of them."

The steady onward march of consciousness, despite the fall, death and disintegration of its vehicles, is repeatedly portrayed in these passages. Life is indestructible. Form is continually destroyed. Consciousness, which is born of their union, unfolds and ascends throughout the succession of Manvantaras.

Thus the Lord saved Israel that day out of the hand of the Egyptians; and Israel saw the Egyptians dead upon the sea shore. *(Ex. 14:30)*

"Day" in the sacred language symbolizes the Manvantaric period, while the seashore is the threshold or interspace between manifestation and dissolution—Pralaya. Manvantara is ending, and as its last moments run out, relics of outgrown, outworn, cast-off bodies litter the margins of the universe, or the worlds on which forms have been produced and have thereafter evolved. Consciousness retains the developed faculty of employing vehicles, even though their limitations have been completely outgrown. In this sense the Israelites "saw" the Egyptians dead on the seashore.

The initiate on the threshold of Adeptship reviews his or her whole human past—all the personalities through which, life after life, the person has evolved and from which he or she has arisen, and all the varied experiences from which knowledge has been gained. Wisdom and power are perceived, examined, and then finally discarded as limitations upon consciousness. No vestige of regret, desire or attachment must remain in the consciousness which, on the threshold of liberation, is about to leave its humanity behind forever. Every perfected human being has thus renewed, reviewed—and in a measure relived—his or her past, extracted every grain from the harvest of lives, harmonized every remaining discord, paid every karmic debt, and attained that absolute detachment from life in form that is one of the marks of the Adept. In this sense the initiate sees his or her former lives ("dead upon the sea shore") as the transition is made out of humanity into superhumanity, or progresses to liberation along the "bridge" in consciousness between the human and the divine principles (the dry land).

The Israelites See the Power of God

In verse thirty-one, the Israelites saw what God did to the Egyptians. In the sacred language "to see" is to comprehend and to know as well as to observe. The inner Selves of the vast majority of the human race at Manvantara's close have realized the great design of nature, or the "great work" of the Lord (v. 31). They have long contributed voluntarily to its fulfillment, and now experience the fruits of the eonic pilgrimage through matter and its bondage back to the purely spiritual state.

In terms of allegory and symbol, the "Promised Land" is a state of human consciousness in which all possible knowledge in any given cycle is attained, all power developed, and all wisdom gained. Entrance into the Promised Land—whether naturally by the Race or as a result of enforced evolution by the Adept—marks embarkation upon the very last phase of any evolutionary cycle: for in that closing period a synthesis of the fruits of all experience is consciously possessed. Thus the great work of the Lord is seen. The Adept anticipates this Racial attainment. The passage as initiate through the grades of the greater Mysteries so stimulates the activity of consciousness that form becomes utterly obedient to it, and fully flexible as its servant and vehicle; for initiation, when conferred within the greater Mysteries, includes the drawing down of interplanetary power into the Monad-Ego of the candidate. Indeed, all the powers and Intelligences of the Solar System become available to each inhabitant of a single Planet who attains Adeptship.

The aid of the solar Logos itself—a synthesis of the whole—is sought and received, and all this is concentrated by the hierophant upon the Ego and the personality of the initiate. The effect varies according to the responsiveness of the candidate, but since every candidate in the greater Mysteries has passed through long trial, training and a scientifically designed test, a very great measure of response is assured. The consciousness is then both expanded and deepened. The limitations of the preexisting state are overcome, and this results in universalization of consciousness. Inner stability and strength are also greatly increased. In consequence the creative, involutionary and evolutionary processes are observed and comprehended. In scriptural language, "that great work which the Lord did" is "seen."

All preliminary study, meditation and self-spiritualization have contributed to this attainment. The threads of every past endeavor, life after life, are gathered up and woven into that figurative strand or rope of power, wisdom and knowledge up which the Ego climbs to the universal source of power, wisdom and knowledge—which is "the Lord." Humanity achieves this naturally in the course of its orderly progression through the cycles. The Adept has reached the goal in advance of the humanity of the Globe as a whole. Earlier individualization from animal group consciousness, and greater intensity of effort, have in most cases—though not in all—combined to produce this earlier flowering of a single plant in the garden of a Planet.

In verse thirty-one the work of God is said to be performed upon the Egyptians. In the cosmic sense the Egyptians here stand for rhythm-imbued, universal substance, the weft and warp upon which the great design is woven. The fully illumined ones see the unfolding and the weaving of that design. The consequence of attainment to this state of knowledge and wisdom is complete accord with the designer, and full cooperation in the process of weaving.

To believe in God and the servant Moses is to know directly the Divine Mind in nature, and its innumerable embodiments and activities throughout the evolutionary field. Such knowledge most certainly moves to awe, but not to fear, for no one can fear that of which one knows oneself to be a part. Awe is inspired by the vision of the cosmos and its life, mind and law. Expansion, however, is the effect of the vision and not the constriction ordinarily associated with fear. In this cosmic sense Moses is the Universal Mind, and all those officials in and by whom it finds expression and direction throughout the total field. Moses is thus a cosmic lawgiver behind whom stands Cosmic Law, indicated by God. To believe in Moses is to believe in the order of things, and to fear God is to obey God, not from dread of retribution but from recognition of the beneficence both of law and of conformity to it. This condition and this action accurately describe the Adept, who is above all things the servant of universal law.

So the great chapter of the Exodus ends. So the allegory of the ten plagues is concluded. Each portrays a phase and an experience on the downward and upward arcs of the creative cycle, and these last verses describe in the phraseology of the mystery language part of the attainment of humanity and universe, in terms of both life and form, at the close of the long pilgrimage.

Bibliography

Allen, James. *Book of Meditations*. Tirunelveli, 1963.

Arnold, Edwin Sir. *The Song Celestial: A Poetic Version of the Bhagavad Gita*. Wheaton, IL: Theosophical Publishing House, 1975.

Atreya, B.L. *Yogavasishta and Modern Thought*. Benares: Hindu University, 1934.

Besant, Annie. *A Study in Consciousness*. Adyar, Madras, India: Theosophical Publishing House, 1980.

Blavatsky, H.P. *Collected Writings*. 15 vols. Compiled by Boris de Zirkoff. Wheaton, IL: Theosophical Publishing House, 1966–1991.

_____. *The Secret Doctrine*. Adyar, Madras, India: Theosophical Publishing House, 1938.

_____. *Theosophical Glossary*. Los Angeles: The Theosophy Company, 1973.

_____. *The Voice of the Silence*. Wheaton, IL: Theosophical Publishing House, 1992.

De Purucker, G. *Occult Glossary*. Pasadena, CA: Theosophical University Press, 1972.

Devas and Men: A Compilation of Theosophical Studies on the Angelic Kingdom. Adyar, Madras, India: Theosophical Publishing House, 1977.

D'Olivet, Fabre. *The Hebraic Tongue Restored*. Trans. by N.L. Redfield. New York: The Knickerbocker Press, 1921. Reprinted by Samuel Weiser, 1976.

Fuller, J. F. C. *The Secret Wisdom of the Qabalah*. London: Rider, 1976.

Hodson, Geoffrey. *The Kingdom of the Gods*. Adyar, Madras, India: Theosophical Publishing Company, 1952.

_____. *Lecture Notes: The School of Wisdom*. Adyar, Madras, India: Theosophical Publishing House, 1955.

_____. *The Miracle of Birth: A Clairvoyant Study of a Human Embryo*. Wheaton, IL: Theosophical Publishing House, 1981.

_____. *Occult Powers in Nature and Man*. Adyar, Madras, India: Theosophical Publishing House, 1955.

_____. *Reincarnation: Fact or Fallacy? An Examination and Exposition of the Doctrine of Rebirth*. 2nd rev. ed. Wheaton, IL: Theosophical Publishing House, 1972.

_____. *The Seven Human Temperaments*. Adyar, Madras, India: Theosophical Publishing House, 1968.

_____. *Through the Gateway of Death.* Adyar, Madras, India: Theosophical Publishing House, 1986.

Hodson, Sandra. *Light of the Sanctuary: The Occult Diary of Geoffrey Hodson.* Manila, Philippines: The Theosophical Publishers, Inc., 1988.

Jinarajadasa, C. *First Principles of Theosophy.* Adyar, Madras, India: Theosophical Publishing House, 1956.

Levi, Eliphas. *The History of Magic.* London: Rider, 1982.

Mayers, F.J. *The Unknown God.* Birmingham, England: Thomas's Publications, 1948.

Powell, Arthur E. *The Solar System.* London: Theosophical Publishing House, 1920.

Preston, Elizabeth W. *The Earth and its Cycles.* London: Theosophical Publishing House, 1930.

Radhakrishnan, S. *The Reign of Religion in Contemporary Philosophy.* London: Macmillan, 1920.

Scott-Elliot, W. *Legends of Atlantis and Lost Lemuria.* Wheaton, IL: Theosophical Publishing House, 1990.

Stephens, James. *Collected Poems.* London: Macmillan, 1931.

The Zohar. Trans. by Harry Sperling and Maurice Simon. Soncino Press, 1931.

Index

Aaron, the Levite, 213, 223–226, 238, 240, 241
 esoteric powers, 225
Abraham, 142, 188
 God of, 201, 207, 218
 and Sarah, 181
Absolute, xv–xvi, 113, 258
 Being, 196
 cosmos emating from, xv, 15
 emanation from, 5, 20
 existence, xv–xvi
 ray of, 5
Adam, 198
 alone is androgynous, 30, 41, 71
 ate of fruit, 33, 35, 38, 41
 creative Spirit, the, 40
 cursed by God, 33
 fall of, 37
 in Garden of Eden, 29, 41
 Monad, 46
 offspring of, 36
 rib of, 29, 30–32
 sleeps, 29, 30–31, 71
 as Spirit, 35
Adam and Eve, 216
 as creative agencies, 41
 descendents of, 43
 expelled from Garden, 33, 43
 in the Garden, 30, 54
 as Monad-Ego, 46
 personify separation of sexes, 30
 symbolize Lemurian Race, 43
 symbolize physical body, 44.
  See also Eve

Adam-Kadmon, 247
Adept(s), xiii, 23, 85, 174–175, 188–279 *passim*
 Brotherhood, 182
 candidate, 45, 84, 108, 110, 124, 206
 Hierarchy, 54–55, 67, 182
 investigators, xiii
 as master builder, 269
 nirvanis, 259–260, 261
 research by, xiii
 teachers, 59. *See also* Initiate; Master
Adeptship, 90, 119, 124, 188, 225, 238, 244, 249, 250, 259, 260, 275
 ascension into, as, 152
 candidates for, 269, 276
 path of, 150
 teachers, 257
Adi, 44
Adonai, 7
Ageless Wisdom. *See* Wisdom, Ageless
Ahamkara, 102, 238, 245, 248, 254, 256, 259, 274, 275, 276
Ain, xv
Akasa, 222
Akkadians, 39
Alchemists, xiv
All
 the eternal, xv
 self-existent, xv, 5
Allegorists, 39
Allegory(ies) (of), 262, 271, 273

282

Theosophical Heritage Classics

present well-known theosophical works, which
are made available in popular editions.

Theosophical Heritage Classics are published by
The Theosophical Society in America, Wheaton,
Illinois 60189-0270, a branch of a world organization dedicated to the promotion of the unity of
humanity and the encouragement of the study of
religion, philosophy, and science, to the end that we
may better understand ourselves and our place in
the universe. The Society stands for complete
freedom of individual search and belief.